Language and Culture

Language and Culture

David L. Shaul
Bureau of Applied Research in Anthropology
N. Louanna Furbee
University of Missouri, Columbia

Prospect Heights, Illinois

For information about this book, write or call:
Waveland Press, Inc.
P.O. Box 400
Prospect Heights, Illinois 60070
(847) 634-0081

Figure 6 (p. 220) from *Native Latin American Cultures*, ed. by E. B. Basso, "Weeping as a Meta-signal in a Mexicano Woman's Narrative," by Jane H. Hill, Indiana University Press. Reprinted with permission.

ISBN 0-88133-970-9

Printed in the United States of America

7 6 5 4

For

Jane M. Rosenthal

Contents

Preface

We began this book out of the conviction that it was needed. We wanted to write a book that examined the relation of language to culture (as well as the use of linguistic structure as a model for other cultural systems), one that drew on primary sources, synthesizing classic and influential arguments and examples with newer themes and views. We wanted a compact and readable volume that could be used in "language and culture" classes (or as a module in surveys) at the undergraduate and graduate levels, yet would be accessible to the general reader. We wanted a work that clung to what we saw as the core of language and culture studies, one that avoided seductive detours into such worthwhile topics as sociolinguistics, pragmatics, the origin(s) of natural languages, or historical linguistics. We did not want an abbreviated introduction to linguistics, however concise and well written.

This does not mean that concise surveys of linguistics are not welcome, that language and culture should be segregated from cognate topics, or that discussion of ancillary fields is not useful to language and culture studies. We only mean to put forth an introduction to language and culture that is devoted to this rubric alone. We believe that no other book successfully accomplishes this task.

The impetus for our joint venture was born around the kitchen table of our mutual friend Jane M. Rosenthal, who, with her late husband Robert Rosenthal, often graciously extended the hospitality of their Hyde Park, Chicago, home to us. On this particular occasion (Chicago Linguistic Society meeting, 1986), after a co-authored dinner we produced for the Rosenthals, we mused about how we both wished there were an introduction to language and culture studies and how we had individually started such a project. Jane suggested we collaborate, and so we did.

Twin Themes in Language and Culture

We have each regularly taught language and culture, and our approach is an eclectic survey (ultimately, a fusion) of two related discourses that proceed from Boasian particularism: the relation of language to other aspects of culture and the use of models derived from the study of language structure as ways of analyzing other aspects of culture. The former enterprise is, of course, varying gradations of linguistic relativity that range from deterministic claims to the denial of any effect of language on culture or cognition. It has as a counterbalance a parallel concern with linguistic universals. The latter endeavor is the pervasive influence of structuralism and generativism in cultural anthropology and elsewhere. Both were metathemes during the 1970s, when cognitive anthropology, the intellectual descendent of linguistic relativity studies, came to appreciate the importance of use and acquisition of categories in (con)text. At the same time, cultural anthropologists, literary scholars, and others interested in formal accounts of meaning came to recognize text and context as possible loci of both culture and language, a larger duality of patterning.

It is our view that language and culture studies can be defined as the integrated study of topics that pertain to just these two themes, although language and culture has sometimes been construed as a field very nearly equivalent to that covered by the term "linguistic anthropology," something that includes much of sociolinguistics, language variation, historical and comparative linguistics, multilingualism and communicative competence, ethnography of communication, verbal art, and so forth. For us, however, that more comprehensive definition labels language and culture writ large.

Here, we delineate language and culture writ small, organized by the two metathemes: the tension between linguistic relativity and linguistic universals and the development of a formal account of meaning (a semiotics) for anthropological study with a concomitant consideration of the influence of cultural anthropological issues for the semiotic study of language. The approach we take is historiographic, following the influence of Yakov Malkiel (Shaul), and Michel Foucault (both Shaul and Furbee). Implicit in a historiographic survey is the assumption that current issues and paradigms are better understood in light of the issues and paradigms that begat them. More is involved, however, than mere genealogy. The larger issues in language and culture studies have been fairly constant: the putative effects of language on worldview, the locus of language and culture, the epistemology of the human sciences, and so forth. The ways of looking at these issues have shifted in the development of linguistic anthropology.

Using This Book

We assume that many readers of this book will be students or instructors who have contracted to probe language and culture studies as an entire or partial course of study in linguistic anthropology. At the same time, we welcome readers from neighboring areas of the humanities and social sciences, as well as the general reader who is interested in this area of human intellectual endeavor.

We presume, however, that most readers possess no knowledge of linguistics or anthropology. Thus we alert the reader to important (key) terms by bolding them when they first appear or when they are explained. Each chapter concludes with a list of the key terms that appeared in that chapter. In addition, each key term is defined in the glossary for easy reference. Clarity of exposition and economy of prose are our editorial ideal.

For the reader with limited time, for use in a lower level course, or for a course in which language and culture studies are a module and not the entire course, chapters 1 through 8 (plus the Postscript) will prove indispensable. Readers more familiar with the topic will notice that nearly every classic quote and example is cited here, but they will also note that novel examples, findings, and ideas appear, as well as developments in the field since 1980. Having said this, we must point out that the last three chapters cover recent developments which are abstract and, at first encounter, removed from everyday experience (which they preach about a great deal). They are much more difficult than the rest of the book; patience and review will reward the reader.

The "discussion and activities" section at the end of each chapter serves to broaden the themes and issues discussed in the chapter by stimulating thinking and action on the part of the reader. Readers can peruse the activities in their minds or among friends and colleagues. We have tried to include an abundance rather than a paucity of activities to allow for selectivity on the part of those who actually attempt the fieldwork suggested and to help readers see other fieldwork opportunities. Emphasis is on common, everyday experience in order to situate analysis in a familiar context. Some of the activities introduce material that is treated more fully in the succeeding chapter (another reason for the general reader to at least skim the activities and then think about them).

We know that other arrangements are possible, and that a more encyclopedic depth is a necessary desideratum. Yet a good introduction cannot be an encyclopedia. A topical organization of the material is almost identical to the historiographic treatment used here.

As a pioneering effort, we are sure that our treatment of this field will produce reactions—and, ideally, other book-length treatments that provide different and perhaps more expansive treatments than what we have produced. Language and culture studies, while formulated around central themes in linguistic anthropology, have yet to receive the organic treatment of such fields as sociolinguistics. We hope that this offering is the beginning of synthetic, professional literature in this field.

Acknowledgements

During the years that we worked on the manuscript for this book, many people generously gave their help, more than can be acknowledged here, but we would single out some for special mention. Our colleagues Bertrice Bartlett, Robert A. Benfer, Kay Candler, Joan Cassell, Paul Friedrich, Jane H. Hill, Jim Porter, Barbara Reid, Paul Stoller, and Christina Swanke read part or all of early versions the manuscript and commented on it. The reviews provided by Ben G. Blount and Harriet M. Klein were especially useful to the final development of the book. We want particularly to acknowledge the help of our students, especially Furbee's language and culture classes of fall 1987 and 1990 and Shaul's language and society classes of fall 1987 and 1988 who used early versions of the book, among whom Keith Kelly, Charles Loew, Diana Sargent, Lori A. Stanley, and Mark Vogel were especially fearless. Our colleague Peggy Placier used an earlier version of the book in her language and culture class. Richard Pretto, Paul Mushen, and Phil Qubain gave us valuable data. Peter Gardner, Gwen Layne, Yolanda Murphy, Tom Stroik, and Gil Youmans ran down important reprints and references for us. Mary Porter and Gail Lawrence kept paper flowing. Paula Cavanaugh checked quotations and caught many of our lapses into graceless prose. Michele Poe and Richard Sutter prepared figures. Thanks also to the Gardner School of Gardner, Colorado, and to its principal Julia F. Marchant, who offered us facilities at a critical time.

We are grateful to our colleagues for their support and especially to our intellectual mentors who over the years have encouraged us through their kindness and generosity. We mention particularly the late William Austin, Constance Cronin, A. L. Davis, Paul Friedrich, Eric P. Hamp, Norman A. McQuown, Emory Sekaquaptewa, and Yakov Malkiel.

Work by one or another of us that is reported on in this book has been supported by the National Science Foundation (GS-3192, BNS-8615807, BNS-8818393), the American Philosophical Society, the Fulbright-Hays Fellowship Program, and the Faculty Council of the University of Missouri-Columbia. We are grateful to all these agencies.

Introduction

> Modern cultural theory suffers from a diffuseness so great that it seems to subvert discourse within our scholarly community. Our theories range from sociobiology, at one extreme, through various kinds of materialism and old-fashioned functionalism to theories, at the other extreme, that locate the study of culture in language and meaning. . . . We can draw some comfort from our one tried and tested anthropological truth, which is that: *Things are never the way they seem.*
>
> —Robert Murphy

Language holds an intuitive relation to other aspects of culture. At the very least, language is the means by which we talk about culture. In formulations that relate the two more closely, language can be thought of as a part of culture, not just an entity closely related to culture. In this book, we examine how persons have investigated the relation of language and culture within the larger context of linguistic and anthropological study, how that study has developed, and how current developments have emerged.

Language and culture studies always relate in some important way to one of two themes. The first pertains to the use of models derived from the study of language structure as ways of analyzing other aspects of culture. These models may be scientifically formal, involving rules and "grammars," or more literary, for example relying on identification of linguistic metaphors or verbal skills in nonlanguage realms. In this book, we refer to this enterprise of employing linguistic models for the analysis of nonlanguage phenomena as semiotics. The second theme is a concern with a tension between a pair of related concepts: linguistic relativity and linguistic universals. Linguistic relativity labels the notion that the language of a speaker in some way influences that person's thought. The position of its opposed concept, linguistic universals, is that there are properties common to all human languages. Although linguistic relativity and linguistic universals are opposed concepts, they are nonetheless not mutually exclusive. Linguistic relativity suggests that language actually structures or constrains human thought. Despite the assumption of unvarying properties, the theory of linguistic universals has given us concepts and methods that have been used to explain variation in human culture analogously with variation in human language, as for example, with studies that revealed structure in the many ways that different cultures have for identifying colors or other aspects of the environment, such as animal or plant life.

These two related themes—the extension of linguistic models beyond language into culture and the parallel tensions between linguistic relativity/language universals—define language and culture studies. They are evident from the earliest days of the discipline at the turn of the century and in the work of its pioneers, of whom Franz Boas and Edward Sapir are the parent figures. This book focuses on this, the core of language and culture, rather than attempting to survey the full range of related studies. Certainly those related studies offer fascinating avenues of investigation—work on language variation and other sociolinguistic topics, on historical and comparative linguistics, and on communicative competence, to mention just a few. In sum, they are often labeled linguistic anthropology, or what we might call language and culture writ large. Instead, we develop a closer view of the center of language and culture, a core heretofore not adequately identified and defined.

Anthropologists who deal with linguistic data fit into two possible overall projects: (1) linguistic anthropology, or (2) anthropological linguistics. The latter term implies the practice of linguistics (descriptive of the structure of language, how languages change over time, etc.), but with some reference to cultural concerns. The term linguistic anthropology implies an anthropological activity but one which is mainly concerned with language, primarily deals with linguistic data, or both. In truth, the two terms are of nearly overlapping use since both center on the study of language in such manner that a concern for the cultural contexts in which languages are used is primary in any assessment of the impact of culture on language description, and in theorizing about language. In this book we will use linguistic anthropology to label this area of study. For practical purposes, the following subfields and interests are in the purview of linguistic anthropology:

- origin of natural languages (not obtained via historical linguistics)
- sociolinguistics (micro, macro)

- literacy and the use of writing systems
- language and culture studies

The last field, the subject of this book, is sometimes referred to as ethnolinguistics. Sociolinguistics and literacy studies have an abundant literature, including book-length introductions. The origin of natural languages is restricted to speculation largely, but also has organic texts. Language and culture studies as a field has hitherto not been summarized in English.

Boas and his student Sapir developed what we now think of as the *Boasian program*. This plan called for the systematic investigation of a wide range of human societies and settings preliminary to formulation of a general theory of human nature and difference. It was Sapir who did much of the work of operationalizing the Boasian program. Sapir's contributions to linguistics and anthropology extended far beyond putting his mentor's plan for the study of language and culture into actuality. Boas urged description of the wide range of New World languages, proceeding from collection and study of native language texts, to be followed only later by formulation of general theories of language and culture. Both scholars came to locate language development and change in the individual (Darnell 1990:12), which in Sapir's case especially led him to a concern with language and psychology. According to Darnell (1990:12), it was their attempts to reconstruct culture history from linguistic evidence that took both Sapir and Boas back to the individual speaker/culture bearer and thereby to psychology. In doing so, both rejected overarching theories of human history as explanations, in particular the evolutionary theories of the late nineteenth and early twentieth centuries. The fact that Sapir developed ideas in language, culture, and personality is typical of the ties that language and culture studies have had with related intellectual traditions, from the humanities, social sciences, and natural sciences. Today, as in the past, language and culture studies pertain to all these styles of investigation, and the theoretical competition among them. Many of the disputes concern how individual scholars conceptualize reality, what it is they think they are investigating, measuring, or interpreting. The question is central to deciding among competing claims as to what language and culture should be because ideas about the nature and locus of reality often determine scholars' assumptions about the world as they pertain to the topics with which they concern themselves.

The definition and location of reality is a philosophical question, and theorists entertain various answers to it. Among those answers, one finds reality regarded as

1. an objective, external entity to which human thought relates;
2. the mental construction of any event or context, regardless of whether that event or context has an external existence;

3. a socially constructed and negotiated entity created in the dialogue between persons (or aspects or voices of a single person, or within a person, in response to a text, a painting, a taste, a smell, or a situation);
4. a constantly shifting creation, neither persistent nor enduring, to which an individual relates and with which the individual interacts in comprehending that reality;
5. any individual's construction or interpretation of some event or situation, i.e., a hypothesis as to the actual state of reality;
6. the sum of all such constructions or interpretations made by individuals in a society;
7. in the special case of social or cultural reality, that portion of such constructions that is shared by all individuals in a society;
8. the expression or performance of a cultural act.

Since there is no complete agreement on the nature and location of reality(ies) in language and culture studies, it follows that there is no general agreement on ways to pursue questions relating to this issue; there is no conventional approach or reigning paradigm. Of course, linguistic anthropology and anthropology are not alone in this crisis. All the social and behavioral sciences, and many of the humanities and physical and biological sciences to greater or lesser degrees, are engaged in the same controversies at present. These challenges fall under the general term of postmodernism. Some scholars feel that these problems present insurmountable barriers to achieving general understanding, but we disagree.

These controversies derive from a questioning of the enduring nature of generalizations drawn from observations, especially scientific observations, and a heightened concern with the effect of the observer on the situation observed. Especially distressing to the skeptic is the issue of how an observer may disturb the very phenomenon under investigation through her or his presence, a social version of the Heisenberg uncertainty principle in physics, as well as a concern with the locus and nature of reality itself, as indicated above. It is our view that just as physics has survived the intrinsic inability to make particle observations at the quantum level, so too will the social sciences move on to productive research within the limits developed by its more humanistic critics.

Although there are many possible and acceptable approaches to problems in language and culture, they are not without constraint; scholars demand congruence and a certain degree of replicability of their results if they are to accept them. Nor is it the case that thinkers work without concern for the findings of others, or that one idea of reality is as acceptable as another in all instances. Approaches to "reality" form a continuum, from scientific to humanistic: the nature of the tension between those poles is one of scientific "explanation" vs. humanistic "comprehension." Language and culture studies are at the center of the current debate, and they benefit from their association with the field of linguistics proper, which has a long history of entertaining insights from disparate views and competing frameworks. Thus, today's polarization presents less of a crisis in language and culture than in some other areas of anthropology. As a result, language and culture studies offer some models of integration for the discipline of anthropology as a whole.

At the end of this book, we will discuss more fully the possibility for such integration, notwithstanding the polarization that underlies these difficulties. Here, we raise the issue to alert the reader that we will be developing our own plan of exposition of these concerns later on and to underscore the vital nature of the issue to the larger intellectual community. Our principal approach to the problems presented by these competing approaches will be to discuss current formulations as they unfold in historiographic frame. This book is primarily an introduction to the core ideas of language and culture, and the organization of the volume reflects that focus. We first present a historical introduction to language and culture studies independent of the present various and intriguing current theoretical issues, tracing the intellectual history of the field. Competing claims and frameworks will be treated in the final four chapters, where we offer suggestions for their integration and present the process of integration in language and culture as a model to be considered more widely in the discipline of anthropology. That language and culture should lead in this respect seems particularly appropriate. No other enterprise so directly bears on questions of sociocultural reality as do language and culture studies, for language is mirror to the mind, culture its larger expression, and society its context for revelation. To examine these impels us toward fuller understanding of explanatory accounts, including those of reality.

In sum, the question of what constitutes reality is one that unites philosophy, the arts, and the sciences. Philosophy attempts to provide an answer through asking fundamental questions and trying to answer such questions using a rational approach. Science attempts to investigate the nature of social, cultural, and physical reality by observation, hypothesis testing, and theory building. The arts and humanities may take a more subjective approach to clarifying or defining reality because they are more expressive and emotive in their form, although they may also be philosophical (and in the case of the humanities, use systematic inquiry).

Language has long been connected with culture. The goal of linguistic anthropology is to provide methods and answers to such issues as how language and culture are related, and ways language may structure thought, the degree to which it does so, and how the structure of natural languages may be used as a model for describing other systems.

1

Language, Society, and Culture

> The clearest case [of patterning] is furnished by linguistics, easily that one of all social sciences and humanistic studies which follows the most rigorous and exact method.
>
> —A. L. Kroeber

Human beings are distinguished from other members of the animal kingdom in a number of obvious ways: humans use a wide variety of tools, and they have a strong sense of self-awareness that manifests itself in art. Further, no human group lacks music of some sort, or an ideology that explains the origin of the cosmos and human destiny. Language is interwoven with the rest of this human thought and action.

Humans are structured into groups based on kin and other factors, and each social grouping of community-size or larger has its own sets of values, beliefs and technologies for survival—its **culture**, and its own language or languages. Thus, **language** can mean both the human capacity for **communication** and the individual languages used in a particular sociocultural setting (French, English, Hopi, Thai, and so on).

A simple correlation of *language-culture-society* was the prevalent model of the human order held by the Western world until fairly recently. This scheme even went so far as to equate the language-culture-society complex with race! We will explore the language-culture-society complex through an examination of the ideas that thinkers have held about these phenomena throughout the development of the intellectual field of language and culture. As we will see, a view of the human condition that equates race with language-culture-society—while intuitively appealing for its simple and commonsensical explanation—cannot hold. Yet it is worthwhile to look at this and other outdated views of human sociocultural groupings if we are to comprehend current ideas. First, however, let us look at what "language" is in a narrower sense of the term: how **sounds** are related to **meaning**, and what characterizes the structure of spoken language (rather than its written reflection), starting with how words are organized, and how they are combined into sentences.

Language as a Self-Contained System

The phenomenon of **linguistic** diversity has long fascinated humanity, and many peoples throughout the world have a Tower of Babel myth. Speakers of a language tend to regard any unfamiliar language as being chaotic since they cannot understand it. In truth, however, every natural language involves two separate systems that interact simultaneously to produce **speech**: the **sound pattern**, and the meaning, or **semantic pattern**. We will explore each in turn.

Consider the words below. Which of them are characteristic of English? Which are not actually English words, but could be English?

bnick	click
slick	shtick
blick	grick
zrick	

The words *slick*, *click* and *shtick* all exist as words in English; the last may sound odd because it was borrowed from Yiddish as a part of New York City culture and then spread into the mainstream of North American English.

The "words" *blick* and *grick* sound like they are English, yet they do not exist as actual English words. They are what are called **lexical gaps**. That is, they fulfill all the requirements for the arrangement of English **consonants** and **vowels** into sequences that sound like English words on the model of *black* and *grip*, for example, but they have no associated meanings, or **semantics**. They are in a sense potential English words awaiting association with the meaning system.

Intuitively, there is something very different and odd about *bnick* and *zrick*. They are pronounceable; if you haven't read them aloud, try it. However, both words sound odd because they are violations of the formula: English words don't begin with *bn-* or *zr-*.

Among the acceptable clusterings of consonants that do occur at the beginning of an English word are the following clusters, with an example for each.

sp	spit	sm	smile
st	stack	spr	spring
sk	skit	str	street
sn	snap	skr	scram

Note that *skr* is often spelled as *scr*. English spelling does not always correspond neatly to the sounds represented.

We can abstract a formula for the word-initial consonant clusters given above. It might look something like this:

$$\# \text{ s} + \begin{Bmatrix} \text{p/t/k} \\ \text{m/n} \end{Bmatrix} + \text{(r)}$$

Formidable at first sight, this *rule* is just a way of generalizing about the "facts" of word-initial consonant clusters in English (# indicates here the front of the word). It condenses the information in the list of words above, and it makes a prediction about what forms native speakers will accept as sounding native-like and which sequences they will not. The formula is read as follows: All English initial consonant clusters begin with *s*; *s* may be followed by *p*, *t* or *k* (with a possible *r* after them), or it may be followed by an *m* or *n*. But wait. Not all English words that begin with a consonant cluster start with *s*.

What about such English words as *pluck*, *clam* (*kl*), *tree*, *prance*, and *crane* (*kr*-)? And how about words like *slash* and *slay* that begin with *s* but are followed not by *p*, *t*, *k*, *m*, or *n*, but by *l*? Clearly, the formula would need to be revised to account for these new facts because they also characterize acceptable English words. What we have shown is how an analyst makes a generalization (**hypothesis**) and then tests it, revising when the prediction is inadequate, and then retesting. At the same time, we might wonder why no words begin with *tl*-, even though there are words such as *battle* where the *tl* cluster appears inside the word. As the analyst works out the sound pattern of a language, he or she will note the inventory of clusters and include information on those like the English *tl* that are restricted in the positions they can assume in a word.

Although all languages have such restrictions on combinations of sounds, the specifics of the restrictions vary by language. The inventory of sounds—apart from their groupings—also may vary considerably from one language to the next. When attempting to discover the sound inventory of a language and how it patterns, language analysts describe sounds using a phonetic classification system based on the ways sounds are articulated in the vocal tract. (A version of these classification systems and the principles underlying them is introduced in Appendix I, "Phonetics.") **Phonetics** constitutes a field of study in its own right and is concerned with the sounds (called **phones**) of languages, their production, acoustic properties, and physiological correlates. Phonetics can be pursued independently from an effort to understand the sound patternings of languages, which is called **phonemics**.

To explore further the units of sound, we may also note that the sound pattern of English has two fundamental groups: its consonants and its vowels. The human vocal tract can produce many more consonants and vowels than are used in English or any other language. English only uses eleven vowels, three vowel clusters (**diphthongs**), and some thirty consonants. Consider the following words:

bit	mat	pit
kit	meet	pick
tit	mitt	pill
mitt	mate	pin
sit	moat	pig
zit	moot	ping
nit	met	piss

In the first column, there is a frame (__it) in which only the initial consonant changes. Note that the presence of each initial consonant signals a different meaning. Now look at the next two columns. Note how there is a constant frame in the second (m__t), where only the vowel varies, and in the third (pi__), where only the final consonant changes. The presence of a different vowel or consonant in the three sets signals different meanings. Their presence distinguishes between different words with different meanings; for example, *bit* and *kit* mean two different things yet the words themselves are distinguished only by having different first sounds.

If we were to look at several hundred simple English words, discounting compound words like *blackboard* or *blackbird* and loan words like *shtick* and *tsetse*, we could determine the basic set-up of the English sound pattern: (a) the set of distinctive (meaning-determining but not meaning-bearing) consonants and vowels (**phonemes**), and (b) the ways these fundamental sound units are put together into root words.

Not all languages have sound patterns identical to that of English. Many differ in the consonants and vowels they have. For example, Kabardian (spoken in the Caucasus) has only two vowels, and over sixty consonants! Languages also vary in the ways they put consonants and vowels together. Some languages, such as Japanese and Hawaiian do not allow consonant clusters at all; others, such as Bella Coola, allow very large numbers of consonants to cluster.

There is another way besides arrangements of phonemes in which languages organize sound—this is the "melody" that all spoken languages have, the **intonation**. Intonation is used to gather words together into groups (**phrases**, sentences), or to indicate the **function** of a sentence. Read the following sentences out loud.

The red one, that's the one I want.

Hector went to bed?

Hector went to bed.

Hector went to bed !!

Notice how the punctuation marks we use signal breaks in the over-all melody of the sentences, rising or falling. These melody differences also signal the function of sentences whose sequence of words are identical; in the last three sentences of the example above, the words and their sequences are identical (Hector went to bed), but the first is a question (*?*), the second a statement (.), and the third an exclamation (*!!*). The intonation system of any natural language is complex—it is sufficient here to notice that it exists as a higher level of organization than single sounds or the ways phonemes aggregate to form **syllables** or **roots**.

We may conclude this very preliminary discussion of the sound patterns of language (we have looked mainly at English) by observing that language structure is hierarchical: thus the analyst starts with small, indivisible units and creates larger and larger analytic units.

Sounds (consonants, vowels = phonemes)

MAKEUP

syllables, roots, words, which

MAKEUP

phrases, intonational groupings.

Note also that the structure of a language is not random. Each language has its own set of consonant and vowel phonemes, its own way of putting these together into syllables, roots, and words, and its own way of grouping these intonationally into phrases and sentences.

Furthermore, the sound pattern of a given language, in theory at least, is independent of the semantic (meaning) pattern of the language. There are five important sources of evidence for this: (a) existence of lexical gaps; (b) word or language games, such as Pig Latin and Double Dutch; (c) puns; (d) slips of the tongue, and (e) glossolalia. Recall that lexical gaps are nonoccurring but potential "words" in a language (like *blick* and *grick* in English); that is, they are plausible words of a language (in that they fit the rules for sound combination) but do not actually exist as conventional words. Frequently, commercial firms exploit lexical gaps in seeking names of new products or trademarks. That way, their product has a native sounding name, and the new product name is naturalized into the language as if it had always been there.

Word games (or **language games**) such as Pig Latin or Double Dutch exist in many cultures. In such games, the syllabic and root structures of words are deliberately manipulated, establishing the independence of the sound pattern. In Pig Latin, the general rule is to take the first consonant or consonant cluster of a word, move it to the end of the word and add *-ay*, e.g., *igpay atinlay* 'Pig Latin.' With a vowel-initial word, *-yay* is added to the end, e.g., *amyay* 'am.' In some dialects, *eemay* 'me' and *eebay* 'be' are routinely used in place of *iyay* 'I' and *amyay* 'am.'

Imay eebay eeking*sp*ay igpay atinlay.

I (me) be (am) *sp*eaking Pig Latin.

Note that the *sp* cluster moves as a unit to the end of the word. Sometimes, consonant clusters are split up, when the last consonant in an initial cluster is an *l* or *r*; for example, *rimpshay* 'shrimp,' or the *r* might be doubled, *ringstray* 'string.' There are many slight differences in versions of Pig Latin spoken in different regions. The interesting fact is that the sounds of the language (phonemes), not letters of the alphabet as commonly thought, are what are manipulated, revealing the sound pattern of the language; for example, one says *ouldshay* not **houldsay* for 'should.' (The * indicates that a linguistic expression is unattested, either because it violates some grammatical rubric, as is the case in this instance, or because it is a hypothetical form, as would be exemplified by the reconstruction of a historically earlier form for which there was no direct evidence, i.e., no written expression.)

Puns are another source of evidence from word play. Consider the following pun spoken by a University of Chicago professor in a lecture on the success of the institution's undergraduate college. "[T]he phoenix [symbol of the University] had to get up off its ash and start flying again" (S. M. Tave, *University of Chicago Magazine* June 1991:15). In this example, the *sh* sound, which closely resembles *s*, is substituted for the *s*, yielding a more acceptable form of a familiar expression. The pun is especially effective because, of course, the phoenix is a mythical bird believed to rise from its own ashes, so there is a **semantic**—that is, meaning—dimension at play in addition to the **phonological** one.

Syllabic structure is also accidentally manipulated to make a more familiar and socially more acceptable phenomenon: **slips of the tongue**. Classics here include the examples "Let me sew you to your sheet" (for "Let me show you to your seat"), and "tips of the slung" for the name of the phenomenon itself. These exemplify a kind of slip of the tongue known as a Spoonerism, named for W. A. Spooner (1844–1930), an English clergyman whose speech often contained such slips (one of his actual examples is "our *qu*eer old *d*ean" for "our *d*ear old *qu*een"). Since these are presumably mistakes rather than cultivated behavior (as is the case with puns), we have even more credible evidence for the separateness of the sound pattern of English from the semantic pattern, because slips of the tongue are automatic, not conscious.

Another interesting line of evidence for the separateness of the sound pattern of English from its semantic pattern is the phenomenon known as **glossolalia**: speaking in tongues. Glossolalia is an ecstatic form of prayer, usually achieved under a trance-like state. The words and other structures of glossolalia are not understandable by the congregation, but they tend to be modeled strongly on the native language of the speaker, whatever that language may be (Malony and Lovekin 1985). Despite this fact, both speaker and listeners have the impression that the glossolalic speech represents an entirely different language.

We may conclude from our limited examination of English and a few other languages that sound patterns: (a) are not random, (b) are organized in a hierarchical manner, and (c) are somewhat independent of the semantic pattern with which they are paired.

But what is a semantic pattern? The answer to this question lies in the traditional use of the term **grammar**. Consider that a speaker of English can add endings (*-s*, *-ing*, *-ed*), to **verbs** (words that express action or state of being) and so we have: *walk*, *walks*, *walking* and *walked*. Note that with some English verbs, we can also have forms in *-en* (*eat*, *eaten*; *bite*, *bitten*). Our common sense as speakers of English tells us that *-s*, *-ing*, *-ed*, and *-en* are added to verbs. Note that although we can make **adjectives** (words that express a state or condition of quality) from verbs by adding *-(a)ble* (*eat-able*, *walk-able*), we cannot then add verb **suffixes** to the resulting adjectives (**eatabling*, **walkabled*). The point is that some of the endings that are attached to English verbs modify the basic **grammatical** meaning of the verb (from present tense to past tense, for example), while others transform the verb to which they are attached into something other than a verb, in the case of *-able* from a verb to an adjective. Once a verb like *eat* has been changed into an adjective (*eatable*), it can no longer be treated as a verb; for example, have tense markings added to it. What we distinguish as a word, then, has its own internal structure.

Each language has certain characteristics that are unique to that language. At the same time, there is a limit to the variation among languages. **Constraints** on what is possible in the grammar of a human language, and the similarities among languages, are the **linguistic universals** that help to define human language. Nonetheless, the range of variation in languages is very great. Some of the ways languages vary are outlined in table 1.

Languages differ in the ways they map information onto forms that the sound pattern has provided. Compare the Spanish verbs below with their English counterparts.

Singular		**Plural**	
habl-o	'I speak'	habl-amos	'we speak'
(habl-as	'you speak'	habl-an	you/they speak'
habl-a	'she/he speak'		

Where Spanish uses suffixes, English uses separate words. Yet the information is the same.

Table 1. Some Ways Languages Differ

	Sounds	**Words**	**Classes**
Inventory of Units	Kinds of phonemes	Words and parts of words	Specific constructions
Arrangement	Permitted sequence of phonemes	Internal arrangement of parts of words (e.g., *kindly* not **lykind*)	Word order
Meaning	Intonation	Word meaning	Kinds of sentences (e.g., question command, declaration)

Formerly, English used to have a system for marking present tense that was similar to that of Spanish.

Singular	**Plural**
I speak-e	we speak-en
thou speak-est	ye speak-en
she/he speak-eth	they speak-en

Something like this would have been current in London speech in 1300. However, this older English example only partly resembles the Spanish one. The **plural** (more than one person) forms are all the same; the hearer must use pronouns as clues to identify the subject, whereas in Spanish the verb word carries the distinct personal pronoun information for the first **person** plural as well as the **singular** (one person) forms. Now we may turn to an even more dramatic example. Look at the example below (Boas 1911:25) and see if you can analyze it as easily as the two examples immediately above.

a - n - i - a - l - o - t

present tense I him her to away give

What does this single word mean in English? The language is Chinook, and the gloss is 'I give him to her'. Notice that every word in the English analysis is represented as a single sound in the Chinook word.

Another example (Sapir 1921:70) from Chinook reinforces the idea that languages can vary strongly in grammatical structure.

```
            i - n - i - a - l - u - d - am
           /   \  |  /   /   \    \     \
past tense I it her to away  give go to
```

The meaning of the second Chinook "sentence" is 'I came to give it away to her'. The *l* marker in both examples signals that the preceding *a*, 'her,' is the **indirect object** (to her)—the recipient of the **direct object** "it'—not the direct object, which is the immediate affectee of the action of the verb. How can human languages be so different in their semantic structure? This question has intrigued scholars at least since the 1700s.

Think back on what we said about sound patterns. English uses combinations of its consonant and vowel phonemes called **words** to express what Chinook expresses in a single string of consonants and vowels, in a single word which is also a sentence. The disparity is startling. **Anthropological linguistics** tries to answer the question of how human languages can differ so much, when we are all endowed with the same neurological equipment. The result of this way of looking at language—and it is not an exclusive view—is that language is seen as a pervasive pattern for other aspects of culture. Models of human behavior that have been developed from **linguistics** have come to be applied to other aspects of culture. Since linguistics was formerly an almost exclusively anthropological enterprise, one can well imagine that scholars with such broad interest in human custom would be drawn to associate linguistic and cultural phenomena according to a single account.

Every language has as the basis of its vocabulary a set of semantic primes called morphemes. **Morphemes** are the smallest units of meaning in a language. For example, the notion 'give' in English is expressed by *-d* or *-t* in Chinook, by *maqa* in Hopi, dat^{y} in Russian, and *ha:'awi* in Hawaiian. Some of these morphemes are a single consonant; others are a sequence of consonants and vowels arranged according to the sound pattern of the particular language. Words (defined by the sound pattern according to primary accent and timing), consist of one or more morphemes. Consider the following English words: *give*, *thank-ful-ly*, *anti-dis-establish-ment-ar(y)-ian-ism*. (The dashes are used to separate morphemes.) The morphemes that make up these words cannot be further divided into meaningful parts.

The semantic system of a language consists of a set of basic semantic units (morphemes) and ways of combining these primary elements into words, phrases, and sentences (according to a set of syntactic requirements). The semantic pattern, like the sound pattern, has a set of fundamental elements and ways of combining them hierarchically into units of increasing complexity.

This unusual sort of communication system, which distinguishes humanity from other animal species by virtue of its complexity, is cogently captured in the phrase duality of patterning, a way of conceptualizing the nature of human language. According to **duality of patterning**, independent elements within one system are building block units in a neighboring system. So a phoneme, an independent element of the sound system of a language, is itself an ingredient of a morpheme, the relevant unit of the semantic system; morphemes are composed of phonemes. It is interesting that both patterns are used at the same time: when one speaks a human language, two complex (and largely unconscious!) systems are being simultaneously intermeshed.

Up to now we have concerned ourselves almost exclusively with language. Now let us examine what is meant by the twin terms culture and society. For now, we will content ourselves with a simplistic view of these two terms.

Language in Relation to Culture and Society

Our English word "culture," comes from Latin *cultura*, 'cultivation, agricultural field.' The idea is that human beliefs (as opposed to the organizations of humans that articulate them in a given social group) form a basis for everyday behavior. (This refers to automatic, unconscious behavior.) The description of cultures is called **ethnography**.

Consider the biological family. It is universal: one must have parents and may have siblings. Yet the resultant social relationships are named differently in different human groups, and actual behaviors vary accordingly. There are three main kinds of kinship naming-behaviors: bilateral (like our own), patrilineal, and matrilineal. In a matrilineal system, one belongs primarily to one's mother's family; in a patrilineal system to the father's. In most Anglo-American kinship systems, one belongs to both one's mother's and one's father's families. Even though the association to the father's family may be somewhat stronger (or more persistent), since we traditionally take family names from our fathers, we nonetheless consider all members of both parents' families equivalently related. An "aunt" on mother's side is no more or less close to us than an "aunt" on father's side. Cousins on both sides are considered to have the same relationships to us; for example, often it is considered inappropriate to marry a cousin regardless of which side the cousin comes from. Such a kinship system as ours is called bilateral since the relationships are symmetrical on both sides of the family.

Behavior often varies accordingly. For example, in a matrilineal system one might be prohibited from marrying cousins on mother's side of the family—especially children of mother's sisters since those persons are members of one's own family. They may even be called by the same terms one uses for one's siblings. At the same time, one's cousins in father's family are not related to one in the same way as mother's relatives and may be regarded as preferred marriage mates. In matrilineal systems of kinship, mother's sisters may be called by a term that is the same or a variant of "mother" since the core meaning will be "woman member of my family in the next elder generation," whereas father's sister will be distinguished by a term that means something more like "female member of my father's family in the next elder generation." In patrilineal systems, such situations are reversed since one belongs to one's father's family but not to one's mother's.

Perhaps the most famous definition of culture is the following by one of the founders of **anthropology**, Edward B. Tyler. Culture, in his words, is "that complex whole which includes knowledge, belief, art, morals, law, custom, and any other capabilities and habits acquired by man as a member of society" (1871:1). A culture, then, is also shared and learned knowledge. A **society** is the actual grouping or array of humans that share the same large body of belief and knowledge. The actual organization of these persons is a **social** problem. The behavior directed towards fathers or mothers or their relatives in a culture, esthetic beliefs about them, and the symbolic values of their roles are **cultural** rather than social.

Not all aspects of a culture are shared equally, however. In every human society, specialized knowledge is a power base: the adults know more than the young, the initiated know more than the novices. Language is also shared unequally in a given society, as part of that society's culture. Adults lack current teenage slang or the **folklore** of childhood, lay persons are excluded by the jargons of various occupations, people from different geographic areas and classes may be expected to differ somewhat in their use of the same language.

The study of the systematic relations of language and social groups is called **sociolinguistics**, which relates language(s) and varieties of a single language to communities of language users (**speech communities**) or smaller groups (networks). The **linguistic repertory** of a speech community is seen as consisting of one or more distinct linguistic varieties associated with social grouping by class, gender, residence, occupation, age, region, and so on, making up multilingual and multidialectal communities. (**Dialects** are mutually intelligible varieties of a language.) Moreover, each linguistic variety used within a speech community has numerous styles; that is, there are ways of using a given variety according to such factors as politeness (neutral, casual, rude, polite), gender (male, female), age (child, teenager, adult, old person), occupation (Dr. Jones, Father Williams), and so on. Study of the use of language in actual **contexts** (the sociocultural as well as linguistic environments in which communication events take place) according to such factors as politeness, gender, and age is called the **ethnography of speaking**. Excellent introductions to sociolinguistics and the ethnography of speaking include, among others, Trudgill (1974), Labov (1973), Hymes (1964), Saville-Troike (1982), and Gumperz (1982).

A member of a speech community will belong to several of its networks and will vary his or her speech according to setting, time, status, or role of speaker and addressee. The analysis of conversation or other forms of discourse helps to illuminate what makes up each speaker's **communicative competence**: Not only must a member of a speech community know the sound pattern and semantic pattern of each of the community's languages, he or she must know how to use language appropriately within that society.

This conception of language differs markedly from the autonomous view traditionally held by theoretical **generative** linguists (see chapter 7). The **autonomous** view (that language may be exactly and neatly analyzed apart from considerations of use and sociocultural context) is reflected in a well-known (and often cited) quotation from Noam Chomsky (1965:3): "Linguistic theory is concerned primarily with an ideal speaker-listener, in a completely homogeneous speech-community, who also knows its language perfectly. . . . " This position has been strongly criticized by sociolinguists (Hymes 1971, Labov 1973). Although it is necessary to isolate the sound pattern and semantic pattern of each linguistic **code** (system for conveying messages) in order to produce a description of each code (a grammar), it is also necessary to take communicative competence into account if one is to understand the use of the language as well as its structure.

The autonomous view of linguistic abilities is idealized; it assumes that language exists in a vacuum, and it avoids sociocultural contextual meaning (the issue of language in context is discussed at length in chapter 7). It is worthwhile to note how meaning is intimately linked to the use of linguistic knowledge. Read the following situation and text. What does this single utterance reveal about linguistic knowledge?

situation: (sportscaster comment, Superbowl)
utterance: "You have to be possessed of a strong arm."

The vocabulary item *be possessed of* implies a personal, nonacquired quality. In the following examples, the question mark (?) indicates a sentence that might be questioned by a native speaker as less than natural; recall that the asterisk (*) indicates a sentence that a native speaker would not accept.

He is possessed of a sound mind.
?He is possessed of a strong arm.
*He is possessed of a lot of money.

In these isolated examples, *sound mind* works well because it is a characteristic of an entire human organism. The example *a strong arm* is an inherent part of the human body (*money* is not). The arm, however, does not seem characteristic of the whole organism, but it works well in the sports example above because the speaker is asserting the importance of the quality for the activity of football. This single example shows how actual use of linguistic knowledge depends both on context and on **linguistic categories**. Both contexts and the categories that occur in them are the central data of **language and culture studies**. Linguistic data are inseparable from context and the problem of selecting appropriate linguistic categories to code reality. By ignoring the problem of context, **autonomous linguistics** (the position that language is not related to culture or society) attempts to avoid complexity, and in so doing it often has produced examples that have been vulnerable to the criticism of being artificially constructed or underexemplified. The controversies surrounding the goals of autonomous linguistics are discussed at length in Newmeyer's *The Politics of Linguistics* (1986; especially chapters 5 and 6).

Our task here is to consider the relationship of the linguistic system of a social group with other cultural systems and to examine the use of models of language as models of culture. A full investigation of sociolinguistics and the **ethnography of communication** falls outside that goal. Nonetheless, social aspects of language use are important to our enterprise and will be drawn on from time to time. Culture as shared-and-learned knowledge may be seen as subsystems of knowledge (kinship, social organization, legal systems, medical practices, music, and so on), as well as the fundamental set of beliefs and commensurate values that interrelate the whole. There may be integration of belief(s)-value(s) with these more formal subsystems; for example, a myth may assign political superiority to patrilineal or matrilineal descent. Such an ideal will be reflected in kinship and social organization, as well as in symbolic action rituals. As such, comparing the sound pattern and semantic pattern of a sociocultural group's language is different from a direct comparison of either of these language subsystems with the group's kinship pattern, religious pattern, and so on, in that the latter are more nearly products of complex integrations, the primary elements of which are much more difficult to define.

Caveat Emptor

In any of the social sciences, a person is confronted with several traditional dilemmas: the psychological reality of social phenomena, the problem of predictability, and the nature of **normative** behavior. It is difficult to study things that are stored in the human memory. How do we know what people really know? The answer is not necessarily to equate culture and language with behavior. We can observe language and other behavior, but **norms** are an analytic outcome of these observations. They are one of several kinds of generalizations one can make about observed behavior. They may be thought of as hypotheses about behavior. Such cultural and linguistic generalizations may be inferred from statistical patterning of events within a definable group.

The systematic investigation of a phenomenon in order to derive theories to predict novel instances is the heart of the **scientific** endeavor. In applying the concept of science to social phenomena, one realizes that it is impossible to predict how a given individual will actually behave in a given situation. The remedy here is to consider a cultural or linguistic description valid if it predicts behavior that is accepted by natives as normal. We cannot reliably say exactly what a person will do or say in a given instance, but we can make formal definitions of the range of acceptable behavior for some situations. Furthermore, we can attempt to formulate a definition of the **strategies** by which individuals create and innovate behavior. Clearly, one does not produce identical behaviors in response to a particular action, just as one does not give set answers to questions (exempting, of course, ritualized exchanges, such as meetings and greetings: "How are you?" "Fine! How are you?", etc.). What we do, however, is cobble together appropriate actions into larger action expressions, linguistic and otherwise, from a ready repertoire, responses that are appropriate, that are sometimes novel and that incorporate our immediate and more distant experiences. It is as though what is psychologically most relevant is the fact we seem to have **rules** (strategies) for creating appropriate behavior on the fly, so to speak, rules of creation or production rather than rules that either label particular kinds of behavior in particular contexts as acceptable (that is, give a formal account of the system), or produce specific behaviors in particular contexts. (See chapter 8 for a further discussion of rules and strategies.)

Thinking along these lines, we can imagine that an individual in a human group must know the culture of that group to get along in it. Yet, does that single person know *all* the culture of that group? Or, a part of it only? Is it in that individual where a culture resides? The problem of the individual as the locus of culture versus the idea of shared norms is a conundrum: Is language or culture a single, monolithic entity that is shared by all members of a society or speech community? Which point of view is more satisfactory, the individual or the collective?

> Because each individual creates his own version of what he understands the languages of his fellows to be, the degree to which his version approximates their individual versions must depend, aside from his own aptitude for learning, on the opportunities he has for discovering significant differences in his and his fellows' speech. (Goodenough 1981:36)

> Because language learning is a process of imperfectly approximating rather than perfectly duplicating the speech of others, there are bound to be competing forms, competing styles of pronunciation, and competing patterns of semantic and symbolic usage within what is perceived as a single continuing, local language tradition. (Goodenough 1981:39)

The same remarks could be made about culture learning and culture sharing. One solution is Ervin-Tripp's suggestion (1967) that people behave as if they were following rules (generalizations about behavior) with the possibility of social and cultural constraints on such generalizations. Studies conducted in the fields of **cultural anthropology** and linguistics sometimes concentrate on the individual as a reflection of culture (biography, autobiography, longitudinal studies), but they most often focus on the beliefs or norms of a group, however imperfectly these are shared. Nonetheless, the role of the individual as creator of observed behaviors is a persistent concern in the social sciences. The integration of individual within the whole underlies much stimulating thinking.

The problems of **epistemology** (the nature of knowledge and how we know what we know) in the social sciences alert the reader to the nature of making systematic inquiry into the obviously complex relationships between language and social structures (sociolinguistics) and language and cultures (language and culture studies). Having outlined the complexity of the structures of natural languages and of how they relate to social structure, we can now turn to the central problem of the book: language and culture studies. We examine the linguistic thought of Franz Boas (1858–1942), one of the founders of the discipline of modern anthropology, and of persons influenced by him, especially Edward Sapir (1884–1939), who was both the chief interpreter and executor for Boas' intellectual program, and one of the people who shaped **linguistic anthropology** (sometimes referred to as **ethnolinguistics**) as we know it today. Deciding the locus of culture and language was as much a problem at the time of the origins of language and culture studies as now, and it is important that both Sapir and Boas eventually resolved the controversy about the locus of language in favor of the individual, situating language development and change in the individual (Darnell 1990:12). Sapir, at least, saw culture as an individually situated entity as well.

Summary

Every human language uses a certain number of vowel and consonant phonemes which are combined to make up syllables according to the syllable formula(s) of the language. Intonational patterns are the next higher level of the sound pattern.

Syllables (and single phonemes, in some languages) are used to make up morphemes. Morphemes include roots, prefixes, and suffixes, which are used to make words, which in turn make up phrases or sentences. Morphemes and higher order combinations of morphemes make up the meaning or semantic pattern of a language.

Languages can vary in an infinite number of ways, which represents a way of looking at human language called *linguistic particularism* (see chapter 2). Cultures also vary in an almost bewildering number of ways, thus cultures may also be seen from the point of view of **particularism**. The idea that each culture is valid, despite being idiosyncratic, is called *cultural relativism. Linguistic relativism*, however, means something slightly different which is the topic of the next few chapters.

Both languages and cultures are systematic to a large degree, and are thus observable and describable. Human societies are also organized, observable, and describable. The systematic description of language is called linguistics. The description of cultures is called ethnography, which is itself the subject matter of cultural anthropology.

The description of phenomena such as language, culture, and social organization thus depends on normative behavior. This view of social phenomena tends to see language and culture as collective, rather than the property of individuals. Yet, the view that the individual is the locus of language and culture is equally valid.

Discussion and Activities

1. The following English words repeat part or all of the word in the second half. This is called **reduplication**. Sort through the words, trying to describe what the function or functions of reduplication is/are in English. Imagine you are tutoring someone from another country who presents you with these data and asks you as a native or fluent speaker to help in making sense of them.

so-so	teeny-tiny
hush-hush	itsy-bitsy
mishmash	betwixt and between
helter-skelter	wiggle-waggle
namby-pamby	gangbang
yackety-yack	she-she
fiddle-faddle	walkie-talkie
tutti-frutti	gew-gaw
tick-tock	hocus-pocus
tiptop	zigzag
froo-froo	muckety-muck
ho-hum	yin-yang
wishy-washy	criss-cross
see-saw	raggle-taggle
rat-a tat-tat	din-din
goody-goody	pooh-pooh

Is a unified account of reduplication possible in English? Is reduplication a single category in the language?

2. Read through the following list of words. What do they have in common?

snub	snout
snit	snoop
sneer	snot
snap	snack
snarl	

What meaning can you assign to *sn*-? Linguists have traditionally considered any meaningful partial in English of a size less than a syllable to be a **phonaestheme.** What does the phonaestheme in the list of words mean?

Now look at the following list of words. Do they have the same phonaestheme as the words above?

snare	snooze
snatch	snuff
sneek	snug
snitch	snow

Is there only one *sn*- phonaestheme in English, or several? Now look at the following list of words that begin with *sm*-.

smack
smile
smell
smirk
smart
smother
smash
small
smoke
smut
smuggle
smooth
smite
smear
smarm

How many phonaesthemes are there in this list? What is the meaning (of each)?

What sort of categories are English phonaesthemes? What do they tell you about **reality** as it is comprehended by speakers of English?

3. What is meant by duality of patterning? Can you think of systems other than language that are structured with duality of patterning?
4. Do language, culture, and society tend to co-occur? That is, does each distinct human society have its own distinctive culture and language? There are examples of this model, as well as notable exceptions.
5. Will all the speakers of the same language share enough common culture to foster peaceful and cooperative relations between all speakers of that language?

Key Terms

anthropological linguistics
adjectives
anthropology
autonomous
autonomous linguistics
code
communication
communicative competence
consonants
constraints
contexts
cultural
cultural anthropology
culture
dialects
diphthongs
direct object
duality of patterning
epistemology
ethnography
ethnography of communication
ethnography of speaking
ethnolinguistics
folklore
function
generative
grammar
grammatical
glossolalia
hypothesis
indirect object
intonation
language
language and culture studies

language games
lexical gaps
linguistic
linguistic anthropology
linguistic categories
linguistic repertory
linguistic universals
linguistics
meaning
morphemes
norms
normative
particularism
person
phonaestheme
phones
phonetics
phonemes
phonemics
phonological
phrases
plural
puns
reality
reduplication
roots
rules
scientific
semantic
semantic pattern
semantics
singular
slips of the tongue
social
society
sociolinguistics
sound pattern
sounds
speech
speech communities
strategies
suffixes
syllables
verbs
vowels
word games
words

2

Linguistic Particularism and Its Outgrowths

> Judging the importance of linguistic studies from this point of view, it seems well worth while to subject the whole range of linguistic concepts to a searching analysis, and to seek in the peculiarities of the grouping of ideas in different languages an important characteristic in the history of the mental development of the various branches of mankind. From this point of view, the occurrence of the most fundamental grammatical concepts in all languages must be considered as proof of the unity of fundamental psychological processes.
>
> —Franz Boas

Franz Boas, one of the founders of North American and world anthropology, came to the study of human beings from the natural sciences. Trained in physics, optics, and geography, his dissertation was on the color of sea water. His Arctic interests won him a place on an expedition to Baffin Land, where he encountered Eskimos and became interested in their culture. By the 1890s, he had immersed himself in the study of the cultures and languages of peoples of the Arctic and Pacific Northwest. His linguistic interests led him to train scholars systematically to study language scientifically in the field, along with other types of anthropological observation, and through the influence of his students, he shaped the character of North American anthropology. By 1908, he had brought together a collection of grammars of Native American languages that was published in 1911 as the *Handbook of American Indian Languages*. The "Introduction" to this work served as an introduction to linguistics and linguistic anthropology for several generations of students and remains an important source for linguistic anthropology today.

Culture and Its Relation(s) to Language

Culture usually has little direct connection with the sound pattern of a given language. Recall that the structure created by a sound pattern is used to convey meaning through the arrangements of phonemes. The sound pattern of a language is a vehicle for conveying information about something other than sound; it conveys meaning. Since culture consists of ideas, beliefs, and concepts, the content of culture is less likely to be connected to the sound pattern of a language than it is to its semantic pattern (its **vocabulary** and **syntax**—the latter being the way of arranging morphemes into phrases or sentences). Suppose a language has the category of dual (two persons) in addition to singular and plural. Pronouns, nouns, verbs and even adjectives might be marked in some way to show that one (singular), two (dual), or three or more (plural) things are being talked about. If coding these categories (singular/dual/plural) on the verb were obligatory, then one might expect that category of number could have some symbolic meaning in the culture where the language was used, although this would not automatically follow. The question of how or whether grammatical categories like number interface with cultural categories is an open one.

Vocabulary is the area of language having the most direct connection with other cultural systems. So intuitively aligned is vocabulary with culture that vocabulary lists have formed the entire approach of language maintenance and renewal programs in some American Indian communities where English is replacing the native language. Under this "language and culture" approach, culturally important vocabulary in the native language is taught to classes, with the grammar being largely ignored. Some typically relevant **domains** include names in the native language for items of material culture important to old lifeways, religious articles and concepts, personal names and clan names, environmental characteristics important to traditional subsistence, and so forth (Eastman 1979a, 1979b; Palmer 1988).

The equation of words with culture is intuitive: If a concept or category is important in a culture, then it probably is named, and this is the task of the vocabulary. Certain aspects of social environment (kinship and other modes of social organization) and physical environment have obvious relations to certain sets (domains) of related vocabulary items. The classic example here is the set of Eskimo words for 'snow.' Boas (1911:21–22) gives four different words for 'snow':

aput	'snow on the ground'
qana	'falling snow'
piasirpoq	'drifting snow'
qimuqsuq	'a snow drift'

His intent was to show how different aspects of the same phenomenon could be coded as different words in the same language. Popularization of his example, however, became anthropological folklore, and eventually general folklore, due to the popular equation of words with culture. Many secondary sources advise their readers that Eskimos have "many" or even hundreds of snow words (Martin 1986). Ironically, Eskimo and English are actually parallel in how they code 'snow.' Martin shows that the West Greenlandic Eskimo language has a more limited number of root words for 'snow':

> In West Greenlandic [Eskimo], these roots are *qanik* 'snow in the air; snowflake' and *aput* 'snow (on the ground)' (Schultz-Lorentzen 1927; cf. Boas's data). Other varieties have cognate forms. Thus, Eskimo has about as much differentiation as English does for 'snow' at the monolexemic level: snow and flake. That these roots and others may be modified to reflect semantic distinctions not present in English is a result of gross features of Eskimo morphology and syntax and not of lexicon. Any consequences that those grammatical differences may have for perception or cognition remain undocumented. (Martin 1986:422, n.2)

In a discussion of Martin's paper, Pullum (1989b) further reviews the persistence of such misrepresentations and the irresponsibility of "experts" in their dissemination.

Snow is, of course, a very important factor in Eskimo life, and is reflected in grammatical modifications to basic vocabulary, but not in an astronomical number of morphemes for 'snow.' English, on the other hand, also augments its two basic vocabulary distinctions (*snow* and *flake*) with a word stock which skiers cultivate in pursuit of their sport (*powder*, *corn*, *crud*, *bullet-proof*, *crust*, *death cookies*, *champaign powder*, *machine tilled*, *ball-bearings*, *sugar*, *corduroy*, etc.); all are metaphoric extensions rather than basic lexical forms. There are nonetheless a number of domains (kinship, numerals, colors, flora, fauna), where the relation between language (vocabulary) and culture can be investigated methodically and in depth, even over time, as in studies of the environment or homelands of prehistoric peoples conducted through study of surviving vocabularies in the languages that descend from that of the earlier group. (This relation of vocabulary with culture, both at a single time and over time, is the subject of the next two chapters.)

The Origins of Linguistic Particularism

We begin here with an examination of Boas's program of linguistics in anthropology. For Boas, language was a complex comprised of sounds that were combined into "groups of ideas."

> From what has been said it appears that, in an objective discussion of languages, three points have to be considered: first, the constituent phonetic elements of the language; second, the groups of ideas expressed by phonetic groups; third, the methods of combining and modifying phonetic groups. (Boas 1911:35 [1966:31])

Although Boas didn't have the idea of duality of patterning, it is clear from this statement that he analyzed languages hierarchically in levels: the sets of consonants and vowels (phonemes), the set of ideas expressed by arrangements of phonetic elements (the language's set of morphemes), the way of combining morphemes (syntax). Although he lacked the terms phoneme and morpheme, it is clear that he had worked out these ideas as concepts.

Boas was startled by the differences in linguistic structure between English and the Native American languages he studied. Recall that sometimes every consonant and vowel in a Chinook word may correspond to a whole word in English. Careful examination of many aboriginal languages led Boas to the doctrine of **linguistic particularism.**

> It seemed particularly desirable to call attention . . . to the essential features of the morphology [word structure] and phonetics of American languages. . . . [K]nowledge of [their structure] has been obscured by the innumerable attempts to represent the grammars of Indian languages in a form analogous to that of the European grammars. (Boas 1911:v)

Each language, then, is particular or unique in its structure. Although Boas is now noted chiefly for championing particularism, it must be borne in mind that he was interested in uncovering **universals** of human language as well. In fact he used the Eskimo snow example not to illustrate a difference between English and Eskimo but to point out a similarity between the two (Martin, 1986:418). Boas's general position on similarities is characterized by the following statement: "[T]he occurrence of the most fundamental grammatical concepts in all languages must be considered a proof of the unity of fundamental psychological processes" (1911:71 [1966:67]). Moreover, some concepts were bound to be in any given culture, as Boas indicated when he wrote that particular groups of concepts could be expected in particular language families. "The characteristic grouping of concepts in American languages will be treated more fully in the discussion of the single linguistic stocks [i.e., families]" (1911:71 [1966:67]). He considered that some linguistically coded concepts could be characteristic of the cultural traditions of a geographic area (North American languages as opposed to Australian ones, for example), and that still other linguistically coded concepts were peculiar to single languages or to particular language families.

For Boas, the structure of a language reflected **psychological reality**. That is, facts about the structure of a language indicated the basic tools of thought. The purpose of the *Handbook*'s introduction was "to describe as clearly as possible those psychological principles of each language which may be isolated by an analysis of grammatical forms" (1911:v). Language was considered an especially good reflection of the cultural reality of native concepts because it is largely unconscious. According to Boas, "[L]inguistic phenomena never rise into the consciousness of primitive man, while all other ethnological phenomena are more or less clearly subjects of conscious thought" (1911:63 [1966:59]). Obviously, a language could not possibly encode every single aspect of the social, physical, and psychological environments of a human community. Such a vocabulary would be impossibly large. Instead, every language linguistically encodes "chaotic reality" in a unique way. "[E]ach language has a peculiar tendency to select this or that aspect of the mental image which is conveyed by the expression of the thought" (1911:43 [1966:39]).

The set of morphemes of a given language (for Boas, "distinctive phonetic groups"), constitutes a basic classification of reality. "Thus it happens that each language, from the point of view of another language, may be arbitrary in its classifications; that what appears as a single simple idea in one language may be characterized by a series of distinct phonetic groups [morphemes] in another" (1911:26 [1966:22]). It would be impossible to make up separate roots for everything encountered in the real world. Only a small set of concepts will be linguistically encoded as morphemes. In order to conceptualize those aspects of reality not named by the lexical primes or conveyed by the grammatical primes, combinations of morphemes, whether compounds (*black-bird*, *black-board*) or derivations (*human-ity*, *complex-ity*, *nice-ity*), serve to create an open-ended set of names for events, states, and entities in the real world. Because the vocabulary of a living language (its **lexicon**) is potentially infinite, interest in linguistic particularism was mostly confined to how languages differed in core grammar (the essential grammatical categories) and basic terms (nouns, verbs, adverbs, and adjectives that are **monomorphemic**, i.e., made up of a single morpheme). It is through core grammar and basic vocabulary that Boas sought to discover deeper psychological categories.

The Boasian Program—Boas and Sapir

As Boas became better acquainted with the rich linguistic and cultural resources on the North American continent, he responded to the diversity he encountered with a program for both examining that variety and documenting those societies which in the late nineteenth century were undergoing radical changes due to increased pressure from European domination. The result was Boas's plan for a salvage linguistics of American Indian languages and a salvage recording of the diverse cultures of the continent. He saw the two efforts as intertwined. A basic tenet of his program was the need to approach a culture through the language of its people, not through translation via an alien language. This doctrine put a burden of language learning and analysis on all fieldworkers, not just linguists. It led to two important substantive results: a host of grammars of American Indian languages and the accumulation of countless culturally relevant texts in these languages. In addition, it assured that novice fieldworkers were trained in linguistic methods, even if their interests lay in other areas of anthropology, a fact that encouraged interdisciplinary sharing between linguistics and anthropology and contributed to the uniquely North American character of the anthropological enterprise as it developed.

With his insistence on the requirement that a culture be studied via texts in its native language, and his concern for the particular grammatical categories in each Native American language, Boas behaved in a manner consistent with his training in natural science. He saw ethnological study as a part of geography, which he called "cosmography" after Von Humboldt. This he set apart from "physical science" (for example, geology, meteorology, and even psychology), which he saw as cumulative and admitting of lawlike statements. Cosmography, on the other hand, involved description of particular phenomena in ways that reached "for the subjective and experiential truth of the individual phenomenon" (Silverstein 1986:69) apart from its place in a system. Thus, from its earliest days, anthropology was situated as an enterprise engaged in study "springing from an affective impulse that puts it close to art" (1986:69). In his concern with faithful renderings of individual cultures through their native language texts, Boas set anthropology on a course of interest in the possible relations holding between language and culture.

Boas held the first chair of anthropology and ethnology at Columbia University and created there the first program for training anthropologists. Through that position, he saw the creation of the first generation of professional anthropologists in the United States, persons of enormous importance to the developing discipline, such as A. L. Kroeber, Margaret Mead, Ruth Benedict, Ruth Bunzel, Ralph Linton, Leslie Spier, Robert

Lowie, and most importantly Edward Sapir. Boas also was in a position to initiate an overall plan for anthropology through these students. Always a forceful father figure to his students, he deployed them to pursue studies of interest to larger issues that fit within his program, and he influenced their later placement in the emerging profession. Unquestionably, Boas was the organizational leader of American Indian linguistics, as well as anthropology, but it was his student Edward Sapir who developed into its theoretician, and eventually became the interpreter of Boasian particularism.

Sapir's vision eventually surpassed that of Boas in the creation of North American linguistics. Although always concerned with culture and cultural issues, Sapir's primary concern lay with linguistic study. As such, over the years, he tended to pull North American linguistics more uncompromisingly toward its establishment as an autonomous enterprise distinct from anthropology. The tension persists today in the discipline, as for example in the ongoing controversy over whether the annual Conference on American Indian Languages should meet with the American Anthropological Association or should convene with the Linguistic Society of America. Even early in the conduct of their collaborations, Sapir differed with Boas over important topics. When Boas planned for the *Handbook* and its succeeding volumes to present brief grammatical treatments of American Indian languages that would be accessible to nonexperts, Sapir found the format too restrictive and insisted on larger treatments (Darnell 1990:22). When he was working on his Takelma grammar, Sapir began to formalize his ideas about the importance of a native speaker's intuitions, through his concept of "pseudo-sounds" (a precursor of the concept of the phoneme), and came to give greater and greater weight to the validity of a single speaker's grammatical system, because for him, the individual (as a psychological entity) was the locus of grammar. Boas, on the other hand, thought that the grammar of the individual was a distortion and sought a single grammar that represented the shared knowledge of all speakers. This fundamental difference of opinion signaled the start of Boas's and Sapir's intellectual divergence over the next 20 years, although it is important to realize that the two collaborated and shared major goals, even though they disagreed about particular conceptualizations. Furthermore, they continued to influence one another's ideas.

Trained in Germanic languages and literatures, Sapir carried out an Indo-European tradition in American Indian linguistics, although he accepted the Boasian ideal of the centrality of the text for linguistic analysis. Sapir's *Language*, written in 1921, was a Boasian paradigm statement for language study (Darnell 1990:96–98), and once he had made Boas's approach better known through it, Sapir urged Boas to make his own statement of general ideas, especially those on culture, history, and psychology. For his part, Sapir contended that language was inseparable from thought and gave as much importance to style and literature as he did to aspects of language that were more traditionally associated with natural science, what Sapir would have called "conceptual science." Nonetheless, the framework in which Sapir worked was "an exemplar of the specifically Boasian historicist and cosmographical point of view, down to the very descriptive tools—the 'concepts . . . taken out of the quarry of conceptual science'" (Silverstein 1986:71). Indeed, even his form of argumentation was Boasian, and his work in the descriptivist tradition of Boas. Sapir is often considered the greatest descriptive and synchronic linguist of the century. Thus, even as Sapir critiqued and refined the Boasian program, none surpassed him in either the speed or number of superbly executed grammars of American Indian languages conducted according to Boasian ideals of description.

To appreciate how Sapir actually put linguistic particularism into practice in North American linguistics, let us look at the evolution of the concept of "sound patterning." The concept originated with Boas in an 1889 paper in which he mentioned that speakers tended to hear a second language through the phonetic patterns of their first language. Over the next several years, Sapir elaborated on this idea, giving it specific reference to the individual's psychological conception of the sound system. In *Language* (1921), he spoke of it as an "unconscious sound pattern" (174). In succeeding years, he further worked out the specifics of the idea of the phonemic principle, culminating in his claims of psychological reality for the phoneme (1933). Thus we can see something suggested by Boas, being developed, grounded, and given theoretical integrity by Sapir.

Sapir and Boas grappled with the position of linguistic and cultural study vis-à-vis the scientific/historical **continuum** (roughly corresponding to today's scientific/humanistic continuum). They agreed on locating both language and culture as individual, psychological phenomena, but whereas Boas tended to approach the study of American Indian languages and cultures from a natural science frame, Sapir leaned more and more toward what we would think of as **humanistic** approaches. His position on the locus of culture and the consequent implications for its study became sharpened in a response he wrote in 1917 to A. L. Kroeber's paper, "The Superorganic" (1917), and an exchange of letters he had with Kroeber in the same year on the issue. Kroeber had argued, in opposition to both Boas and Sapir, for a view of culture as an entity apart from any of its culture bearers, something with a character, history, and trajectory of its own, independent of the people characterized by it. It appears that both Kroeber and Sapir were in agreement on the role of particular intellectual approaches to the study of culture; for example, that psychological study need be separated, and in fact, much of the investigative work of both men was historical (i.e., humanistic). Kroeber wrote in a November 4, 1917, letter to Sapir, ". . . it's a safe bet that my actual work will always be literature" (Golla 1984:260). Nonetheless, they disagreed on the nature of the culture each studied, whether it was external to the society and its individuals (Kroeber's view) or situated within the individual psyche (Sapir's and Boas's view).

The Boasian program for the study of culture took the native language of a culture as the primary source for cultural data. Beyond this practical consideration of language, which produced the "Introduction" to the *Handbook* and the theoretical constructs of the phoneme (the "phonetic elements" most significant to a native speaker) and the morpheme ("distinct phonetic groupings"), the Boasian ideal of investigating the nature of human beings saw language as the only window of the mind. To investigate the underlying, universal psychic unity of humanity, the anthropologist had to get beyond linguistic and cultural particularism. However, the early phases of this project were largely descriptive (and thus particularistic). Once anthropologists realized that the basics of language (phonemes, morphemes) were somehow psychologically real, they became attracted to the doctrine of **linguistic relativity**—basically, the idea that different languages, having different structures, have different psychological effects. If a given language was a major part of a culture, and was relativistic in effect, then all of a given culture was relativistic. Between 1920 and 1960, a great portion of the anthropological enterprise was descriptive. Particularism and **cultural relativism** were important twin themes of this period. A search for cultural universals, however, had emerged in the 1930s. The tension between a search for universals and particularism ("science" versus "humanism"), as well as the twin tensions between individual versus group as the locus of language and culture have remained as permanent fixtures in linguistic anthropology and other anthropologies. The early importance of language in cultural studies resulted from the fact that languages are to some degree neatly structured, and this structure is discoverable. Anthropologists turned to language in general as a **model** for other subsystems of culture as well as to actual languages for clues to aspects of culture that are psychologically real.

In the language and culture tradition, descriptive work leans toward the "pure conceptual science" in Sapir's terms (or toward "physics" in Boas's terms). Language description is **synchronic** (at a single stage in time), or even achronic (beyond historical considerations). **Diachrony** (a comparison of the same language[s] at two or more different times) in language and culture studies tends to admit lawlike generalizations, such as the evolutionary sequence of basic color terms (see chapter 4). Such generalizations are held to be valid at any time and are cast scientifically; for example, they include studies of psychological relevance of a set of terms, or sociological parallels of such a terminology, or perhaps studies of equivalent structures or processes in language and other cultural systems.

The descriptive synchronic linguistic work remains largely scientific, although it is surely influenced especially by functional studies. Such work retains a near reverence for the importance of **text**, in proper Boasian tradition. Beyond using studies of texts as data for making descriptive (scientific) linguistic statements, however, conventional presentations of text studies are challenged now by the humanistic critique. Texts are also shaped by performance conventions. Some artistic expression, such as the plastic arts, are also treated as texts for humanistic study. The critical issues dividing today's scientific and humanistic synchronic studies have to do with the conceptualization of reality that the analyst accepts.

On the other hand, in language and culture studies, diachronic study has included the fairly cleanly "scientific" work of language classification (firmly in the descriptive tradition). It also has involved reconstruction of lifeways from linguistic evidence (**time perspective**). Also bear in mind that both Sapir and Boas situated language development and change in the individual. "[R]econstruction of culture history led both Boas and Sapir back to the individual, and thereby to psychology" (Darnell 1990:12).

Summary

The concept of linguistic particularism gave rise to the idea that if most **naive thinking** is language based, and each lexicon is a particular cutting up of chaotic reality, then one's native language colors one's thought. This view, known as linguistic relativity, led to the investigation of the relation of the parts of language (the sound pattern and the semantic pattern) to culture.

The sound pattern of most languages has little to do with any of the cultural systems of its speakers. The exception here is **onomatopoeia** and other types of **sound symbolism**. Of the semantic pattern of each language, the morphemes and other **lexemes** of its vocabulary (lexicon) have the most direct connections to culture. The grammar, like the sound pattern, has less obvious connections to culture. The relation of semantic pattern to culture is the topic of the next two chapters.

The other relationship of language to culture grew out of the study of language structure. This view, called **structuralism** (see chapter 5) or **semiotics**, is the application of the hierarchical model of language structure to cultural systems like social organization, fads, music, etc. The interest in structuralist analysis of culture began in Europe and spread to the United States in the middle of the twentieth century.

The fascination of linguistic relativity in North America and the invention in Europe of structuralism as a method of analyzing culture led to an initial concentration on psychological reality. Both linguistic relativity and structuralism tend to see the individual as the locus of culture. It was not until theoretical interest shifted to the search for universals that linguistic anthropology took on a more collective focus.

Discussion and Activities

1. Try to think of how you would apply the concept of duality of patterning to the following cultural systems.

   desserts

   bachelor(ette) parties

   television commercials

   football games

   These cultural systems each have an outer **form** (shape or design) and an inner meaning. Is the meaning the same thing as the function in each case?
2. Why would scholars interested in linguistic particularism be more committed to the individual as locus of culture and language than to a collective approach to language and culture studies?

Key Terms

continuum
cultural relativism
domains
diachrony
form
humanistic
lexemes
lexicon
linguistic particularism
linguistic relativity
model
monomorphemic
naive thinking
onomatopoeia
psychological reality
semiotics
sound symbolism
structuralism
synchronic
syntax
text
time perspective
universals
vocabulary

3

The Whorf Hypothesis

> The *mental individuality* of a people and the *shape of its language* are so intimately fused with one another, that if one were given, the other would have to be completely derivable from it.
>
> —Wilhelm von Humboldt

Edward Sapir carried forth his mentor's ideas about linguistic particularism: although all languages had carefully structured sound patterns and semantic patterns, each was structured differently. In executing Boas's program, he influenced these ideas, but took care to maintain the distinction between language and culture. Recall how a culture might be conceived of as a set of different systems (kinship, other social organizations, legal system(s), ritual, medical practices, etc.) that all articulate the same set of fundamental beliefs and values. In much the same way, a language may be seen as the intermeshing of two distinct parts, the sound system and the semantic system (duality of patterning). The separate components of a language, when brought together, result in linguistic behavior. Sapir was aware of the distinctiveness of language and culture, and warned about directly comparing the two.

> Nor can I believe that culture and language are in any true sense causally related. . . . If it can be shown that culture has an innate form, a series of contours, quite apart from the subject-matter of any description whatsoever, we have a something in culture that may serve as a term of comparison with and possibly a means of relating it to language. But until such purely formal patterns of culture are discovered and laid bare, we shall do well to hold the drifts [discrete patterns] of language and culture to be non-comparable and unrelated processes. (Sapir 1921:218–19)

Yet increasingly throughout his career, Sapir expressed the idea that there was some relation between language and culture. "[Language] defines experience for us by reason of its formal completeness and because of our unconscious projections of its implicit expectations into the field of experience" (1931:578). Why, on the one hand, does he warn us not to compare language and culture, and why, on the other hand, does he postulate some intimate connection between these two? Answers to these questions take us into the history of Western philosophy.

Language and Knowledge

Epistemology has intrigued Western thinkers at least since the time of the ancient Greeks. The key to knowledge seemed to be language, and it was this fact that prompted the Greeks to study the structure of their own language. Space prohibits discussion of the whole of the debate about the relation of language and thought through the course of Western philosophy, but we need to consider the period of the latter 1700s, for the intellectual ancestors of Boas and Sapir are from that particular period, the Age of Enlightenment.

The English philosopher John Locke (1632–1704) thought of words as conventional signs. For him language was a medium for exchanging information, a mere vehicle for communication, and an aid to memory. The French student of Locke, Condillac (1715–1780), extended his teacher's ideas about language in *Traité des sensations* (1754). He took the position that language was not only a vehicle for thought, but that thought was based in language. Intuitive knowledge of reality was sensation, the impulses transmitted to the brain by the senses. It was language that transformed sensations into knowledge by reducing complexities of the real world, **chaotic reality**, to **grammatical** and **lexical categories**, (see chapter 4 for a detailed discussion of lexical categories) thus providing a means of conceiving and calculating ideas about reality.

This discourse stimulated interest in the origin of languages on the part of Rousseau, Herder, and other philosophers of the Enlightenment: Humans differed from all other animal species by being capable of thought; thought was facilitated by language, another exclusively human trait. It remained for a student of the next generation to ask that if language were the basis of all human thought, what consequences can differences in grammar or vocabulary have on the worldview of native speakers?

Wilhelm von Humboldt (1767–1835) held that each language had its own inner form. He thought that the word structure (**morphology**) of each language held the key to the knowledge of its speaker's worldview. Von Humboldt studied languages that were exotic to him, for example,

Kawi (Old Javanese); he even traveled to do fieldwork on Basque, a language having no known linguistic relatives, that is still spoken in the Pyrenees Mountains between France and Spain. The title of von Humboldt's major work is revealing: *On Language: The Diversity of Human Language Structure and Its Influence on the Mental Development of Mankind.* Von Humboldt's idea that language shaped thought probably reached Sapir through his training in Germanic languages and literatures, but its importance was reinforced through his studies with Boas. Boas was exposed to the idea from H. H. Steinthal, a teacher of his at the University of Berlin (Koerner 1992). For Sapir, the intriguing relation was not between language and culture, but between language and knowledge or thought. Language, for Sapir, was a key to a sort of social psychology. This shared view of reality was distinct from culture per se.

Benjamin Lee Whorf, a celebrated student of Sapir's, interpreted Boas's linguistic particularism and his interest in psychological reality in a different way than did his teacher. For Whorf, mental **categories**—whether named (**overt**) or not linguistically coded (**covert**)—were the basis of culture itself. Linguistically coded categories (grammatical or lexical) were a key to understanding the basis of human behavior. These were categories like past tense, progressive aspect, plural number, masculine gender, animate, and so on, some of which we will examine in examples discussed in the next chapter. In Whorf's words:

> We cut nature up, organize it into concepts, and ascribe significances as we do, largely because we are parties to an agreement to organize it in this way—an agreement that holds throughout our speech community and is codified in the patterns of our language. The agreement is, of course, an implicit and unstated one, *but its terms are absolutely obligatory*: We cannot talk at all except by subscribing to the organization and classification of data which the agreement decrees. (Whorf 1956: 213–14)

Because he held that language was not only the basis of thought, but also of culture, Whorf concluded in some of his publications that language shapes culture. In others, he only argued for an association between language and thought, culture or experience (Lucy 1992a, 1992b).

His essential argument of the stronger position is as follows: Assume that language is the basis of all thought. Each language is particular in terms of its grammatical and lexical categories (its semantic pattern). Native speakers are unconscious of the categories their language has, so habitual thought (not careful, calculated thought) by a linguistically naive native speaker will be cast in terms of the categories that his or her language has available. In other words, one's native language determines how one perceives reality, or prescribes one's **worldview** (fundamental beliefs and essential values that derive from them). This worldview issue is often called the **Whorfian hypothesis**. Another term in popular usage for the thesis is the Sapir-Whorf hypothesis. However, this latter term is not accurate, because, as we have seen, Sapir did not subscribe to the strong (**deterministic**) version of the hypothesis sometimes espoused by Whorf.

Related to this discussion of the Whorfian hypothesis are the terms linguistic relativity and **linguistic determinism,** because they label ideas through which the hypothesis and its consequences have been interpreted. Linguistic relativity refers to the view that language may influence thought, especially habitual thought, and that there is at least some association between habitual behavior, experience, culture, thought, and language. This weaker view does not insist on language having a causal priority in these associations. On the other hand, the stronger claim is deterministic: language shapes thought. Curiously enough, one finds both of these positions espoused in Whorf's own writing (Hudson 1980:104), although only the weaker accords with Sapir's thinking. Sapir did regard language as the primary influence for the individual, although he accepted that, for society, culture might influence language. Thus, language might carry a category just because of its cultural saliency, yet in terms of an individual in that society, it is the language that dictates that the category be used.

Before turning to empirical work on the Whorfian hypothesis, a number of objections to the thesis must be considered. The most obvious critique involves asking whether thinking can be independent of language. As mentioned previously, there is some evidence favoring a separation of linguistic capacity from at least some other types of thought. Fluent mathematicians, skilled musicians, and proficient logicians all have mastered various language-like systems (mathematics, a music theory, some sort of logical calculus) and are able to think in terms of them. But what of everyday examples common to most people? The phenomenon of "having something on the tip of one's tongue," the intention of saying something before uttering it, daydreaming, reacting emotionally, or aesthetically—all of these examples of types of thinking are ones human beings can express without the mediation of language. Yet all of these types of experience may involve manipulation of concepts (thinking, transforming of sensory impressions into recognition and understanding).

Whorf assumed that language use was largely for exchanging information, a view congruent with the major thrust of theory at the time. That is, he concentrated on the literal value of linguistic expressions. Recall, however, that language has many more functions in a speech community than just to impart information (greetings, maintaining group identification, emotional and artistic expression, entertainment, etc.). Even if one's attention is restricted to literal meaning (**denotation**) and not affective meaning (**connotation**), it is helpful to distinguish between *language as* *knowledge* and *language as a tool for thought*. Language may be used for problem solving, or in formulating a new concept. Once the problem is solved, or the new idea linguistically encoded, a new category is present in the language user's mind. If it is an overt category, it has a name, a linguistic label. Other problems in testing the Whorfian hypothesis are: formulating testable hypotheses and testing lexical as opposed to grammatical categories. (For critiques of the Whorfian project, see J. Hill [1986b], Schlesinger [1991], Koerner [1992] and Lucy [1985, 1992a, 1992b]).

Defining the Whorf Hypothesis

As mentioned previously, the term linguistic relativity refers to a weak or mild "reading" of the Whorfian thesis: Some discrete aspects of a language (lexical and grammatical categories) may affect the way native speakers of that language perceive, categorize, remember, and even think about the world. This position, of course, assumes that nearly all human thought is done by means of the habitual and unconscious use of the basic categories provided by the language. The stronger claim, linguistic determinism, may be rejected from the start, because if one's native language truly controlled a speaker's total cognition, translation or explication from one language to another would be impossible, nor would it be possible to do the critical thinking needed for formulating concepts not easily codable in language.

It is on linguistic relativity, the milder claim, that Whorf concentrated his scant empirical work. He was interested in both lexical and grammatical categories in actual languages and meant to compare them to actual cultural patterns observable in the community speaking the language. The lexicon (all the morphemes of the language and their conventional combinations, **idioms** and other larger-than-one-word expressions) and the grammatical apparatus (syntax, or **morphosyntax**—word and sentence structure) constitute the semantic pattern of a given language. Imagine being confronted with an object new to you; it might be, for example, one of the tools used by dental technicians to clean teeth. If you were asked to name this tool, your response might follow one of several strategies.

1. You give the correct (i.e., conventional) name—the "scaler."
2. You don't know the name but recognize the object.
3. You use "thing-a-muh-jig."
4. You try to extend single words that you know to name the object.

5. You try to describe the use or appearance of the object in a roundabout way.
6. You coin a term for the object.

In situation (1), it would be likely that you have some familiarity with dental equipment and are not a lay person. In situation (2), you have seen the object before (perhaps you have observed the tools in your dentist's office in the past); you have a covert (unnamed) category. In (3), you call the object by a general name for objects you do not know. In (4), you try to name the object with single words you already know, and in (5), you describe the object at length (possibly in a paragraph). In (6), you create a name of your own to label the covert category, making it an overt category. Any time one uses conventional vocabulary items (lexemes), be they single morphemes, single words, or phrases, one is employing linguistic knowledge that is already "in place" in one's mind. When one searches for single lexemes to describe a concept that has no conventional name, or when one tries to combine existing lexemes to describe a covert category or a new item of culture, then one is using language as a tool of thought. These two approaches (language-as-knowledge and language-as-a-tool-for-thought) represent use of the lexicon alone or the lexicon together with the syntax. In testing the effects of pre-existing linguistic categories on naive perception of reality, one is testing two different kinds of tasks.

We come then to the problem of forming testable hypotheses. Whorf's thesis has to be turned into a hypothesis which can be tested empirically with data. One must clearly demonstrate a significant correlation between actual linguistic categories and some other discrete form of behavior that is culturally based. Having considered how to operationalize the Whorfian thesis, Brown and his colleagues (1976:128) derived the following testable claims from it.

1. Structural differences between two language systems are paralleled by nonlinguistic cognitive differences in the native speakers of those languages.
2. The structure of one's native language influences the worldview one acquires as one learns that language.

To these two positions, Kay and Kempton add a third.

3. "The semantic systems of different languages vary without constraint" (1984:66).

These represent three "versions" of the Whorf hypothesis. In testing position (1), it is sufficient to find behavioral differences between groups whose respective languages treat the same phenomena differently (examples: kinship, color, reference to time or space).

In testing position (2), one must formulate the "worldviews" of at least two different linguistic groups; there must be some overarching cultural pattern(s) to be observed in several areas of each culture that show differences relatable to the differences in the respective languages. So, for example, an overall cyclic view of time might be reflected linguistically by nonlinear expressions for referring to time, theologically as some type of reincarnation, ritually by rites that return at the end to exactly the same conditions that prevailed at the start, in graphic arts by recursive or never-ending geometric shapes. Taking this hypothetical example, one would have to show that this pervasive pattern is in the lexicon or syntax of the language of the group. However, it would still be difficult to show an actual tie between linguistic and cultural patterns. Most linguistic anthropologists have steered away from such grandiose schemes, preferring to work with well-defined lexical data in testing the positions given above.

In attempting to address position (3), one must not only try to find instances where differential behavior is predictable linguistically (essentially, position [1]), one must also explain any behavioral differences by discovering conditions under which linguistic influence is neutralized. For example, if language A has distinct overt linguistic categories for 'green' and 'blue,' and language B has only a single word ('grue') that labels the ranges of color named by 'green' and 'blue' in language A, then we may reasonably expect differential naming behavior by native speakers when naming colors of the blue-green spectrum. To go beyond claim (1) to claim (3), one must somehow study color perception independently of language usage, and find influence of language on that perception (see chapter 4). The testing of the Whorfian thesis (in its linguistic relativity form) ultimately leads to the question of linguistic and cognitive universals.

Testing the Whorf Hypothesis

Grammatical (morphosyntactic) traits useful for testing linguistic relativity tend to be either optional categories or culturally governed use of obligatory grammatical categories. An example of an obligatory grammatical category in English is **number** (singular or plural). In some languages (Chinese, for example), number is not usually marked on nouns. In others, Hopi for example, number is marked following principles independent of the linguistic system. An example of an optional grammatical category is found in Mandarin Chinese where the plural suffix *-men* may be added to a few nouns referring to close friends or kin. In Hopi, plural marking tactics on nouns (there are seven of them) are applied on the basis of three covert categories of a noun: whether it is human, animate, or inanimate.

If a category is obligatory, and its use not culturally governed, it will always be expressed. If it is always present, there will be no identifiable use of it that can be associated with presence or absence of a cultural factor. Thus, the most basic and widespread categories are of no utility for studying Whorfian effects since they must always be present when using a given language. These obligatory categories of that language are trivial from the point of view of linguistic relativity.

Sapir emphasized that the effect of grammatical categories must be taken collectively.

> Inasmuch as languages differ very widely in their systematization of fundamental concepts they tend to be only loosely equivalent to each other as symbolic devices. . . . The point of view urged in this paper becomes entirely clear only when one compares languages of extremely different structures, as in the case of our Indo-European languages, native American Indian languages, and native languages of Africa. (1931:578)

Sapir expressed the opinion that all languages had a common psychological basis, but that grammatical diversity had to be appreciated (Sapir and Swadesh 1946), thus providing for some sort of grammatically based linguistic relativity. To demonstrate his point, Sapir gave the equivalents of 'he will give it to me' in a number of Native American languages, some word-oriented, some sentence-oriented. The pair below, using a simpler, sentence is representative of the kinds of differences Sapir found:

Yokuts:	ma-m	wa:n-en	lha:-ni
	thee	give-will	that-at

Navajo: n-a-yi-diho-'áá:lh —> neido'áá:lh
thee-transitive-will-give-round-this

Although the English sentence may be translated as a sentence (in Yokuts) or a single word (in Navajo), thus convincing Sapir of some common basis for all human language, he could not help but assume that *radically differing sets of grammatical categories* must have an effect on habitual thought. On the other hand, Sapir did not link linguistic relativity to cultural diversity as Whorf did. Sapir never lived to test his views of linguistic relativity as they touched on grammatical categories. Others attempted to follow his lead, however.

One of the clearest demonstrations of linguistic relativity with respect to grammatical categories is the study of Carroll and Casagrande (1958). In Navajo, verbs of handling things take the size and shape of the object being handled into account. In the example of Navajo above, *-áálh-* refers to round objects. In the following Navajo commands, shape and size are obligatory grammatical categories of **classification**. All of the examples mean 'hand it to me' (Carroll and Casagrande 1958:27).

šań-léh	(long and flexible object)
šań-tíı́h	(long and rigid object)
šań-iłóós	(flat and flexible object)

The first command might refer to a string, the second to a stick, and the third to a piece of paper or cloth. Carroll and Casagrande reasoned that children who spoke Navajo only would tend to group things by shape in tests designed to discriminate simple objects on the basis of color or shape, while Navajo children from the same reservation environment whose native language was English would not. They found that children in the Navajo-only group tended to use shape as a category for grouping at an earlier age than the English-speaking control group. In extending the test, it was found that urban black children behaved like the English dominant group of Navajo children, while urban Anglo children tended to behave like the Navajo dominant children. Carroll and Casagrande were able to explain the urban differences with nonlinguistic situational factors, but concluded that grammatical factors might influence thought, although such grammatical categories might not be the only factors involved.

A rather different line of inquiry involves the use of **counterfactuals** in English as opposed to the alleged lack of them in Chinese (Bloom 1981). Where English has such devices as *if* . . ., (*then*) . . . *would have* . . . ('*if* he had read the paper, *then* he *would have* done such and such') to talk about hypothetical events, Bloom claimed that Mandarin Chinese has no direct equivalents. He gave English-speaking and Mandarin-speaking groups tests involving questions that could be easily handled by overt counterfactuals. In the tests, the English-speaking group did better than the Chinese group. Subsequent discussion (Hatano 1982; Au 1983, 1984; Cheng 1985) has located design errors and translation errors in Bloom's research instrument. For example, the word *yàoshi* means 'if' and is a word very familiar to first-year students of Mandarin. It is used to form conditional sentences in Mandarin, a task that is not usually difficult for English-speaking learners of the language, since the word order of conditional sentences in both languages is the same. Bloom apparently assumed that there was no conditional lexeme in Chinese and so did not construct counterfactual examples using *yàoshi*.

Aside from critiques of the design or conduct of Bloom's study, there are two other ways of testing Bloom's hypothesis: (a) searching for a language with explicit grammatical markers for counterfactuals but with different usage from that of Bloom's English speakers, or (b) identifying usage of English by English speakers that differs from that of Bloom's English-speaking group. The first situation is exemplified by a study conducted by Lardiere (1992). The Arabic language shares with English the characteristic of having explicit marking of counterfactuals. Lardiere examined use of these counterfactuals by Arabic speakers. One of her test sentences was actually drawn from Bloom's study ("If all circles were large, and this small triangle '▲' were a circle, would it be large?") and translated into Arabic. What Lardiere found was that although the Arabic language has counterfactual constructions, Arabic speakers use them rarely. She attributed this finding to cultural preferences, since clearly the cause could not have been absence of a language feature. In reconsidering Bloom's Mandarin materials, she also suggested that the paucity of counterfactuals more likely derived from a cultural proclivity of the Chinese to avoid such nonconcrete, "let's pretend" constructions.

With respect to the second possibility, monolingual populations exist who rarely exploit the English language's grammatical machinery for entertaining speculation and marking hypotheses. One example is presented by children educated in fundamentalist grade schools, where learning is done by rote, and speculation is not encouraged; such children typically have problems with math and science in secondary schools (Heath 1982).

Grammatical markers and constructions are not necessarily independent of cultural factors. For example, it is often claimed that bare **imperatives** (such as, *Close the door!*) are universally avoided and that they are often softened by casting the command as a question (*Would you close the door?*). In Polish, a question used as an imperative is not understood: "English, as compared with Polish, places heavy restriction of the use of the imperative" (Wierzbicka 1991:20).

The **tautology** is another example of a culturally conditioned grammatical category. In English, tautologies (such as *boys will be boys*) emphasize sameness and triviality, whereas in Chinese the same construction ('A is A') focuses on individual differences, and may have unsavory implications ('Men are men, but . . . [he lacks masculinity'] Wierzbicka 1991:423–424). Recall that Whorf sought to relate linguistic categories directly to cultural categories. He was concerned as well with the importance of covert categories. "[There is a] give-and-take between language and the culture as a whole, wherein is a vast amount that is not linguistic but yet shows the shaping influence of language" (Whorf 1956:147).

Earlier we mentioned a hypothetical example given above of a *cyclically oriented* language and culture complex. This is what Whorf thought he had found in the Hopi language and culture. He contrasted that putative language-culture complex with English language and culture as an example of Standard Average European (SAE) culture. Whorf thought that Europeans and Americans conceived of time linearly instead of cyclically. His linguistic data are given in table 2. Note that the overall *linear* model of time in English seems to predict why a speaker of English can apply plural to the concept of 'day,' while a Hopi cannot, or why 'summer' and 'winter' are nouns in English, while these concepts are not objectified and are usually treated as **adverbs** of time (tensors) in Hopi. However, Whorf's observations on noun classes and verb **tenses** (relative time in which action/event took place—present, past, future) in English and his comparison of them with Hopi equivalents are refutable (see the notes in table 2). Further, his ideas about plurality and "cyclicity" seem to hold up only until one examines temporal inference (lexemes referring to time) in Hopi, when it becomes obvious that Hopi is basically like English with respect to its treatment of time.

Table 2. Whorf's English-Hopi Comparative Data

	ENGLISH	HOPI
plurality	ten men, ten days	ten men, *ten days[1]
noun classes	count vs. mass	no mass nouns[2]
cyclicity	'summer', 'winter' (nouns)	'summer,' 'winter' (adverbs)[3]
tenses	present, past, future	no tenses[4]
duration	temporal metaphors of size, distance, or amount	"express[es] intensities, 'strengths,' and how they continue or vary their rate of change" (1956:146)[5]

Notes

[1] According to Whorf, only concrete nouns in Hopi could be pluralized. The Hopi example in the text about beans coming up in eight days contradicts this idea (recall that the asterisk(*) indicates an unacceptable form).

[2] Whorf states that "all nouns have an individual sense in both singular and plural forms" (1956 [1939]:141). Contrary to Whorf's beliefs, Hopi does have mass nouns which, just as their counterparts in English, do not regularly pluralize: *paahu* 'water in nature,' *kuuyi* 'any contained liquid, especially water.' In fact, the primary characteristic of mass nouns in English is that they do not pluralize.

[3] Here, there is perhaps a connection between Hopi culture and a linguistic tendency to treat the seasons and other annual events as cyclic.

[4] Hopi may be analyzed by some people as having tenses; Whorf does so in earlier writings. His later analysis of the Hopi tense forms as "validity forms" was probably motivated by his commitment to the idea of Hopi as a timeless language. See Shaul (1985).

[5] Time adverbials in Hopi (Whorf's *tensors*) are discussed in the text.

While Whorf thought that English (as representative of SAE) and Hopi treated time (*temporal reference*) in fundamentally different ways, given the linear and cyclic models of time that he posited for each culture, he believed that the two languages modeled the concepts of space (*spatial reference*) in about the same way. Malotki (1979) carefully catalogued all lexemes of spatial reference in Hopi and then proceeded to show that each of the spatial terms had a temporal sense (Malotki 1983). In other words, temporal lexemes derive from spatial terms in Hopi, just as they do in English. Thus, if the structure of spatial reference is roughly the same in Hopi and English, so is the structure of temporal reference.

Ura	morivosi	nanalt	taalat	ang	kuyvangwu.
recall	bean seeds	eight	day(s)	along	usually come up

'Recall that beans usually come up in eight days.'

The word *ang* used with the temporal expression 'eight days,' means 'along'; it indicates a line between two points.

Whorf's cultural traits that exhibit cyclicity are much more anecdotal in nature than are his linguistic data. It is worthwhile to mention them here critically; Whorf does not elaborate on them very much himself. Hopi culture puts an emphasis on preparation for events (the Hopi lifeway rests essentially on communal rituals of a cyclic design; preparation usually replicates the entire event). Hopi individuals emphasize mental concentration (thought power) in realizing desired goals (simply a mental form of ritual preparation). Hopi culture is more group-oriented than American culture; one wonders how group orientation fits the overall cyclic model. Hopi culture exhibits little interest in historicity (could this simply be the by-product of an oral tradition coming from a preliterate society?). While these seemingly disparate traits of Hopi culture may relate to a covert cyclic model of Hopi culture, the Hopi language does not lack a word for 'time' (in fact, the Hopi word *qeni* means both 'place/position' and 'time'!). Temporal reference in Hopi does not use a cyclic model exclusively; Hopi does use a linear model for some temporal expressions. There is no profound connection between the cyclical model in Hopi religion and actual grammatical categories in the Hopi language.

Whorf's contribution to the modern interest in cognitive science should not be overlooked. While Boas and Sapir pointed out the typologizing aspect of language, Whorf went further to posit a system with both overt (named) categories and covert (linguistically uncoded) categories that underlie cognition as an integrated means of coding cognitive categories and analyzing experience. Hence, Whorf conceived of the lexicon and syntax of a language as an interrelated structure—as a duality of patterning. Although Whorf's empirical examples of linguistic relativity from Hopi have been discredited, his ideas about language and cognition, while couched in a very opaque and difficult style of writing, remain of interest.

Whorf's thought about language reflects his training in physics: space and time are absolutes (there is more than one way of looking at both constructs). Events and states in the real world may be coded in a given language *only in terms of that language's grammatical categories.* Whorf and Sapir wanted to go beyond the language-specific particularism of Boas and describe how grammatical categories, taken as a whole, constitute a theory of reality. This point is worth considering, in order to show the type of contribution Whorf wanted to make and to highlight the importance of this sort of endeavor to later research.

Western culture has been preoccupied with viewing reality in terms of causation. So, for example, such factors as **animacy** (human, animate, inanimate, abstract) and tense may be analyzed from the standpoint of causation. Human actors are more likely to cause an action or state than other animate (but nonhuman) entities, and so on. The time an action takes place, moreover, is seen from the point of view of the **causer** of the event or state. Let us consider the following example in English in which the focus on causal **agents** differs depending on the way the action is stated.

Situation:

At some point in the course of human history, Shah Jahan "caused" the Taj Mahal to be built.

The Taj Mahal was begun in 1632 and was completed in 1654; some 20,000 persons were involved in the process. If Shah Jahan (and not the architects, master craftsmen, or laborers), is considered the "builder" the following statement obtains:

Shah Jahan built the Taj Mahal.

If we add the dates of the actual process to that statement, the resulting sentence is incongruous:

Shah Jahan built the Taj Mahal from 1632 until 1654.

For one thing, the description *built* indicates a simple, completed action and not a process that lasted 22 years. It also sounds like a single individual actually made the entire building.

If we identify the "causer" as the architect (actually there was a commission), we are more likely to locate our statement between 1632 and 1654, because the architect's viewpoint would most naturally fall between these dates. Thus, statements such as these would follow:

The Taj Mahal was built from 1634 to 1654.

The Taj Mahal will be done in n-many years.

Note that the architect's vantage point focuses on the building or the construction process, not on a person as a prime mover; hence, the building, *not* the architect(s), appears as the subject of both statements. The first statement is after the building took place, while the second is before the fact.

Another instance of variability with respect to causal agents can be seen in differing kinds of discourse, scientific or everyday. The emphasis on causation and causality in Western thought is typical of the writing **style** of the most characteristic product of Western culture, science. Following are parallel expressions, offered by a scholar interested in **nominal** and **verbal styles** of exposition (Halliday 1987:146):

> Experimental emphasis becomes concentrated in testing the generalizations and consequences derived from these theories.
>
> We now start experimenting mainly in order to test whether things happen regularly as we would expect if we were explaining them in the right way.

The first passage is more "scientific" when read, and the following equivalent text imitates everyday language. The emphasis, even fixation, in the scientific style is on processes, neatly ordered by statements of causality, that derive the abstract generalizations (hypotheses, theories, models) that constitute science.

Without fully exploring the details of causality as a theme of Western culture, we may note that Whorf posited the need for studying "reality" as objectively as possible, realizing that any given cultural tradition (science, for example) has bias(es). It is this idea (the subjectivity of all cultural traditions, including science) that was Whorf's most important contribution. Note that physics—Whorf's orientation—has increasingly become less oriented to the cause-and-effect physics of Newton, and even Einstein. The new physics is predicated on the Heisenberg uncertainty principle (Heisenberg 1927), which states that a scientific observation can be compared with a dynamic process that results in only *one* version of a story that could be told from any number of viewpoints. Thus, physics has come to consider the possibility of many-faceted explanations. The abandonment of static models is also typical of contemporary social science (Friedrich 1986).

Whorf was trying to establish a science of human cognition that was sensitive to culture, one that examined systems of human categories. Structurally, these systems would ultimately derive from universals or **near-universals**—what all comparable human category sets (for example, colors, numerals, kin terms) had in common. It was also Whorf's belief that the categories used by a given culture intersected with the language(s) used by that culture. Whorf's goal remains a major concern of cognitive and linguistic anthropology; the interaction of cognitive and linguistic categories has endured as a vital issue.

Looking ahead somewhat, we will consider some data that seem culture specific, and then propose a principled, cross-cultural, cross-linguistic explanation. The point of this exercise is to provide an example of how a universals-oriented study of cultural categories and linguistic categories might be carried out.

In Spanish, there is a tendency to avoid "casting" inanimate objects as subjects (actors) in sentences. A typical construction along these lines in Spanish would be the following:

Se	me	rompió	la	ventana.
Itself	to-me	broke	the	window

This example may translate into English as 'The window broke,' but it is closer in sense to 'The window broke on me.' This latter rendering uses a comparable English category (*'to up and "verb" on someone'*) and is understandable, but odd, at least in some contexts. This is because the English lexeme (vocabulary item) 'to up and "verb" on someone' tends to be used only with reference to living things.

The plant up and died on me.

Bill's dog up and got sick on him just before bird season.

Do these data represent a universal category that is used differently in different cultures? At this point, let us consider the idea of various degrees of animacy (and thus differing degrees of ability to initiate action). From most animate to least animate, we have:

human > animal > plant > inanimate

This continuum reads: "human over animal over plant over inanimate." That is, even though humans, other animals, and plants are all "animate," a human is more likely to cause an action than is an animal, and an animal is more likely than a plant, and finally, a plant is more likely than an inanimate object. The greater the degree of animacy of an entity, the more likely it is to cause an action. The Spanish example given earlier constitutes a circumlocution, a sociolinguistic device to avoid saying, "I broke the window," which is more appropriate when the action is purposive and not accidental. The avenue offered by Spanish is more constrained by the considerations of animacy than is that available in English. Rather than attributing causal qualities to inanimate objects, Spanish uses **indirection** (*'to "verb" on someone'*), whereas English either may use indirection or may "cast" an inanimate as the do-er:

The window broke.
The window broke on me
The window up and broke on me.

Or even,

The window got broken on me.

The most neutral of the above list is the first. The second, third, and fourth imply special circumstances: In the second example, the actual do-er is clearly the speaker 'I' ('I' is coded by the word *me*), who was somehow trying to manipulate the window. 'I' is coded by *me* nearly unambiguously in the second example, but it is so coded only potentially in the third and fourth; for these latter two examples, it is possible to understand that the 'I' did not actually break the window but was directly affected by an already existing fracture. The Spanish sentence (*se me rompió la ventana*) does not have the restricted meaning of the second English example. Instead, it corresponds to the English *the window broke*.

We have considered a reasonably culture-free example for two comparable constructions (linguistic categories) in English and Spanish, but there are still culture-specific conditions on the use of the two comparable structures. Few cross-linguistic or cross-cultural generalizations can be made that do not have to refer to culture-specific or language-specific factors.

Another classic example of animacy as both a cultural and linguistic category can be found in the Navajo verb prefixes *bi-* and *yi-* (Witherspoon 1980). The prefix *yi-* indicates that the first noun before the verb is the actor. So,

man horse *yi*-kick

means 'the man kicked the horse.' The prefix *bi-* indicates that the second noun is the agent. So,

man horse *bi*-kick

means 'the horse kicked the man.' These prefixes actually have the following approximate values in Navajo culture.

yi- 'entity with potential for action'

bi- 'allows self to be acted upon'

This means that in the sentence 'man-horse-kick,' the *yi-* can only refer to the man, because he is higher on the animacy scale than the horse, in that he is a more rational being and thus more likely to be in control of the situation. Consequently,

*horse man *yi*-kick

is semantically unacceptable; a horse—from the Navajo point of view—is not as capable of deciding to kick as a human being is.

Other cultures prefer to put humans in the background as agents of causality. In Samoan culture, for instance, there is a "a linguistic correlate of a more general cultural disposition which tends to prefer descriptions and assessments that focus on the result or consequences of an event or action rather than on the human actor/initiator" (Duranti and Ochs 1990:15–16). In the following sentence from a conversation about providing food for visitors, one person states that "the chicken in our chicken pen died."

Pee mai	le	moa	i	le	maakou	paamoa.
died	the	chicken	in	the	our	chicken-pen

This is preferred to 'we killed a chicken'; by indirection, "a conscious and premeditated act (the killing) carried out by a human participant (the speaker) against an animate being (a chicken) is presented as an apparently accidental event" (Duranti and Ochs 1990:17). Thus Samoan culture prefers not to focus on human agency (or perhaps causality in general), but this is linguistically reflected by indirection (using some indirect way of stating something).

It is not only grammatical categories like number or animacy that are culturally applied to referents in the real world. Some categories like modals and pronouns depend entirely on the context in which they occur for meaning. **Modals** are words, often monosyllabic, that denote condition, intention, probability, and the like; examples include *perhaps*, *should have*, *never again*. A **pronoun** such as *I* or *this one* refers to a real world entity; no fixed meaning can be established for pronoun referents as it can for noun or verb referents since, for example, *I* means whoever is the speaker for a given utterance, and *you* means whoever is the addressee in a conversation. The meaning of a noun, such as *person*, or a verb, such as *run*, is somehow independent of actual contexts. Like pronouns, modals rely on the mutual understanding of hearer and speaker to have their most natural meaning. But it is not enough to show that pronouns and modals are dependent on actual contexts for their meaning; it must be shown that contextual interaction is culturally governed in such a way as to affect pronoun or modal choice. With pronouns, this is not difficult, because many of the world's languages reflect such culturally relevant categories as age, sex, and status. A familiar example is the European distinction between second person pronouns (Brown and Gilman 1960). In most European languages, there is a "polite" *you* and a "familiar" *you*. In practice, the polite pronoun (examples: Spanish *Usted*, French *vous*, Swedish *ni*) is spoken to people of superior social rank and among/between equals who are not kin or otherwise intimately related by friendship or camaraderie. The informal pronoun (examples: Spanish *tu*, French *tu*, Swedish *du*) is used among family, close friends, comrades, and to such social inferiors as children or animals. In fact, the situation may be more complex in a given language. There may be the following types of **honorifics** (pronouns sensitive to politeness levels) in a given language (Brown and Levinson 1978):

1. speaker honorifics
2. addressee honorifics
3. bystander or audience honorifics
4. formality levels in general

In each of these situations, language use is determined by the relative **roles** and **statuses** of participants in speech. The point is that these roles and statuses are culturally defined, so there is an intimate link between grammatical form and culture.

The semantics of modals is messier than that of pronouns; such modal categories as probability and obligation are culturally sensitive, as one might well imagine. The cultural underpinnings of grammatical categories must be taken into account (Silverstein 1976, 1977), whether the grammatical category directly codes context (as with pronouns and modals), or whether it codes only some attributes of context (such as number and animacy).

Two of the major types of modals are epistemic and deontic. **Epistemic modals** express the degree of commitment a speaker has to what is being said. Consider the word *must* in the following two sentences:

He must have been here; there's his hat.
That must be the case.

In these two sentences, *must* codes the relative validity of information (speculation, inference, hearsay). Note, how in other circumstances the word *must* may code the active involvement of someone (the speaker or someone else).

He must come here tomorrow to pick up his hat.
That must be left for the experts.

This latter use of *must* is **deontic**; an active involvement of someone is predicted (whether by obligation, need, or circumstances). From these small examples, it may be seen that the meaning of *must* and other modals essentially refers to contextual factors.

To sum up, there may be no direct connection between grammatical categories and cultural categories. Where there are interrelationships, such a connection is expected (for example, categories dealing with human volition and agency, animacy, politeness), or because the linguistic category depends on context for its meaning (modals, pronouns), or else because the grammatical category or construction has symbolic value. Such instances may involve subtle shifts over time. For example, Australian English is characterized by what appear to be diminutives: *mozzie* 'mosquito,' *barbie* 'barbecue,' *sunnies* 'sunglasses,' *lippie* 'lipstick.' Although such diminutives suggest effeminacy in most dialects of English, their value in Australian culture is exactly opposite. The British attitude of keeping a stiff upper lip was transformed in Australian culture as the ideal behavior (toughness, antisentimentality, comradeship). Ironically, this is symbolized in the noun suffix *-ie* which cuts "things down to size, [and shows] 'mateship,' good-natured humour, love of informality, and dislike for long words" (Wierzbicka 1991:56). There are thus reasons for relationships between grammatical and cultural categories. It is vocabulary, however, that has a much closer (and obvious) relationship to culture.

Summary

Linguistic particularism holds that each language has a sound pattern and a semantic pattern that are distinct from those of all other languages. (The closer two language varieties are in terms of **genetic relations**, deriving from the same mother tongue, the closer their sound patterns and semantic patterns will be.)

The growth of linguistic relativity from linguistic particularism lies in the philosophy of the Enlightenment. This philosophy was humanistic (human-oriented) and held that humanity was capable of progressing towards an earthly utopia by applying reason to all things. This meant, of course, that ultimately reality was explainable by natural or social sciences. Objective inquiry could discover the purpose and origin of everything in human experience.

This philosophy held, then, that human language had arisen as part of the **social contract**. Yet the strikingly different structure of actual language argued against a common origin for human languages, and even suggested that thought processes and conceptualization of the speakers of different languages could be fundamentally different. This view, which originated in the ideas of Wilhelm von Humboldt and was cultivated at the University of Berlin, was brought to the Americas by Franz Boas, the father of American academic anthropology. Linguistic particularism and linguistic relativity, integrated with structuralism in the 1920s, would remain the dominant view of language in the social sciences until after World War II.

Linguistic relativity is often called the Whorf hypothesis, although this program of study was transmitted from Boas to Whorf by Edward

Sapir. In defining the Whorf (-Sapir-Boas-von Humboldt) hypothesis, anthropologists in the 1940s and 1950s attempted to find relationships between language and lexical domains on one hand, and grammatical categories on the other.

Some grammatical categories (such as number, case, and perhaps even tense) may be used by speakers independently of direct connection to other cultural systems. When referring to something that happened in the past, a speaker will use past tense if his or her language has such a grammatical category. If overtly marked **cases** label a noun's relationship to the verb in a language (for example, label a noun as subject-of or direct-object-of a verb), then speakers of that language are compelled to employ them if they are to be understood. Yet some factors such as animacy may be reflected in the degree of control an entity may have as the doer of an action; cultures may or may not prefer to code such information. Thus, while grammatical categories may code relationships that are sensitive to culture, not all cultures (and hence not all languages) will code these sorts of relationships in the same way.

Discussion and Activities

1. How is **politeness** coded in contemporary American English, other than in expressions like *please* and *thank you*? Think about verbs, **helping verbs**, and **interjections**. It may be helpful to try to write scenarios that call for politeness and then ask consultants to create a dialogue, either written or tape recorded.
2. How is **solidarity** expressed in American English? Is it expressed by lexemes, grammatical categories, or both? Think of some examples.

Key Terms

adverbs
agents
animacy
cases
categories
causer
classification
chaotic reality
connotation
counterfactuals
covert
denotation
deontic
deterministic
epistemic modals
genetic relations
grammatical categories
helping verbs
honorifics
idioms
imperatives
indirection
interjections
lexical categories

linguistic determinism
modals
morphosyntax
morphology
near-universals
nominal styles
number
overt
politeness
pronoun
roles
social contract
solidarity
statuses
style
tautology
tenses
verbal styles
Whorf(ian) hypothesis
worldview

4

Linguistic Relativity and Lexical Categories

> [T]he world is presented in a kaleidoscopic flux of impressions which has to be organized by our minds—and this means largely by the linguistic systems in our minds.
>
> —Benjamin Lee Whorf

Lexical categories, coded by various lexemes, refer to entities (**nouns**), events (verbs), qualities (adjectives), and states (adverbs, adjectives) in the physical, social, and ideational environment of a speaker of a language. Lexemes referring to the physical environment may reflect obvious environmental conditions; it is reasonable that there would be names to distinguish local plants and animals, geographical features, and so on. Such language and culture correlations are trivial, in that they are easily explained. It is clear, though, that lexical categories have more to do with social and physical reality than with grammatical categories, since lexical categories directly code **features** of the real world. Recall that lexemes can be single morphemes (*good*), **compound words** made up of two or more morphemes (*good-'un* = 'good one'), words that are **derivations** (*good-ness*, *good-ly*; neither *-ness* nor *-ly* has any independent meaning), idioms (*a good boy* in the sense of 'naughty' or 'mischievous,' *a good old boy* meaning a 'crony'), or other conventional expressions (*good and* _______ , where the blank is filled by any named quality such as *hot*, *tall*, *busy*) and where *good* must precede. The lexicon (the set of all conventional or usual lexemes) is potentially open-ended, because it reflects a changing biological and social world. Any test of linguistic relativity and lexical categories thus rests on lexical primes (morphemes).

The classical examples of relations between vocabulary and culture, **homeland studies** and **loanwords**, come from **historical linguistics**. By making a model of what must have been present in a parent language (**reconstruction**), linguists are able to "reconstruct" earlier stages of a given culture. The enterprise depends upon **methods** of reconstruction such as that called the **comparative method**. Following the comparative method, one compares forms in related languages that all derive from the same ancestor lexeme in a language that was parent to all the later related tongues. These descendents of earlier sounds or lexemes are called **reflexes** of the forms in the ancestor language. The goal is to reconstruct that common ancestor, called the **proto-language**. For example, compare English *father* and Latin *pater*, and English *fee* (from Old English *feoh* 'cattle, property'), with Latin *pecunia* 'wealth.' Where there is an initial *f*- in English (and other Germanic languages), there is usually an initial *p*- in Latin and its descendant languages such as French and Spanish. Such **systematic correspondences** may be tabulated, and eventually the original morpheme may be reconstructed; such reconstructions are marked with an asterisk indicating that they are hypothetical and unattested (**pətér*, **péku*). Even a single **cognate set** (for example, a set of "cousin" morphemes, each of which is a **cognate** of the other in that they derive from a common ancestor and have similar meanings) allows one to infer past cultural conditions: the Indo-Europeans, the linguistic ancestors of the Germanic and Latin peoples, must have had cattle, and these must have been in part the basis of wealth in their culture and daughter cultures. Witness the parallel (but independent) developments in Germanic and Latin: **péku* 'cattle' comes to mean 'wealth.'

Homeland Studies

Homeland theory (sometimes called linguistic archaeology or linguistic paleontology) uses reconstructed floral and faunal terms to infer the relative geographic range of the species with which the speakers of a prehistoric language were familiar. A ready example comes from study of the Keresan languages. The common ancestor, called pre-Keresan, is a reconstruction based on comparison of the various descendent languages. Pre-Keresan floral and faunal terms (extracted by gloss from Miller and Davis 1963) reveal a biome common to much of western North America. Two species, however, may be analyzed as **critical species**: mesquite and various quail species. Mesquite (Nabhan et al. 1979) is perhaps the most desirable wild seed food in the American Southwest. However, mesquite is not a reliable resource where there are consistent killing frosts, even though it may survive in favorable microclimates as far north as Idaho because its seed pods are borne on the most recent wood. Killing frosts every year would preclude reliance on mesquite as a primary resource, and it would not likely be coded as a single morpheme. This restricts productivity in the Southwest to the hot lowlands, where quail is also the most abundant. All this suggests that the pre-Keresan speech community was familiar with this valuable resource (there is a single root for it in pre-Keresan). The neighboring non-Keresan languages (Zuni, Hopi) do not show evidence of antiquity for mesquite fruit as an ancient foodstuff. Hopi has no word for mesquite (Albert and Shaul 1985) and Zuni does not appear to (Newman 1958). Nor does Zuni or Hopi have a single morpheme for it. The speakers of pre-Keresans must have lived in the hot lowlands or an adjacent area before drifting into their present location in northern New Mexico.

Homeland studies, while sometimes inexact in actual species identification, forcefully show that vocabulary and culture are linked. Another branch of historical linguistics, the study of linguistic borrowing, is often called **areal linguistics**. The borrowing of words from one language into another is an additional reminder that no language exists in a social vacuum. A classic case of borrowing is the vast array of words in English that came from Norman French after the Norman Invasion of the British Isles in 1066. Perhaps no single group of such loanwords is more telling than the following domain (Fr. = French).

Native English	French Loanword into English	French Source for Loanword
pig	pork	*porc* 'pig'
cow	beef	*boeuf* 'ox'
sheep	mutton	*mouton* 'sheep'
calf	veal	*veel* 'calf'
chicken	poultry	*poulet* 'chicken'

The native English words (left column) all refer to the animal itself. English clearly did not lack for names for these animals prior to the Norman Invasion. Nonetheless, English did borrow the French term for these same food animals (middle column). Of the borrowed words, however, all have either the meaning of the prepared meat of the animal (pork, beef, mutton, veal), or the meaning of the generalized class of the animal in question (poultry). Thus, although the French source words (right column) duplicate the meaning of the native English terms, the actual loanwords into English took on specialized meanings, primarily the designation of the meat of the animal. This fact is not surprising when one considers that the French language was associated with the upper class of native English after the Norman Conquest, a group who ate more meat than did the English-speaking peasants. Through instances such as these, scholars have become aware of an especially rich relationship between the vocabulary of a language and its cultural situation.

The logical connection of the comparative method in historical linguistics is the practice of employing reconstructed data in trying to push further back into time. Although it is possible to propose **phyla** (language superfamilies made up of language families), the danger here is that there is no known way of distinguishing, at remote **time depths**, inherited linguistic material from borrowed linguistic material (think of the hundreds of Latinate and French words in English, creating sound correspondences between the two languages that exist alongside the native words). Such work on **long-distance** (linguistic) **relations** has been confined to considering inherited linguistic traits. The Nostratic hypothesis (Illich-Svitych 1971, Kaiser and Shevoroshkin 1988) suggests that the following families form a linguistic phylum (a family of families): Indo-European (the family to which English and Latin belong), Afro-Asiatic (including Semitic and ancient Egyptian), Uralic (Finnish, Hungarian and others), Altaic (Turkic, Mongolian and others; perhaps Japanese and Korean), Kartevelian (a language family in the Caucusus), and the Dravidian languages of southern India. The following cognate set is typical of the evidence given for Nostratic:

Proto-Indo-European	*moro	'mulberry'
Proto-Altaic	*mür	'berry'
Proto-Uralic	*marja	'berry'
Proto-Kartevelian	*mar-caw	'strawberry'

There are regular **sound correspondences** among consonants here (*m*:*m*:*m*:*m* and *r*:*r*:*rj*:*r*); there is also a vowel correspondence (*o*:*ü*:*a*:*a*) that is presumably regular. The meanings are roughly on par; only the 'berry' part of the Proto-Kartevelian form is being compared. It should be noted that Indo-Europeanists dispute the form **moro-* (Pokorny 1959: number 749).

Greek	moron	'mulberry'
Latin	morum	'mulberry'
Armenian	mor, mori, moren	'blackberry'

Semantic fuzziness, however, is to be expected in reconstructed data. For example, Proto-Indo-European **ker-* may mean "horn, head; with derivatives referring to horned animals, horn-shaped object, and projecting points" (Watkins 1985:29). Which meaning came first, 'horn' or 'head'?

Even given the possibility of semantic haziness over time and the reality of semantic change and loanwords, proposals for long-distance genetic relationships of languages may eventually be accepted. However, the prospect of connecting such simplified linguistic prehistory (some proposals suggest fewer than twenty phyla for the entire planet) with other prehistory studies derived from archaeology and physical anthropology are hindered by lack of phonetic and semantic clarity. A prominent example is the proposal that the native languages of the Americas belong to just three phyla (Eskimo-Aleut, Na-Dene, and Amerind) and that these three linguistic phyla neatly match proposed archaeological proposals for the peopling of the Americas (Greenberg, Turner and Zegura 1986; Greenberg 1987). The first two groupings, namely Eskimo-Aleut and Na-Dene, are noncontroversial. A wide variety of linguistic, archaeological, physical anthropological and social evidence leads to the association of these two groups with two late migrations from the Old World to the New, Eskimo-Aleut being the most recent, and Na-Dene the previous. However, the twenty or so Na-Dene languages, plus the few Eskimo-Aleut languages, constitute a fraction of the languages of the New World.

The real controversy centers on Greenberg's hypothesis that all other New World languages derive from a single tongue, brought by the people who made the earliest migration to the Americas from Asia. If correct, this would mean more than 2,000 languages, conventionally grouped into about 200 language families, derive from the single tongue, the mother of the language family Greenberg calls Amerind. How could so many languages, indeed *all* the languages from the Sub-Arctic south, have diverged from a single language in the 12,000–20,000 years that have passed since that earliest migration? Greenberg arrived at this conclusion by **mass inspection**. With this procedure, one lists words by language for comparison, and similarities pop out; where look-alikes cluster, one may hypothesize an earlier genetic relationship. Since in comparing data from so many languages one cannot possibly know all the languages adequately to be certain that the correct parts of words are compared, one must accept first of all that there will be many errors, but that the pattern of distribution of these errors will be random, and as such any biasing of the results that they cause will be cancelled out.

A more curious difficulty of the mass inspection method is the near impossibility of presenting sound correspondences so one knows in all instances that cognates are being identified for comparison. Take, for example, the following words for 'rain.'

Maidu	bai
Oti	beia

Capoxo	vui
Mobima	poi

Maidu was spoken in central California; the other three are or were spoken in South America. Although there is similarity in the forms, no regular sound correspondences have been offered for the forms, nor are other criteria given for considering look-alikes to be cognates. Given the relatively finite list of consonants and vowels that can be made by the human vocal tract and the universality of the syllable shape of CV (consonant-vowel), it is possible to propose a genetic connection between any two geographically distant languages. Consider the following, deliberately chosen:

Maori	pa	'hill, stockaded village'
Hawaiian	pa:	'fence, wall, corral'
Lakhota	phaha'	'hill, mound'
Lakhota	pa	'head'

The Maori form (Reed 1948:54) and the Hawaiian form (Pukui and Elbert 1965:272) are cognates; both languages belong to the Polynesian language family which is a grouping that has long been accepted, a kinship demonstrable by their many resemblances in morphosyntax as well as **phonology** (the sound pattern of a language). The Lakhota (or Sioux) words (Buechel 1970:424 and 422) are from a language spoken in the middle of North America which can have no genetic relationship to the Polynesian languages. The resemblances are accidental. Unless constrained, mass inspection can produce proposals for genetic relatedness between almost any pair of languages. Not only does Greenberg not "spell out criteria for deciding when two words correspond closely enough to qualify as a match" (Wright 1991:58), many scholars question his hypothesis about the unity of Amerind as a language phylum.

There are also problems with the data, deriving from the aforementioned difficulties of comparing so many languages that one cannot know them all well. "Many simple mistakes have been found in *Language in the Americas*: words in the wrong language, words with the wrong meaning. Greenberg's detractors . . . almost invariably veer toward their favorite subject: his sloppiness" (Wright 1991:58). This summary of criticism of Greenberg's proposal comes from a disinterested party writing for the educated and cultured lay public; it is indicative of the general reception the work has been given by most linguists who work with Native American languages. Yet, there is a certain appeal to it, especially when one considers the strong evidence from physical anthropological studies that seems to indicate significant differences among the three modern-day groups, the speakers of Eskimo-Aleut languages, the speakers of Na-Dene languages, and the speakers of all other American Indian languages.

Consideration of proposed remote linguistic relationships leads to a methodological dilemma. Greenberg's approach assumes that regular sound correspondences will eventually be lost, although residual cognates will remain (Greenberg 1987:1–37); it ignores the possibility of massive borrowing and language shifts in the past which must have taken place. On the other hand, the Nostratic hypothesis rests on regular sound correspondences that seemingly go far back into time.

> If the sound correspondences proposed for Nostratic are correct, the premise of Greenberg's method is false . . . Alternatively, if Greenberg is correct, the proposed Nostratic sound correspondences must be spurious; they would merely demonstrate the extent to which accidental similarities between languages can be discovered if the concept of similarity employed is sufficiently broad. (Bateman et al. 1990:5)

The comparative method, which has its basis in the social and physical sciences alike, is thus limited in its applications. Most scholars agree that it is not reliable at remote time depths, and the method of mass inspection proposed to plumb remote time depths in its place is problematic too. These methodological problems are but two of several to confront linguistic anthropology; others will arise in the course of future chapters.

It remains to be seen if such extensions of historical linguistics as Nostratic (which relies on regular sound correspondences) and Amerind (which relies on similarity of putative cognates alone) will come to have any significant impact on language and culture studies. Such extensions may have the potential of unifying the study of human prehistory, a potential that has tremendous implications for anthropology. The further back in time, the less possible is exactness and inclusiveness. For that reason, it is unlikely that reconstructed linguistic data will ever tell us about Neanderthal cognition, as some have hoped it would.

Classical Semantics

In the nineteenth century, linguistics scholars concentrated on what lexical relations might contribute to an understanding of prehistory. This emphasis was replaced in the twentieth century by a concern for **synchrony**, that is the study of a language at a particular time, usually the contemporary form of the language. This concern eventually led linguists to the study of languages as removed from social and cultural contexts, and to the approach known as autonomous linguistics. Recall that autonomous linguistics is the position that a natural language, with the exception of its lexicon, is relatively self-contained and independent of culture or society. This position takes its semantic theory directly from the classical lexical semantics of Aristotle. The approach was influential upon anthropological linguists who employ the concept of **basic terms**, which derives from classical semantic tradition. Basic terms label essential items in a semantic domain, such as color or plant life; basic terms are usually a single morphene ('red'), and are not a metaphor nor a loanword (not 'plum' or 'rouge').

The standard view of lexical meaning (**lexical semantics**) comes from Aristotle's *Metaphysics* and has only recently been challenged. The following are the basic assumptions about the nature of lexical categories:

Lexical categories have clear boundaries.

Lexical categories are defined by necessary, binary features.

All members of a category have equal status.

Semantic description would be easy if words and morphemes fit into neat, tidy boxes as Aristotle claimed. Yet as we will see, this simplistic view of a language's morphemes is inadequate.

Consider what belongs in a category, for example, 'cup.' We understand that a cup is used for drinking a beverage, has a semi-circular handle, and comes with a saucer. (Otherwise, it would be a 'mug.') But what about an egg cup, or the handleless cups that are used to dispense coffee from a vending machine? Do saucers only belong to teacups? What about the relative size of a cup? (Soup cups are wider than ordinary cups.)

Clearly, the category 'cup' does not have crisp, stateable, definite boundaries. This lack of clear boundaries is called **fuzziness** in the recent literature of lexical semantics. Lexical fuzziness is a criticism of the maxim that lexical categories have clear boundaries. Two classic studies of food and beverage containers are Labov's (1973) and Kempton's (1981). Both studies show how such fundamental concepts as 'cup' and 'bowl' vary depending on size, function, and ratio of width to depth.

One way to define such distinctions among lexemes is through the use of **semantic features**. Characteristics, such as [wide] and [has handle], would be candidate semantic features to distinguish members of the lexical set that includes 'cup,' 'mug,' and 'bowl.' Semantic features are definite, stateable attributes of a given term. For example, consider the terms 'dog' and 'cow.' Both name animals that are mammals. Thus both [animal] and [mammal] are necessary semantic features of these terms. However, the necessary defining features must also differentiate the lexemes from one another. Dogs are [canid] or [canine]; cows are [bovine]. We could use these terms to define other kinds of animals.

$$\left.\begin{array}{l}\text{fox}\\ \text{wolf}\\ \text{coyote}\end{array}\right\}\quad [+\ \text{canid}]$$

ox [+ bovine]

Horses, donkeys, and zebras would be [+ equine]. The features [canid], [bovine], and [equine] can be easily and exactly specified.

The problem is, however, that if we define the terms of a domain, say familiar animals, we must make a **features matrix** that is potentially infinitely long.

dog

[+ animal]
[+ mammal]
[+ canid]
[- bovine]
[- equine]
[- feline]
[- porcine]

In making an exact definition of 'dog' with semantic features, one must specify an almost endless list of what traits a dog is and isn't (as noted by the + and -). It is therefore not economical to define a morpheme by making such a **componential analysis** of each term, though the idea is appealing because of the exactness involved. At the least, one requires a theory that places greater value on some features (or types of features) than others, and inclusion in such a list of possibly relevant features would then have to be motivated on external grounds such as the universality of certain features, how easily they might be learned by children, or how psychologically relevant they might appear to native speakers. Such a theory leads one far from the apparent simplicity of componential analysis.

Another problem with such a componential analysis is that it is hard to determine what constitutes a necessary feature, from the point of view of defining the features themselves. For example, one can easily see that the following subfeatures define such features as [canid], [bovine], and the others used above.

[+/- whiskers]
[+/- horns]
[+/- cloven hoof]
[+/- snout]

Clearly, these have the advantage of defining animals as collections of physical attributes. Since these characteristics make up such concepts as 'canid' and 'bovine,' they may appear more basic and thus preferable as semantic features. Yet how does one know how native speakers of English conceptualize 'dog' and 'cow'? Do they use prototypical images of the whole animal, or do they define by specific physical attributes? Perhaps some such features are more salient to speakers than others. Just what is a necessary feature?

Another problem with the autonomous view of lexical categories is that of linguistic knowledge versus what autonomous linguistics would term "nonlinguistic knowledge." The problem lies in determining how much information constitutes a linguistic definition of a term. A classic example here is *bachelor*. This term might be given the following features matrix:

bachelor

[+ human]
[+ adult]
[+ male]
[- married]

The presence or absence of a feature like [human] or [married] contributes to a definition of *bachelor*. Since these are **binary features**, they do not allow for gradient or scalar representation. Binary features present several difficulties, but especially problematic is the selection of which binary features to use (the possible use of [- child] instead of [+ adult], or [- female] instead of [+ male]. Apart from this difficulty, the analysis looks satisfactory as long as we stick to denotative or literal meaning.

When we look at connotative (figurative, extended) meaning, however, the situation becomes more complex, and less amenable to analysis using binary features. Consider the following terms, which are members of the same domain as *bachelor*:

spinster
bachelor of arts
bachelorette

The use of *bachelor* in academic degrees is a specialized problem (the problem of **polysemy**, two or more distinct but related senses of the same term).

But what about *spinster* and *bachelorette*? We could analyze each of these as the following:

[+ human]
[+ adult]
[+ female]
[- married]

Yet, what is the difference between the two? Do we just add another feature to distinguish the difference? Just how much cultural knowledge can we add to our set of features for a language?

Suppose we added the feature [+/- young] to differentiate between the two female terms. We could do this to avoid giving sexism a connotative interpretation that might be present in Western culture, thus keeping the analysis as autonomous as possible. Yet will we end up with a set of features that will apply to all languages? Put another way, are there languages spoken in cultures that lack sexism? (Furthermore, is sexism universally similar where it exists or fairly culture-specific in each case?)

Consider the following domain:

fake	phoney
bogus	ersatz
sham	artificial
mock	imitation
false	

It has been claimed that there are no true **synonyms** in English. This set of related vocabulary items share a core meaning, but their connotative meanings separate them. The features needed to define them systematically and unambiguously comprise a large set that must utilize a great deal of cultural knowledge.

Another problem with semantic feature analysis is that not all members of a category have equal status. For example, the days of the week are not of equal value as examples of the category "day of the week." Pause for a moment and think which days of the week are most important in contemporary culture.

You probably thought of Monday, Friday, Saturday, and Sunday. This is because Monday is a start of the work week, and Friday is the beginning of the weekend. Most leisure and family activity is planned for weekends, and Monday is even dreaded. This folk theory of the week is supported by conventional wisdom.

Work was hell today; I thought it was Monday.

T.G.I.F. (Thank God It's Friday.)

The weekend is just a two-day coffee break.

Thank goodness it's a three-day weekend.

The fact that some days of the week are *conceptually* more important than others shows that not all members of a category have equal status.

This example also shows another problem about lexical categorization. This problem is the possibility of inherent organization of a domain of vocabulary. The lexeme "day of the week" illustrates this problem nicely: the days of the week are actually structured into a two-part model:

Friday/*Saturday-Sunday*/Monday

the other three days

The days belonging to the weekend are italicized; essentially, they are a single unit. Friday and Monday buffer the preferred time zone of the weekend, and the other three days are inconsequential in the conceptual scheme of things, except perhaps in those circles that label Wednesday as "hump day," the mid-week day that gets one over the first part of the week and toward the next weekend.

Another problem ignored by theories based exclusively on Aristotle's ideas is that of context. Words and other items of vocabulary do not just exist by themselves. They are learned and used in actual contexts. Pronouns and modals (and most adverbs) are tied to context; they get their meanings from the sentence in which they are used (and that sentence is part of a conversation or other text). Consider again the word *fake* and its **slotmates** in the list above. The differences between *sham*, *bogus*, *fake*, and *phoney* are all tied to the contexts in which they are used. One could say that all mean something like 'inherently and deliberately false.' Yet this account would not solve the problem of differentiation among them, or the existence of so many terms for essentially the same thing. The central, core meaning of 'false' among the members of this set is probably peripheral to the meanings and usage of these words. It cannot be accidental that better thesauruses have example sentences to disambiguate and illustrate the many sets of supposed synonyms of English.

Basic Terms

It is primarily basic terms that have concerned scholars interested in possible relations between language and culture. A basic term is monomorphemic (it consists of a single morpheme). It is of high frequency of usage, and it has a fairly specific reference. To understand what is meant by basic terms, we turn to biological classification.

Everyone who has taken a course in biology knows that plants and animals are classified by biologists as to genus and species. For example, 'willow' is the genus (**generic**) *Salix*, which is the Latin word for 'willow.' A 'weeping willow' is *Salix babylonica*, which translates as 'Babylonian willow' (referring to the exile of the Jews in Babylonia at the time of Nebuchadnezzar). The **species term** refers to a basic kind of willow tree, whereas the **generic term** has a more general meaning. A **specific term** refers to a variety of a basic (species) kind.

Suppose that someone named Thompson hybridized a special kind of weeping willow. This hybrid would be known as a varietal: *Salix babylonica* var. *Thompson*. A three-level model is thus possible: generic (genus), basic (species), specific (varietal). This same sort of nomenclature (system of naming) may be applied to referents that are not biological.

furniture	(generic)
chair	(basic)
dining room chair	(specific)

Generic terms are semantically vague, and may be grammatically unusual. For example, generic terms in English are not count nouns: this means they do not have the category of number.

*three furnitures
*some furnitures
*a furniture

Just as generic terms in English cannot show singular or plural, specific terms are usually **compound terms** made up of more than one word (dining room chair).

Other languages may code the generic/basic distinction differently from the way it is coded in English. For example, German has a so-called gender system. This means that all the nouns in the language are labeled as "masculine," "feminine," or "neuter" for grammatical purposes (regardless of natural gender, or even the possibility of having sexuality at all). It turns out that the neuter gender (marked by the word *das*) typically is assigned to generic terms.

das Obst	'the fruit'
das Gemüse	'the vegetable'
das Metall	'the metal'
das Tier	'the animal'
das Fahrzeug	'the vehicle'

In German, basic terms are monomorphemic, as are basic terms in English; they also typically have masculine or feminine gender, not neuter. Specific terms, as in English, are compound words; they may have any gender. Thus, German, which carries gender distinctions for all nouns, employs the gender category in characterizing generic, basic, and specific terms, whereas English cannot use this distinction since it has limited gender marking (Zubin and Koepcke 1981).

This concern with basic terms (as opposed to generic and specific terms, but especially in their contrast to generic terms) will structure what we have to say in the next sections on color terminology and folk biology.

Color Studies

Let us turn to work on the relation of lexical categories to culture, one which bears more strongly on the issue of the tension between linguistic relativity and language universals. Recall how Boas conceived the morpheme list of a language to constitute a self-contained, complete classification of all "reality" known to a given culture. All other concepts had to be named from this fundamental set. It is small wonder that lexically based studies of linguistic relativity have relied on basic terms (single morphemes of restricted application that are not loan words). Those domains of basic terms (for example, kinship, color terms, types of plants, domesticated animals, etc.) that can be conveniently and objectively studied are the areas where the most research has been done. In general, languages may differ in how they treat the same objective domains (we will consider the domains of color and folk biology here). Still, there are universals to be found when large numbers of languages are sampled with respect to their basic terms for a given domain. Studies of color terms in particular were interested in "what limits common human biology sets on possible intercultural variation" (Kay, Berlin and Merrifield 1991:13). (See Witkowski and Brown [1977] for an early view of the search for lexical universals, and Blount and Schwanenflugel [1993] for a more recent review of theories of the **categorization** of color and other domains.)

In 1969, Berlin and Kay proposed that **basic color terms** are added to any language according to a universal sequence. The general interpretation of cross-cultural terminologies prior to the Berlin and Kay publication was that such terminologies were of near infinite variety and culturally determined (Lenneberg and Roberts 1956); differences in color terms was frequently cited in support of the Whorfian hypothesis.

Berlin and Kay found that if one knows how many basic color terms a given language has, one can predict the areas of the color spectrum to which they will refer. Note we are talking of two kinds of entities: basic color terms and **basic color categories**. Basic color terms are the color names of a language that in general are (1) a single lexeme (not *hot pink* or *bluish green*), (2) not a metaphor (not *plum* or *turquoise*), and (3) not a borrowed word (not *ecru* or *beige*). These are terms such as the English words *red*, *green*, *blue*, *yellow*, etc. Basic color categories, on the other hand, are the ranges of color in the color spectrum that are named by particular basic color terms. The color categories are in some sense the actual "colors," whereas the color terms are the names of those categories. The primacy of basic color terms over nonbasic ones is reflected in the linguistic behavior of speakers. Basic terms will be recalled earlier in a list than will nonbasic ones, there will be greater agreement on them, and people will recall them more often. All these factors combine to make basic terms psychologically more salient than nonbasic ones (Smith 1993, Smith et al. 1995).

Berlin and Kay (1969) discovered that basic color terms tend to be added to a language in a predictable sequence. Table 3 gives that basic sequence in simplified form. If a language has two basic color terms, it is a Stage I system. Such systems consist of two categories, one naming the white-warm categories (the union of white, red, and yellow) and the other naming the dark-cool categories (the union of black, blue, and green). If a language has three basic color terms (Stage II), they will be roughly translatable as *black / dark*, *white / light*, and *red* since they will label those categories on the color spectrum. If a language has four basic color terms (Stage III), the fourth will label either the category *yellow* or *grue* ('green-blue'). In Stage IV languages, there are five basic color terms; in Stage V languages, the *grue* color category has split into *green* and *blue* with their associated basic color terms labeling the two. Stage VI languages have added a label for a *brown* category. Thus, although languages slice the color spectrum differently, there is an order to how they do it. And, not only is there a predictable order, but that order was found to be correlated with facts of the physiology of color vision. The simplest color terminologies, for example that of the Dani (Heider [Rosch] 1972a, 1972b), include only two basic color terms.

Table 3. Evolutionary Sequence of Development of Basic Color Terminologies in Languages

Stage	**Stage II**	**Stage III**	**Stage IV**	**Stage V**	**Stage VI**
black/dark (cool)	black	black	black	black	black
white/light (warm)	white	white	white	white	white
	red	red	red	red	red
		yellow	yellow	yellow	yellow
		grue	grue	green	green
				blue	blue
					brown

Note: Languages share common features of color naming, and differences in color naming that exist between languages are not random. A Stage III language will have either *yellow* or *grue* but not both. A Stage IV language splits *red* into *yellow* and *red* categories. A similar split of *grue* into *green* and *blue* typifies a Stage V language. Stage VI languages add *brown*. Stage VII languages add one or more of the following, in any order: *purple*, *pink*, *orange*, *grey*.

Source: Berlin and Kay 1969

The sequence of the evolution and development of basic color terms was found to be grounded in the neurophysiology of color vision (McDaniel 1972, Kay and McDaniel 1978). The six basic color terms of Stage V represent a naming of light and dark, plus a labeling of the four response states of the opponent cells of the optical pathway (McDaniel 1972, Kay and McDaniel 1978) which process visual input into responses to red, yellow, green, and blue (Hering 1920; DeValois, Abramov, and Jacobs 1966;

DeValois and Jacobs 1968). The neurophysiological correlation provided counterevidence to arguments leveled against the evolutionary theory of basic color terminology that were based on causal notions from cultural differences. The primary distinction is between light and dark, which is represented in Stage I languages that have only two basic color terms—one for *warm* colors and one for *cool* colors. Next, the *warm* category is split, giving Stage II languages in which *red* is partitioned out of the *warm* category and labeled with a basic color term. Then either the *yellow* area is further separated from the *red* category and labeled, or the initial partition of the *cool* category occurs establishing and labeling a *grue*. Notice that the sequence establishes the "primary" colors—*red*, *green*, *yellow*, *blue*—as more important and the development of their labeling by basic color terms as less variable than what is observed with the "secondary" colors—*brown*, *purple*, *pink*, etc.

In the years since its initial formulation, the evolutionary hypothesis of basic color terminology has been widely tested, and to date, the Berlin and Kay evolutionary sequence and its implications have largely withstood this testing, although details of the original model have been criticized and revised along with improvements in method (Rosch 1973; Berlin and Berlin 1975; Kay and McDaniel 1978; Kay 1975; Burgess, Kempton, and MacLaury 1983; Kay, Berlin, and Merrifield 1991; MacLaury 1987a, 1987b, 1991). The model has found further support in its grounding in the physiology of human color perception (McDaniel 1972, Kay and McDaniel 1978, see also Hering 1920), and in studies of the acquisition of color terminologies by children, where the pattern of a child's learning of basic color terms was found also to follow the evolutionary sequence (Harkness 1973; Dougherty 1975, 1977; Mervis, Catlin, and Rosch 1975).

A revision of the model (Kay and McDaniel 1978), however, precluded a category combining yellow with green. This revision was subject to criticism when it was learned that the Salishan languages (Pacific Northwest coast of North America) "have developed a yellow-with-green category, which has displaced a green-with-blue category . . . Yet yellow and green are separated by greater perceptual distance than green and blue" (MacLaury 1991:42). Thus, even substantiated "universals" are statistical, and may have exceptions.

What has been conceptualized as a pattern of adding basic color terms and categories, evolutionarily and acquisitionally, perhaps should instead be interpreted as a pattern of partitioning of the color sphere. McDaniel (1972) has suggested such an interpretation based on values for the two qualities of warm-light and cool-dark. Thus, Stage I of the sequence represents partitioning of the color sphere into two categories: warm-light and cool-dark. The principle that McDaniel proposes is that a new distinction will always develop first in the set that is [+ arousing] (warm-light) (see also Kay and McDaniel 1978:638–41). Apart from cultural relativistic ones, other explanations for part or all of the variety of basic color terminologies found in the world's languages center on the role of context (Lucy and Shweder 1979, Shweder 1984) or on biological differences, such as differences in pigmentation of the eyes (Bornstein 1973a, 1973b, 1975; Furbee 1992; Furbee et al. 1996), or on "vantage" or point-of-view (MacLaury 1991, 1992a, 1992b).

Keeping in mind that the evolutionary sequence is also a language acquisitional sequence; it appears possible that basic color terms may provide a test of the hypothesis that an individual's language is lost in the reverse of the acquisitional sequence, a position held by some aphasiologists (Jakobson 1941, Emery 1985). Preliminary tests for such patterned loss of basic color terminology were conducted with Broca's aphasics, Wernicke's aphasics, patients with Alzheimer's disease, and normal controls using a variety of nonverbal and verbal tasks adapted from those used by the World Color Survey. The results of those tasks generally supported a conclusion that aphasic and Alzheimer subjects had loss of basic color terminology in a reverse of the evolutionary and acquisitional sequence (Furbee 1985b).

Equally interesting in the aphasia study, however, was the nature of the variation revealed in different trials for one of the tasks used with the normal, aphasic, and Alzheimer subjects. In that task, the idea of a basic color term was defined for subjects; then subjects were asked to name basic color terms in the absence of color stimuli. Terms recalled early in the listing were regarded as more salient than those given later. Thus, the earlier a term was recalled, the more salient it was judged to be. Saliency so measured was used as an indicator of a term's being high in the evolutionary sequence.

When naming basic color terms, subjects revealed strategies for remembering, none of which produced exactly the hypothesized evolutionary sequence. Subjects did tend to begin with an arousing primary red or yellow, as predicted by the theory, but they then followed one of three patterns for remembering.

In one pattern, some subjects continued around the color sphere through the arousing colors into the cool colors, thence to the point at which they began. This pattern was named the Hue Neighbor Strategy (figure 1a). An example is a list given in an order such as red, orange, yellow, green, blue, purple. A second strategy was the Dialectical Strategy (figure 1b). Using it, a subject would name an opposite to the previously named category, bouncing from a term for an arousing primary category, to a term for a cool primary category, back to arousing, and so on. An example is the sequence red, green, yellow, blue, orange, purple. The third strategy was as follows: after naming an initial basic color term, for example red, sometimes subjects named next all the terms which labeled categories that had belonged with the first named term in an earlier evolutionary stage. This variation was called the Ur Category Strategy (figure 1c). An example would be naming the primary red, then the derived orange before the primary yellow, after which moving to blue and green and finally giving purple.

Figure 1 **Three Color Naming Strategies**

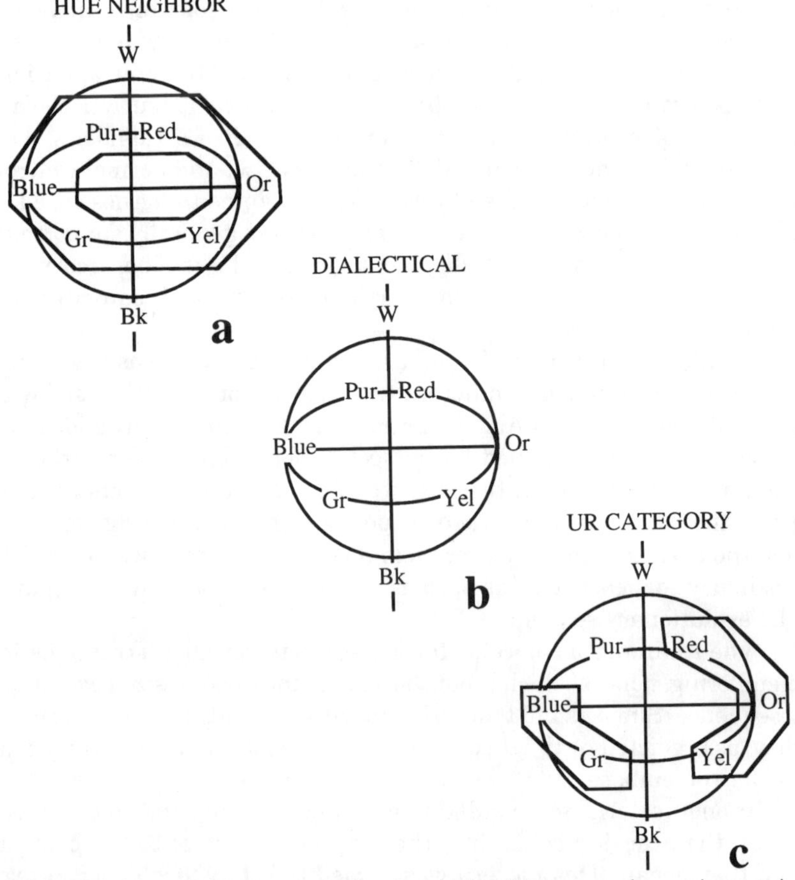

(a) Hue Neighbor Strategy, according to which a list in an order such as red, orange, yellow, green, blue, purple might be given.
(b) Dialectical Strategy, according to which a subject would name an opposite across the color sphere to the previously named category, giving, for example, a sequence such as red, green; yellow, blue; and then, orange, purple.
(c) Ur Category Strategy, according to which after naming an initial basic color term, for example red, subjects named next all the terms that labeled categories which had belonged with the first named term in an earlier evolutionary stage; for example, red, orange, yellow.

The results of these color studies were interesting because they revealed a recapitulation of the evolutionary sequence. In addition, both sets of results suggest that the evolutionary and acquisitional sequence may nonetheless emerge only collectively, rather than in any single individual. At the same time, the strategies for remembering color terms, reflecting as they do reliance on the cognitive representation of the color sphere, give us an insightful explanation of variation based on cognitive abilities.

It is important to note that all cultures can describe all colors. For example, a culture such as that of the Tojolabal Mayans, whose language has a basic color term for a *grue* category (*ya'š*) will distinguish between 'leaf-colored *ya'š*' and 'sky-colored *ya'š*,' or some similar descriptive combination (Furbee 1976). While there is abundant evidence that persons from different languages and cultures categorize colors differently, there is very little to suggest that they might actually perceive colors differently (except, of course, for individuals who are color blind). One small pilot study has indicated that eye color might slightly affect color perception (Furbee 1992, Furbee et al. 1996); if that is true, it supports a proposal by Bornstein (1973a, 1973b, 1975) that persons with light eyes might see color somewhat differently from persons with dark eyes.

Figure 2 shows the results from the pilot study conducted with ten English-speaking male subjects. The perception of color did appear to be related to eye color; five of the subjects had blue eyes and five had brown eyes. The task used to study this possible difference in perception was one in which 13 color chips, representing the **focus** (the best example of a category) of 10 basic color *categories* for English speakers, plus three other nonfocal chips (*chartreuse*, *beige*, and *turquoise*), were presented in randomized sequences of all possible triples—a triadic sorting task. The subjects were asked to judge which pair of each triple most resembled each other; for example, given color chips that represented the categories *red*, *blue*, and *yellow*, subjects tended to judge the pair *red-yellow* as more alike than either of the pairs *red-blue* or *yellow-blue*.

Figure 2 derives from an individual differences nonmetric multidimensional scaling analysis of the results of the experiment. Figure 2 shows the scaling of the aggregated results from the ten subjects for Dimensions I and III; Dimension I, the horizontal, can be labeled as "saturation of pigment," and Dimension III, the vertical, seems to indicate the arousing/nonarousing or warm/cool dimension. (Dimension II, which is not shown here, distinguished pigmented from nonpigmented colors by grouping the "noncolors" of *white*, *gray*, *black*, and *beige* apart from the "real colors.")

With respect to Dimension III, the warm/cool dimension, the blue-eyed subjects in general tended to use the warm/cool dimension in making decisions about colors more than did the brown-eyed subjects. (Note that

Figure 2 **Results from a Pilot Color Study**

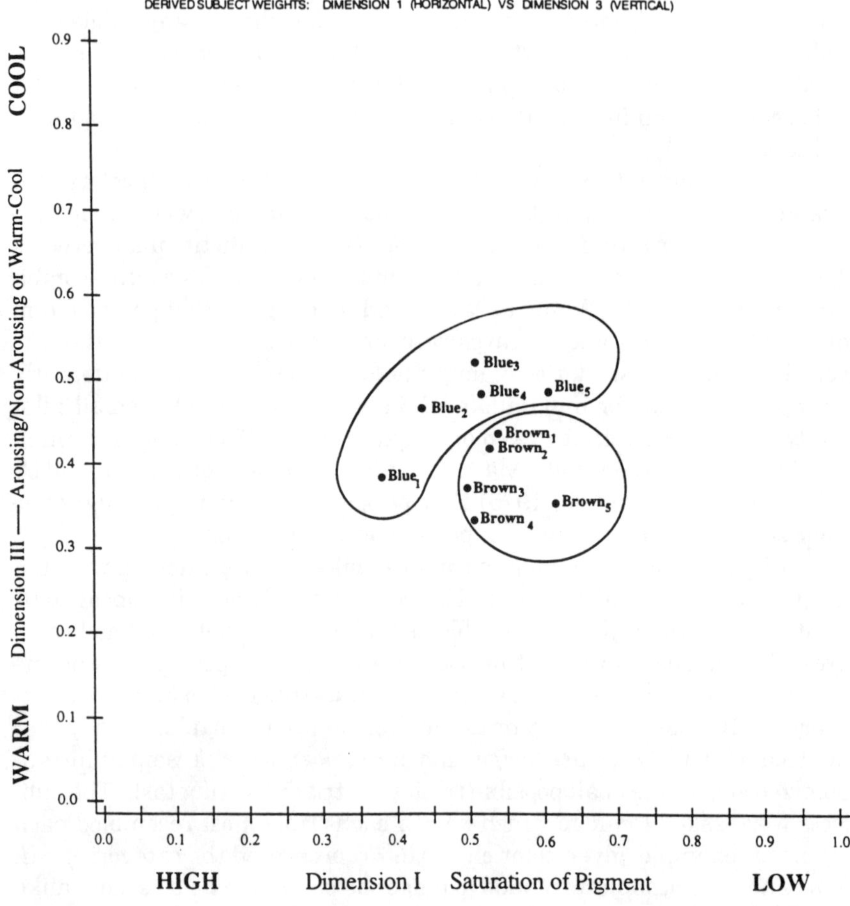

two subjects, one blue-eyed [$Blue_1$] and one brown-eyed [$Brown_5$], wore contact lenses, and both seem to be somewhat outlying from their respective groups.) There are two important caveats here: First, these results are no more than suggestive. Ten subjects comprise a very small sample, and the study would have to be replicated with a much larger sample to make it convincing. Second, it is important to recognize that even if eye color is found to have some influence on color perception, such a finding would not necessarily mean that the cognition of color naming would be influenced by those slight perceptual differences. Such a connection would have to be independently demonstrated.

The same study was repeated with 14 female subjects. Results were compared with those from the male subjects, and gender differences were identified in the performance of men and women on the color tasks (figure 3). Despite the small sample size, this gender difference in color perception supports other recently reported findings that a systematic difference may exist in the color vision of men and women and that it derives from genetic differences between the sexes (Merbs and Nathans 1992, Mollon 1992, Winserickx et al. 1992).

Figure 3 **Comparison of Perception of Colors by 10 Male and 14 Female Subjects**

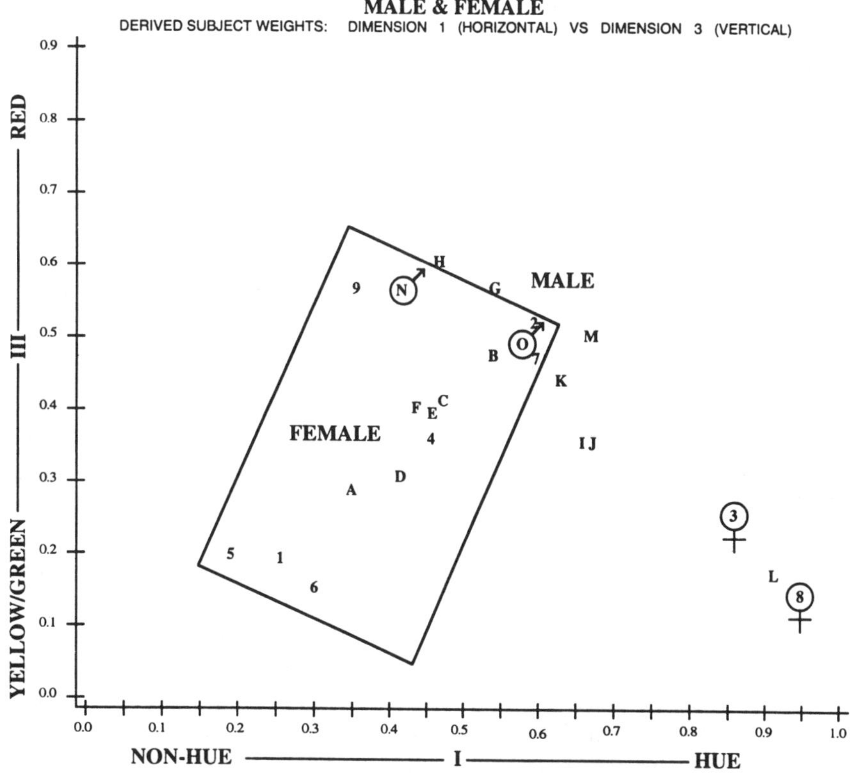

These results have special relevancy when viewed in light of a recent revision of the color theory. MacLaury (1992a, 1992b) proposed that variability in color categorization might better be modeled according to what he terms "vantage theory" rather than by logical representations such as the fuzzy logic model of Kay and McDaniel (1978).

> [Vantage theory] rests on four axioms: (1) people perceive 6 unique hues (white, black, red, yellow, green, and blue), [with] 15 potential pairs [of hues]; (2) the members of each pair are to some extent similar and to some extent distinct; (3) each pair of hues differs in these extents; (4) people attend simultaneously to similarity and to distinctiveness and can reciprocally shift the emphases they place on each; if attention to distinctiveness is strengthened attention to similarity must weaken. (MacLaury 1992a:141)

Vantage theory looks at the differences in color naming as much as similarities within and across languages. "Vantages" can be represented by "coordinates" (comparable to the "dimensions" of the study reported above). The theory assumes that different individuals may compose color categories by paying closer attention to some dimensions than others: "hue, brightness, similarity, and distinctiveness are not the only coordinates by which people compose color categories" (MacLaury 1992a:150). Most languages name colors on the basis of these dimensions, but saturation may also influence the formation of color categories. "Connotative coordinates" are also possible (MacLaury 1992a:150), and may help explain the kind of results Conklin (1955) obtained for Hanunoó categories where the *cool* and *warm* categories connote dryness and wetness respectively.

Color studies exemplify an active area of investigation that has relevance for the study of language universals, which in its original formulation (Berlin and Kay 1969) seemed to present a clean challenge to conventional relativistic formulations. Those findings were substantiated by correlations of cross-linguistic color categorizations with knowledge from the neurophysiology of color vision (McDaniel 1972, Kay and McDaniel 1978) and seemingly coordinated well with suggestions about acquisition and loss of color terminologies (Jakobson 1941; Dougherty 1975, 1977; Emery 1985, Furbee 1985b). Still, investigators found significant deviations from what was anticipated, especially with respect to the brightness and saturation of colors (Stanlaw 1987, MacLaury and Galloway 1988), and out of these exceptions has arisen an explanation of the construction—the varying construction—of color categories (MacLaury 1992a, 1992b). It has become apparent that the explanation of color naming and categorization straddles extreme relativist and universalist positions. Although color studies may still be seen as largely exemplary of universals in language, satisfactory formulation of a theory must attend to the variability that characterizes many reports made from a relativistic point of view.

Studies in Other Domains

Improvements in method have produced a clearer understanding of lexical universals in the domain of color and the centrality of the process of category construction to acceptable accounts. Other **lexical domains** especially amenable to empirical study are terms for flora and fauna. Studies of folk biology were stimulated by the color studies. In revisions of the original formulation of folk biological classifications (Berlin, Breedlove, and Raven 1968; Berlin 1972), the following implicational sequence was found to prevail for the life-form terms for plants in folk ethnobotanical botanical classifications (Brown 1977):

$$\text{no generic terms} > \text{‘tree’} > \text{‘grerb’} > \left\{\begin{array}{l}\text{‘bush’}\\ \text{‘vine’}\\ \text{‘grass’}\end{array}\right.$$

For example, if a language has a basic term for ‘grerb’ (green, leafy, nonwoody herb), it also has a basic term for ‘tree’; if it has a term for ‘bush’ or ‘vine’ or ‘grass,’ it also has a basic term for both ‘grerb’ and ‘tree.’

Brown (1979) found the following scheme to predict basic terms for animal life forms.

$$\left.\begin{array}{l}\text{‘fish’}\\ \text{‘bird’}\\ \text{‘snake’}\end{array}\right\} > \text{‘wug’} > \text{‘mammal’}$$

If a language has a basic term for ‘mammal’ (rodent, large mammal; sometimes, any large animal), it also has a basic term for ‘wug’ (bugs, worms, small reptiles, arachnids, snails, etc.). The sequence implies that all languages have basic terms for ‘fish,’ ‘bird,’ and ‘snake.’ A summary may be found in Brown (1984). (See Ellen [1987] for a critique of Brown's project.)

Additional investigation (Berlin 1972; Berlin, Breedlove, and Raven 1973) has shown that the hierarchical organization of floral and faunal domains is also universally constrained. The following is the most complex hierarchy that may be found in a floral or faunal domain.

I unique beginner (‘plant,’ ‘animal’)
II life-form (‘wug,’ ‘tree,’ etc.)
III generic (example: ‘oak’)
IV specific (example: ‘coast live oak’)
V varietal (‘Thompson's coast live oak’)

Languages often lack basic terms or have opaque terms (compounds where the meaning is not immediately transparent) for unique beginners or life-forms. Further, often there are about 500 lexemes (basic terms) labeling generics. Specifics or varietals are rarely coded by a basic term, being named instead by a modification (compound or derivation) of a basic term naming a generic.

The study of cross-cultural lexical semantics is not limited to concrete referents. Abstraction may be studied in much the same way. For example, Tyler (1984:27) suggested that in Western culture, the notion of 'to see' was used as a metaphor for coding firsthand experience.

Let me see how it tastes.

Oh, now I see . . .

Use of these English language expressions code knowledge derived from other senses. Such proverbs as *seeing is believing* show that 'to see' is indeed the basic metaphor for 'knowledge' in our culture. Tyler then points out that the Dravidian languages of southern India use 'say' and 'do' as the basic way of coding knowledge gained from the senses. However, Viberg (1983), in a cross-linguistic survey of verbs of perception showed that 'see' correlates with 'know' cross-linguistically more than any other verb of perception. As with animacy as a culturally motivated grammatical category, the cross-cultural study of lexical categories (even those referring to abstractions) remains a fruitful area for future investigation.

There will always be some domains or categories where languages tend to agree more. So, for example, the category of 'passerine birds' (perching birds) vs. 'nonpasserine' are largely valid across languages because of an essential characteristic (perching) that is salient to all classifications of birds (Boster and D'Andrade 1989). Such categories as 'soul' are less likely to be as close semantically across languages and cultures because abstract terms are more symbolic, being divorced from the physical world. So, for example, Wierzbicka (1989:45) notes that "*soul* can always be translated into Russian as *duša* [the closest Russian equivalent to English *soul*], while the reverse is not true." The Russian term does not fit into the mind/body frame of reference of the English term. The issue of comparability will always persist in the study of lexical categories.

Within many language communities, the relativistic impact of words is exploited in the field of advertising. Words formed with morphemes from Latin, for example, give an American trade name or product name an air of sophistication (Room 1982), although those from other languages may have the opposite effect (for example, the French soft drink name *Pschitt* would not sell well in the Anglophone world for at least two reasons, and the American car name *Nova* was a poor choice in Latin American countries since *no va* means 'it doesn't go' in Spanish). The way the product or trade name looks or sounds is obviously important: an industry devotes itself to analyzing the English morpheme list from the point of view of form (sound or written appearance) and meaning (Mamis 1984, Trachtenberg 1985) in order to create favorable linguistic effects. Names such as *Compaq* (for computers), *Die-Hard* (for batteries), *Acura* (for a luxury car) attest to the success of commercial applications of lexical relativity. This shows that linguistic relativity is indeed a phenomenon to be reckoned with, despite the interest in lexical universals that has grown out of Whorfian studies.

The study of lexical universals that emerged from investigation of linguistic relativity and lexical categories has remained an active area of research. A number of cross-linguistic implicational universals have been discovered. While it is assumed that these cross-linguistic lexical universals are somehow innate, it has been shown both that a Whorfian effect may be observed empirically (Kay and Kempton 1984) and that cognition may occur independent of linguistic use.

Summary

Linguistics during the 1800s was largely concerned with genetic relations between languages. Linguists tried to reconstruct the grammar and lexicon of the ancestor language (proto-language) of each **language family**, inferring the homeland of each reconstructed family and identifying the loanwords present in each. Such reconstructions pertained to the creation of a **culture history** for a language or language family. Eventually, it was hoped that the original human proto-language could be reconstructed, and ultimately the origin of human language uncovered. The goal of reconstructing so distantly using the methods presently available is generally held to be unrealistic by most present-day scholars. The study of linguistic particularism, in the form of historical linguistic reconstruction, actually led the way to the study of linguistic universals.

In trying to test linguistic relativity, anthropologists and linguists in the 1950s and 1960s focused on psychological reality, choosing domains such as kinship, color terms, and folk biology to study. This is because these domains are easily verified from outside any particular language.

It was found that there were linguistic (and cognitive) universals in the way categories were organized in all languages. A distinction between basic terms, generic terms, and specific terms emerges from the study of lexical universals. This suggests that categories that are lexically coded are organized in domains hierarchically. Generic and basic terms tend to be monomorphemic, and generic terms may be grammatically odd. Specific terms are usually compounds or derivations. The following issues remain open to further discussion: the cognitive organization of grammatical categories, the influence of context on the learning and use of categories, and whether linguistic and cultural categories are binary in nature. These issues will be examined in later chapters.

Discussion and Activities

1. How does the hierarchical model of generic, basic, and specific terms apply to color studies and folk biological terms? Is the relationship of this model the same to each domain? What does this tell you about human cognition in general?
2. Each class member should collect 20 full-page advertisements from newspapers and magazines. Sort all of the ads into domains. How is each domain reflected linguistically? Is it possible to generalize about the relation of language and culture in North American culture from these domains?
3. Analyze the following lexical domain:

cheat	nick
bilk	pinch
chisel	steal
fudge	embezzle
rip off	rob

   What semantic features do each of these terms have in common? What assumptions must a speaker have in mind in order to use each of these appropriately? Can you organize this domain in terms of the generic, basic, and specific model?

4. Put the following words on cards.

margarine	eggs	cereal	bread
paper cups	sugar	canned corn	saucers
soap	potatoes	corn chips	green beans
cleanser	pie pans	milk	plastic knives
dish towel	tin foil	baking powder	coffee
tea kettle	potholders	napkins	waxed paper
can opener	fresh fruit	spatula	window cleaner
garbage bags	rice	chili powder	measuring spoons
asparagus	peanut butter	salt	black pepper
cutting board	strainer	deodorant	bandages
mouth wash	dog food	blender	garden seeds

   Each student should ask four consultants—two men and two women—to sort the cards into "aisles" of a supermarket, and then have them label each aisle. Get the age, shopping expertise, educational background, and income bracket for each consultant.

5. Pool each class member's data from (4). What categories emerge from the data? Are they general or basic terms? Do men differ from women in the way they conceptualize the supermarkets? Does education, economic class, or habitual shopping experience influence categorization?
6. Have class members, perhaps as teams, visit three or more supermarkets in your area to see where stores actually place these items. Do stores agree in their categorization? How does this jibe with the intuitions of your consultants?

Key Terms

areal linguistics
basic color terms
basic color categories
basic terms
binary features
categorization
cognate
cognate set
comparative method
componential analysis
compound words
compound terms
critical species
culture history
derivations
features
features matrix
focus
fuzziness
generic
generic term
historical linguistics
homeland studies
language family
lexical domains
lexical semantics
loanwords
long-distance relations
mass inspection
methods
nouns
phonology
phyla (sing. phylum)
polysemy
proto-language
reconstruction
reflexes
semantic features
slotmates
sound correspondences
species term
specific term
synchrony
synonyms
systematic correspondences
time depths

5

Structuralism and Semiotics

> If I use ivory chessmen instead of wooden ones, the change has no effect on the system; but if I decrease or increase the number of chessmen, this change has a profound effect on the "grammar" of the game.
>
> —Ferdinand de Saussure

There were two major consequences of the linguistic particularism of Boas in language and culture studies. The first, as we have seen, was linguistic relativity. The second was structuralism, a particular approach to the analysis of language and other sociocultural systems involving the identification and definition of elements in particular systems of arrangements by the relations holding between them. Structuralism was implicit in much of Boas' work, although it was Ferdinand de Saussure (1857–1913) who made the approach explicit for language.

To give an example of the structuralist approach, let us return to how Boas conceived of a language as consisting of a set of consonants and vowels (phonemes) that coded linguistically the fundamental concepts of the language (morphemes), and combinations of such groupings (words, simple sentences). Both Boas and Sapir were concerned with the increasing complexity of linguistic units. In English, for example, given the syllable shape CVC (C = consonant, V = vowel), only certain consonants may appear as the first consonant or the last consonant. Keep in mind the notational conventions for the pertinent units used in phonological study: square brackets, [ ], indicate phones (**speech sounds**), the actual sounds that can be grouped differently in different languages into phonemes. Phonemes are indicated by being written between slashes, / /, and are the fundamental sound units of a particular language. Examine the following list of English words written phonetically (in terms of actual speech sounds):

[bæŋ]	'bang'
[kæt]	'cat'
[bæt]	'bat'
[mæt]	'mat'
[næt]	'gnat'
[hæt]	'hat'
*[ŋæt]	(impossible combination)
*[kæh]	(impossible combination)

Notice that the problem with *[ŋæt] and *[kæh] has to do with their first and last consonants, respectively. [ŋ] (= *ng* in spelling) may not appear as the initial consonant of English words, and [h] may not appear as the second consonant in such a CVC English word. Certainly, the combinations [ŋæt] and [kæh] are easily pronounced by native English speakers; when singing, English speakers often substitute [ŋ] for word-initial [n], for example. Further, both [ŋ] and [h] are phonemes in the language, as shown by the following **minimal pairs**: /bæŋ/ 'bang' vs. /bæn/ 'ban'; /hæt/ 'hat' vs. /sæt/ 'sat.' Any given language uses only a subset of all the consonants and vowels (phones) that are producible by the human vocal tract. Furthermore, the selection of sounds and the preferred arrangements of those sounds in a given language are highly variable. Thus, both the sound inventory and way a language puts the sounds together into "phonetic groupings" or phonemes are relatively **arbitrary**.

Moreover, the arbitrary nature of the linguistic system pertains also in the case of the morphemes of a language. Recall that the morphemes of a language are the fundamental units of meaning of that language. The set of concepts that a language employs as its fundamental view of reality (its morpheme list) is just as arbitrary as the set of sounds it puts together into its phonemic inventory. Why is one language, with regard to basic color terms, a Stage IV language and a neighboring language a Stage V language? There is no facile answer. Higher-stage systems tend to be found in societies that have more complex social and political organization, but such a correlative observation is not usually explanatory in and of itself, although it does suggest a possible line of inquiry for seeking cause. Furthermore, there is usually no logical relationship between the form (actual pronunciation as a string of consonants and vowels) of a given morpheme and its content (meaning).

dog	(English)
chien	(French)
Hund	(German)

perro	(Spanish)
pòoko	(Hopi)
gogs	(O'odham [Papago])

A domestic canine is not actually associated with these sequences of sounds, nor does it resemble any of them. The relationship between the concept dog and any of these sequences is arbitrary. There are, however, a number of exceptions to the generalization that the relationship between a linguistic sign and its referent is arbitrary (Friedrich 1979a). One is onomatopoeia, in which a linguistic form imitates the sound that it represents; for example, *cock-a-doodle-doo* or *ding-dong*. Another is sound symbolism. Symbolic forms have connotations that illustrate their meanings rather directly, for example, *sizzle* or *flap*. Nonetheless, the instances of nonarbitrariness are few and relatively unimportant although interesting.

The way morphemes are put together into words is also arbitrary. Consider the following English data.

walk-ed	*ed-walk
walk-s	*s-walk

Some of these morpheme sequences are unusual because of the fact that English marks tense arbitrarily as a suffix and not as a prefix. Now consider the forms *go-es* and **go-ed*. The latter form is also impossible but not because it violates the arbitrary order for construction of English verbs as did the unacceptable forms in the preceding list that are marked by the asterisk (*). **Go-ed* is impossible because the past tense of 'go' in English is irregular (*went*). The arbitrary order for constructing English verbs—the rule for regular verbs—is:

Root + Tense

That is, one does not mark tense (relative time an action takes place) in English at the beginning of a word.

The word order used to structure words into sentences is also arbitrary. In English, the basic word order is SVO (Subject-Verb-Object). (Note that **object** here refers to the direct object, although as we have seen previously, objects may also be of other kinds, for example, indirect.)

I saw the dog.
S V O

In other languages, such as Scottish Gaelic or Hawaiian, the word order is VSO.

Chunnaic	mi	an	cu.	(Scottish Gaelic)
saw	I	the	dog	
V	S	O		

Ua	'ike	au	i	ke	'i:lio. (Hawaiian)
past tense	see	I	direct object	the	dog
V		S	O		

Other languages, for example, Tojolabal Maya, have a VOS basic word order:

Kila	ts'i'	ke'n.
I-saw	dog	I
V	O	S

In addition, SOV (e.g., Hopi), OSV (e.g., Xavante) (see Derbyshire and Pullum 1981), and OVS (e.g., Hixkaryana) (Derbyshire 1985) basic word orders are known. Why don't all the languages of the world have a single basic word order? There is, again, no easy answer. An SVO word order would be incorrect in Gaelic or Hawaiian, though it is the proper one in English. The orders SOV, SVO, and VSO, however, account for an overwhelming number of the world's languages. Principled reasons for this fact are to be found in linguistic typology, functional grammar, and theories about natural language processing. For example, information in conversation tends to be given in an order such that previously mentioned or known information appears before novel information is introduced. If someone said,

> "Mary went to the store,"

they might include the word "store" in a further description of what she did at the store:

> "And, at the store, she bought the best cookies I've ever eaten."

The new information follows the old information. In this manner, new information is placed in relation to what is already known or "on the table for discussion." Thus, there is a functional reason for the subject-before-object orders (SOV, SVO, and VSO) found in the vast majority of the world's languages.

There are nonetheless ways of varying basic word order for information management.

> A: Well, what did she break?
>
> B: It was the chair (that she broke).

In this exchange, several topics (including *chair*) could be in Speaker B's mind. The frame "*it was* ________ *that*" allows the object *chair* to be moved forward and focused from among other possibilities.

A language is also structured in increasing orders of complexity. To review,

sound level: CVC
word level: verb + tense
sentence level: Subject + Verb + Object

These units increase in size and meaning; note that this view obscures the notion of duality of patterning and the idea that the sound pattern of a language is independent in some respects of the semantic pattern.

These orders of increasing complexity are called **levels**. In a given language, one may expect to find a sound level, a word level, and so on. The structuring on each level is arbitrary for the most part; there is a conventional or usual order that must be observed. The fact that every language has systematic structure was one of the facets of language that interested Boas and Sapir, although they thought of the systematic structure of each language as being unique to that language; that is, they had accepted the doctrine of linguistic particularism. This view stimulated research on linguistic relativity, as we have seen, and is implicitly **structuralist**.

The Systematic Structure of Language

It was Ferdinand de Saussure who systematized Western thought with respect to the structure of languages. The son of a well-placed family of scientists in Geneva, Switzerland, Saussure made notable contributions to historical linguistics at the age of 18. He is usually remembered, however, as the father of modern linguistic theory. His lectures on general linguistics from 1907 to 1911 were published in 1916 after his death as *Cours de linguistique général* (1959[1916]; first translated into English in 1958 as *Course in General Linguistics*).

Saussure realized, like Boas, that language was structured hierarchically in levels. Saussure stressed the arbitrariness of human language (and behavior in general), noting that all linguistic meaning came from the system of language itself and not from some external system. Saussure organized his thoughts about linguistic structure in terms of several **dichotomies** (paired opposites). The most important of these are syntagmatic and paradigmatic relationships.

Syntagmatic relationships are relationships of sequence or combination. For example, given the CVC formula used to structure some English morphemes, one may substitute (insert, put in) almost any English consonant in the first slot other than /ŋ/ as the first C. Given the CCVC formula for some morphemes in English, one notes that there may never be two successive nasal consonants. Sequences like **mnit* are impossible, though some languages do allow two nasals together initially:

Dakota *mni*, 'water,' which was borrowed in the English word *Minnesota*. Note how English restructured the word after borrowing it by inserting a vowel between the *m* and the *n* in keeping with the English constraint against beginning a word with an *mn* sequence.

Formulas of inclusion specify **paradigmatic** relationships, that is, relations of membership in a set; for example, in CVC, C stands for some set of consonants not some particular consonant; in the formula SOV or VSO, S stands for a set of subjects not a particular subject. There are formulas for structures on every level of language, and there are constraints as to what items may be substituted into a given slot in a formula, regardless of whether the formula is one that pertains for sounds, for morphemes, or for words. For example, each personal pronoun in the following set—*I*, *you*, *he*, *she*, *it*, *we*, *you all*, *they*—stands in paradigmatic relation to each of the other pronouns in the set because any one of them, but only one of them, may appear as the subject of a particular sentence.

For Saussure, human language, even though arbitrary, was not random. It existed as patterned behavior. Moreover, this highly complex patterning was organized in levels of increasing complexity, each level having its own set of primitive elements (having paradigmatic relations) and ways of structuring the elements into usual orders (formulas specifying syntagmatic relations, those relations holding across elements in a sequence). Yet there is more to Saussure's theory of language than the doctrine of nonrandomness. Saussure observed that human language can be thought of as arranged according to a hierarchy. The structure at each level stands in a hierarchical relationship to those structures in neighboring levels. All such structures may be analyzed in terms of paradigmatic and syntagmatic relationships. For example, a morpheme can be thought of as a product, which is composed of primitive elements (phonemes) that were themselves the products of an analysis of phones at a lower level. Those phones were the primitive elements of that phonetic level below. Furthermore, for Saussure, as for Boas and Sapir, language was psychologically real.

Language is habitual and largely unconscious, yet highly structured. In describing the structure of a language, one is essentially describing a kind of knowledge that is beyond the consciousness of its speakers. One uncovers such out-of-awareness knowledge by observing actual speech and identifying patterns in it within the levels and according to the system of syntagmatic and paradigmatic relations holding among the elements. That actual linguistic behavior Saussure termed **parole** (speech, message). He gave the name **langue** (language, code) to the unconscious knowledge that underlies parole. Thus, like Sigmund Freud and Émile Durkheim, Saussure posited in humans various kinds of unconscious but highly structured knowledge. Saussure's theory of human behavior, derived largely from his thinking about linguistic structure, is called structuralism. It was meant to be applied to other areas of human endeavor. He envisioned a science of symbols (semiotics) which would include language as well as other sociocultural systems.

It is important to note that the elements on each level contrast with each other through the paradigmatic relations. In English verbs, for example, one of the markers (*-s* / *-ø*, *-ed*, *-ing*, *-en*) must be present on the verb. These markers constitute a paradigmatic set and a system of contrasts. The absence of one of the elements implies the presence of one of the others.

-s/-ø	present (e.g., *she walk**s**, I walk*)
-ed	past (e.g., *he walk**ed***)
-ing	progressive (e.g., *we are walk**ing***)
-en /-ed	completive (e.g., *they have prov**en**, you have walk**ed***)

From the point of view of this simplified array of the English tense and aspect system (the system is more complex, though this general outline is true), events are analyzed (1) as happening in the present with no comment about completion or lack of it, (2) as having happened in the past without any comment about the progressive or completive nature of the event, (3) as ongoing, or (4) as completed. This constitutes a basic theory of how events happen in the world. A member of this arbitrary set (the **paradigm**), when attached syntagmatically to an English verb at the word level, may be thought of as expressing a set of contrasts, with the four elements describing every possible human action with respect to tense (relative time of action) and **aspect** (relative manner of action). Since the set "slices up the picture" completely (it is meant to cover all possibilities), it defines itself and requires no clarification from outside the system. Each element has meaning only with reference to the other elements in the set with which it has paradigmatic relations, and each element in the array stands in paradigmatic relation with each of the other tense and aspect elements.

One can regard this definition of the meaning of an element in a set as arrived at by contrast with each of the other elements in that set; these contrasts form a series of **binary oppositions**. The *-s* that marks the present tense in English is defined as such by its paired contrast with *-ed* (the past tense marker), with *-ing* (the progressive marker), and so on. This definition by contrast provided by paired binary oppositions is the keystone to structural analysis. According to structuralism, nothing has meaning unless it contrasts with some other element. Each noun, for example, may be thought of as having meaning only in its contrast with each of all other nouns: *father* contrasts (and so "means") with *mother*, *lawyer*, *dog*, *daddy*, and so on.

Structuralism and Human Behavior

The notion of a structuralism as a mutually defining set of primes may be extended to other types of human behavior, such as chess, football games, and dinner parties. We will consider such events in terms of syntagmatic and paradigmatic relations, and in terms of underlying knowledge (langue) and actual behavior (parole). **Competence** is that capacity and knowledge held by an idealized speaker/hearer. It is a psychological construct that can be compared to the more sociological construct of langue. **Performance**, on the other hand, refers to an actual use of such knowledge and is comparable to parole in the same way that competence is comparable to langue. The goals of many formal theories of grammar relate primarily to competence, but for some theories, especially functional ones, performance is seen as the primary or initial subject of study; the account of competence emerges from it.

Saussure succeeded in making explicit the principles by which language is structured at each level, although, as we have seen, the germ of structuralism is implicit in the work of Boas and is the basis of the doctrine of linguistic particularism. Saussure's *Course* also insisted that language (langue) was largely unconscious knowledge and that this **deep** knowledge could only be glimpsed through actual instances of language use: speech (parole). In insisting on the psychological reality of linguistic knowledge, Saussure also had to confront the problem of individual versus shared norms.

This characterization begs the old questions of what language is, what culture is, and what society is. As we have seen thus far, language is highly structured; each language consists of a sound system (set of consonants and vowels; syllable and morpheme formulas) and a semantic pattern (lexicon of morphemes and lexemes derived from them; patterns for constructing words, phrases, clauses, sentences). Culture is also distinctive. This term can imply erudition or sophistication (ballet, symphony, art opening, etc.), distinctive ethnic practices (Chinese New Year, Polish-American dancing, etc.), or the life-way of a people. This last sense is the primary anthropological meaning of the term culture. If one expands the notion of life-style to a group level (life-way), one notes that there may be many distinctive systems in one's (or one's group's) culture: institutions for social organization, economic transactions, legal means of settling dispute and intergroup problems; a cosmology to explain human origin and destiny in nature; religious, ritual, and medical systems. One also finds seemingly scattered things that must be part of a culture: superstitions, characteristic modes of dress, food, housing; interpersonal distance; and gestures. A working definition of culture as all shared, learned knowledge permits several important principles to emerge. Culture, like language, is essentially knowledge. It must be transmitted to newborn or adopted members of a social group; it is *traditional*.

The only real evidence for culture is actual behavior. Not all anthropologists consider culture to be knowledge: some locate it in behavior, some in artifact, and some in society. The location of culture (and language) dictates the nature of one's theoretical construction and understanding of these issues, but for now, we will follow Boas and take culture to be knowledge.

After an initial phase of describing Native American cultures that seemed to be dying out, the students of Boas (Kroeber, Sapir, Bunzel, Benedict, Mead, and others) pointed out that culture seemed to consist of a multiplicity of traditional systems (kinship, other social organizational mechanisms such as societies and moieties, legal codes, religious doctrine, ritual, folk biology, folk medicine, etc.). Did cultures possess any basic principles that underlay the discrete systems that seemed to make up culture? For example, a commitment to atheism on the part of a society might be expected to influence social organization, political and economic systems, life-crisis rituals (birth, coming of age, marriage, death), and public art. Anthropology searched in the 1920s for themes that ran through the various systems of a given culture, much as Whorf saw an overarching cyclic model in Hopi culture and language.

The search was for themes deriving from a culture's basic beliefs and values that pervaded all cultural systems. Fundamental beliefs imply fundamental values. For example, an atheistic society might just as well exhibit a hedonistic philosophy instead of one committed to a struggle for an earthly utopia. Consideration of how basic belief-value systems affect individual or group personality will not be discussed further here, although the issue of whether there are covert categories, knowledge, or principles that crosscut cultural systems—including language—will remain a consideration.

Revising our view that culture is a collection of systems of knowledge that may ultimately relate to basic worldview, we are still confronted with the issue of the shared nature of cultural systems. That is, which is the locus of culture, the individual or the group to which that person belongs? As noted earlier, one solution to this dilemma is to posit culture as knowledge that guides human behavior and action. To understand an individual's culture is to be able to predict what is culturally appropriate behavior in a particular situation, not to predict what the person actually will do in every single instance. One may think of cultural knowledge as that shared by all participants in the society (that is, as a subset of all knowledge in that society) or as a sum of total knowledge; the latter approach would imply some account as well of both the variation and the means by which individuals interact since they have slightly varying bodies of cultural knowledge.

Thus, we are led to a second dilemma, the degree to which cultural knowledge is shared. In a multilingual society, one might reasonably expect that individuals would vary in fluency in the various codes (languages, or dialects of a single language) used in that society. Although all Navajo Indians share a common socioeconomic organization and worldview, not all speak Navajo. Some of those who do speak Navajo speak no English, yet all have to deal with the Anglo world via the English language. Similarly, Navajos vary in religious practices: individuals may be Seventh-Day Adventists, members of the Native American Church, or Catholics, they may subscribe to the native religion that centers on elaborate curing rites (called "sings"), they may have no specific interest in religion, or they may follow yet some other belief not named. Some may practice a mixture of these religions. Individual Navajos vary in their knowledge of the traditional religion; only curers, patients, and others that have participated directly in a "sing" have direct experience with the native religion. Consequently, individuals vary in what and how much they know about traditional Navajo practices. One way to address the problem of cultural knowledge as shared norms is with the criterion of **mutual intelligibility**. Much as two linguistic varieties are considered dialects if speakers of one can understand the other variety, we may analyze the differential knowledge of individuals with respect to a given cultural system as one of dialect or **idiolect** (individual version of a cultural system). For example, Navajos trained as native religious specialists ("singers" who know one or more ceremonies or "chants") might be said to have a different "dialect" of traditional Navajo religion than does the average Navajo.

Similarly, investigation of the beliefs about illness and disease has revealed patterned variation. One such study was conducted with Tojolabal Mayan Indians, who live in southern Mexico. When a group of 33 Tojolabals were consulted for detailed study of their ideas about illness and disease, and especially about the etiology of disease, certain patterns of similarities and differences were found in their conceptions. Their ideas were examined through an interview, the preparation for which involved a careful, structured elicitation of information in a manner that protected against introducing ideas about the subject matter from the investigator's point of view. Such methods assure that the questions to be asked are relevant to the persons whose ideas are being studied. Results from the 33 persons whose knowledge was particularly closely studied revealed that there were about three subgroupings within the 33. These subgroups were termed "diseasealects." In general, the cognition of individuals within one of the three "diseasealects" differed less from each other than did the aggregate score of each diseasealect from the aggregate score of each of the other two diseasealects (Furbee and Benfer 1983, Furbee 1985a). Further, the diseasealects invite one to look for formal rules by which to relate them, as one might relate dialects by rule, and they present possibilities for "sociolinguistic" study. For example, are members of a particular diseasealect predominantly men? Or women? Are the diseasealects representative of persons who live in particular regions? Or do members of a particular diseasealect share some other characteristic, such as knowledge of curing, or wide experience with the non-Indian social world, or extensive travel beyond the areas traditionally considered to be Tojolabal?

What seems to be involved is not simply knowledge in some sort of static, almost dictionary sense, but rather knowledge for reaching comprehension of slightly varying versions of one's own cultural belief, a set of strategies (instead of rules) perhaps for negotiating—even creating—cultural comprehension in rich interactive settings. Thus, one might think of one's cultural knowledge as constantly changing, shifting in response to changing situations.

Saussure had intended that structuralism be the basis of a science of symbols (semiotics). By taking the structural model of syntagmatic and paradigmatic relations, it is possible to discover underlying patterns in any given cultural system, whether organization is obvious (as with kinship) or not readily apparent (as with superstitions). The claim is that human behavior is not random. Social practices that involve the community use distinctions (categories, which stand in paradigmatic relations to each other) alone or in combinations (defined by their syntagmatic relations) to create meaning.

Semiotics (formerly called **semiology**) is the scientific study of signs. By sign, we mean the fundamental elements of a system, its primes. These primary units are structured in conventional combinations. For example, depending on the dialect and region where one lives in the United States, one is likely to have some selection from the following names for meals: breakfast, lunch, dinner, supper. Most of us have only three meals in a day (snacks are not really meals), and we may name them in any of these ways:

Morning Meal:	Breakfast	Breakfast	Breakfast
Mid-day Meal:	Lunch	Dinner	Lunch
Evening Meal:	Supper	Supper	Dinner

Usually, *dinner* names the largest meal of the day, whether it is eaten at mid-day or in the evening, although some native speakers of English routinely name an evening meal *supper* regardless of its size. Let us take the common case, however, and consider what constitutes a dinner, customarily our major meal. For many, dinner means something like the following; the parentheses in the formula indicate optionality:

(appetizer) + salad/soup + entrée, side dish + (dessert)

This formula claims that dinner may start with an optional appetizer which is followed by a soup or a salad, that then the main dish (entrée) is consumed at the same time as the side dish (probably a vegetable, though this is not specified in the formula), and that dinner may end with an optional dessert. Think of the various foodstuffs which are classified as *appetizer*, of how many kinds of soups and salads there are, of how main dishes may harmonize with side dishes, or how many desserts there are. All of the soups stand in paradigmatic relationship to each other; one usually selects only one soup. The same goes for salads, entrées, side dishes, and desserts. For any instance of a meal, the actual selections (cheese and crackers + Caesar salad + pork chop with peas + baked Alaska, for example) stand in syntagmatic relationship to each other. We have extended the structural model to the cultural category of dinner. Note, however, that dinner may not be the same concept in all cultures; in Chinese dinners, for instance, one serves a soup as the last item in the meal or at the end of a course of the meal. Note also, that there are restrictions in what may "logically" (from a "native speaker's" point of view) appear in the same combination. In North American culture, some foods don't "go together"; sauerkraut and ice cream would be such a conflicting combination.

Knowledge of how breakfast, lunch, dinner, or even a snack is structured is mental knowledge (langue) which serves to generate actual behavior (parole). Where there is meaning (this implies sharing norms in common to some degree), there is a system of mutually opposed elements that may be put into conventional orders or combinations. Structuralism is a way of discovering the modeling of language systems and other cultural systems. The basis of the method is to try to uncover the fundamental elements of a system and work out how they combine to form structures. Note, however, that not all sign systems exhibit the combinatory (syntagmatic) relations. Consider a stop light; there are three elements (red, green, amber) that are in paradigmatic relation with each other, but there is only one slot in the formula. There is essentially no combination. Note, however, that signs may be modified (the yellow/red/green light may be solid or flashing).

Some structuralisms (**sign systems**) are linear. Language clearly is an elaborate **linear structuralism**; one speech sound precedes the next, one word comes before the following word (the exception here is gestural language). Dinner is a linear structuralism, since it proceeds through time. So is Beethoven's Fifth Symphony. Yet, is conventional dress linear? For example, a cowboy hat implies a certain kind of belt, jeans, boots, and a "western" shirt. Rather than being a conventional order, *conventional* *dress is a combination that occurs at the same time*; it is a **nonlinear structuralism**.

Sign Systems

Before going on to discuss various applications of structuralism, it is necessary to clarify what is meant by the term **sign**. Largely the work of the American philosopher Charles Peirce (1839–1914), the usually accepted theory of signs rests on a typology of three terms: icon, index, and symbol (see Peirce 1940).

sign = icon, or index, or symbol

An **icon** is a sign that bears a direct resemblance to the thing to which it refers (its **referent**); **index** indirectly indicates the referent, and a **symbol** has no physical resemblance or relation to its referent at all. For example, a drawing or pictograph of a flame would be an icon for the concept 'fire,' while an index for 'fire' might be a picture of smoke or actual smoke. The sound sequence /fayr/ (English *fire*) is completely arbitrary, and is a symbol for 'fire'; it bears no actual physical resemblance to fire or smoke. As noted in the previous chapter, most cultural and linguistic signs are arbitrary. That is, most linguistic and cultural signs are symbols, not indices or icons. We are therefore primarily concerned with symbols, although it is important to note the existence of the other two types of signs.

There is probably not a single cultural phenomenon that does not involve a system of signs, all of them amenable to structural analysis to some degree. Some sign systems are deliberately constructed by people to categorize fields of knowledge (think of the symbolic systems used in mathematics, chemistry, biology, and logic) or to make useful distinctions (examples: traffic signals, Morse Code, insignia indicating rank, units of measure). Such useful, verifiable sign systems may be called *deliberate* to distinguish them from less conscious sign systems (*nondeliberate*). Sign systems which use one set of phenomena as signs to conventionally interpret another set of concepts may be termed **hermeneutic** (the Greek word for interpretive). The way sign systems are interpreted is usually through analogy; one set is analyzed and understood using another sign system as a model. So, for example, Basso (1967) shows how western Apache terms for human anatomy were extended to categorize automobiles:

wos	shoulder	front fender
gan	hand/arm	front wheel
do'	chin/jaw	front bumper
ní	face	windshield to bumper

číh	nose	hood
k'ai	hip/buttock	rear fender
zé'	mouth	gas pipe opening
bid	stomach	tank
ndą́ą́	eyes	headlights
ts'ǫǫs	veins	electrical wires
jíí	heart	distributor
zig	liver	battery

From this list, spelled according to Perry et al. (1972), it may be seen that the human body has been taken as a convenient metaphor for dissecting a second system, the automobile. Here, we have a straightforward hermeneutic sign system. One set of concepts is signified by reference to another set of signifier concepts. It is not a simple matter of relating an anatomical concept to a car part. Rather, both sets have the same (or at least parallel) internal structure. Both sets have a pair of spherical objects that deal with light ('eyes/headlights') that are positioned on a broad, slanting frontal plane ('face/windshield to bumper'). Both run on substances that are introduced into an internal storage area ('stomach/tank') via a small aperture ('mouth/tank opening'). The utility of this model can be easily understood in context: the introduction of cars into a largely monolingual western Apache speech community.

Similarly, in three integrated Bolivian communities of Quollahuaya Indians, the mountain that dominates the local terrain carries body part names for various of its sections: right leg, belly, right arm, and so on (Bastien 1985; 1987:67–68). This practice resembles the familiar one in English of extending body part terms to topological features: *foot* of the mountain, *arm* or *finger* of the bay, *head* waters of the river. In the Bolivian case, there is further extension of these body part names to label the social groups of the community that are associated with parts of the mountain. Each group, called an *ayllu*, is a kin-based, political entity that also has geographical associations with a different part of the mountain. Thus, the *ayllu* names are also based on body part terms, but probably secondarily from their referring to the parts of the mountain that are so labeled.

Every native culture-bearer in each sociocultural group swims daily in a sea of signs that participate in sign systems. Many of these are out-of-awareness knowledge, but deliberate (empirical or convenient) sign systems are consciously learned, and a person will be aware of the knowledge he or she has about them, for example, about the meaning of traffic signals.

Since we are largely concerned with out-of-awareness knowledge and behavior in this discussion, however, we will concentrate here on folk classifications, hermeneutic sign systems, and sign systems that deal with covert categories. Symbolic anthropology, literary criticism, folklore, religious studies, and other humanistic disciplines have nondeliberate sign systems as a focus of study, as opposed to the deliberate sign systems of motorists and scientists. Nonetheless, some sign systems are not hermeneutic; some are basic, fundamental, primary sets that serve as **signifiers** for themselves (e.g., linguistic labels for body parts) and may serve as models for another set of signs or concepts through such mechanisms as metaphor—for example, extension of body part names to car parts or mountain parts. In the next chapter, we will touch on the semiotics of several domains that are pervasive in human life: food and fashion, gestures (**kinesics**) and social distance (**proxemics**), sacred and mundane ritual, and narrative.

Summary

Natural and social science researchers undertake the tasks of description and classification prior to hypothesis testing and theory building. The terms phone, phonetic, and phoneme represent a claim about the nature of reality, which is the central issue of categorization in language and culture studies. Observable, describable reality is represented by the term phone (speech sound).

There is a limited number of speech sounds that are possible, given the human vocal tract as a sound generating device. The study and systematic description of possible speech sounds is the subject matter of phonetics. (See Appendix I, "Phonetics," for a brief introduction.) Phonetics thus represents a universal condition of the human species, independent of racial variety or cultural background. The analysis of the speech sounds (phones) of a language to discover the phonemes of that language and their patterning is called phonemics.

Cultural systems add another dimension: culture-specific categories do not use all the features or traits of a sign, just as not all possible speech sounds are included in a language as phonemes. (Perhaps this is for ease of processing.)

Another property of native categories is that they are automatic. Linguistic and cultural categories provide a way of dealing with chaotic reality. They are thus automatic, once learned. They allow a person to speak a language in a cultural context without pondering or translating consciously. Native knowledge is thus deep, a sort of competence, a langue as opposed to parole.

The **structural method** (also known as, structuralism) is a way of getting at what natives know. By observing permissible combinations of signs, it is possible to find out what the formulas (**syntagms**) of each system or subsystem are. A formula has various slots (in the case of linear structuralism) or simultaneous members (in the case of nonlinear structuralism). The items that may substitute into each slot or membership position constitute a paradigm.

An important issue that arises from use of the structural method is whether or not native categories are more like rules that are invoked unconsciously, or whether they are more like strategies, conscious or unconscious, that are used as needed. We will return to this issue in later chapters.

Learnability is another issue that arises when one ponders the nature of native knowledge. What is a learnable category? Is there some genetically endowed basis for some or all cultural and linguistic categories? We will also return to this issue.

Discussion and Activities

1. From the point of view of North American culture, analyze the structure of the following television genres. Do they have the same or similar structures? Do the structure(s)' features have cultural significance?

    sit-com
    talk show
    game show
    late show
    soap opera
    mini-series

    Abstract from your structure(s) a set of features that you think North Americans would recognize and apply to the analysis of these terms, once they were told what the features were.
2. Have class members gather data on the television genres in (1) above from a variety of consultants. Then give the consultants the set of features agreed upon in class and ask them to analyze each term. How do the results from your consultants compare with one another and with the analysis of the class?

Key Terms

arbitrary
aspect
binary oppositions
competence
deep
dichotomies
hermeneutic
icon
idiolect
index
kinesics
langue
levels
linear structuralism
minimal pairs
mutual intelligibility
nonlinear structuralism
object
paradigm
paradigmatic
parole
performance
proxemics
referent
semiology
sign
sign systems
signifiers
speech sounds
structuralist
structural method
symbol
syntagmatic
syntagms

6

Signifiers in Syntax

> In dealing with the songs of cultures that do not employ the Western tempered tonal system—where the intervals between notes are smaller (microtonal) than our half-steps; where, consequently, Western concepts of harmony are in complete variance with the character of their melodies; where the methods of performance differ from Western practices—the suggested chords will hardly convey the true character of the melody. They are, at best, approximations. Indeed, the tunes themselves, as transcribed into Western notation, are approximations of the original performance.
>
> —Charles Haywood

It is a common folk theory in North America that music is a universal language or code. This notion, from the nineteenth century, holds that the psychological base is the same for all members of the human species. Yet differences between cultures (and hence ultimately differences between similar sets of cultural categories) are strikingly obvious, causing much concern in modern complex societies such as that of the United States, over questions of integration of multicultural perspectives.

It was hoped by Saussure that a science of semiotics could eventually describe the basis of human cognition and categorization. Structuralism provided a way of discovering what natives know, and it is still valuable as a way of indicating what categories or features are important to natives. Once sufficient comparative data had been accumulated from the vast variety of languages and cultures of the world, Saussure and his followers presumed that it would be possible to entertain hypotheses about how the human mind works, despite the effects of local cultures, to create unique expressions. This procedure brings to mind the hope of nineteenth-century linguists who sought to discover the origin and nature of all human languages by studying language families and reconstructing proto-languages. In this chapter, we postpone the search for universals of linguistic and cultural cognition in order to examine structuralism in more depth.

Semiotics All around Us

Sign systems may exist in two ways: as elements that may paradigmatically fill slots in a conventional order (examples: language, dinner) or in a conventional combination (appropriate combination of foods or clothing). So, for example, for many North Americans, breakfast consists of something like the following sequence.

"juice" + (breadstuff) + main dish/side dish + (dessert)
coffee _ _ _ _ _ _ _ _ _ _ _ _ _ _ _

For the "juice," fruit may be substituted. Breadstuff might include toast, grits, sweet rolls, or cereal. The main dish (everything from eggs to French toast to a large cut of meat) is often accompanied by breakfast meats, toast, or potato products on the side. Coffee (or perhaps tea or cocoa) is partaken throughout. An optional dessert of sweets or fruit may follow, in which case the breadstuff course is often not presented. The meal may be abbreviated to the first two steps (appetizer + breadstuff), with the likelihood that the appetizer will be juice; this is referred to as continental breakfast.

Although persons familiar with North American culture may want to quibble with the details, they are likely to see a very familiar linear structuralism in the system of signs that make up 'breakfast.' The elements themselves, however, do not have symbolic value. Here we can say that the **structure** has a primary meaning for 'breakfast,' whereas no element within the structure can mean 'breakfast' in the same way. This observation is clear when we consider that those elements (bread, coffee, meats) can also participate in the "structures" that mean 'lunch,' 'supper,' 'snack,' and 'dinner.'

It is just as possible for the elements in a conventional order to have symbolic value. The so-called 'backwards dinner' (dessert + entrée + soup/salad + appetizer), a popular U.S. recreation in the 1950s, is a modification of the basic 'dinner' order, but no single element has a symbolic value on its own. The Jewish Passover meal—the seder, on the other hand, is a ceremonial meal consisting of elements, each of which does have a symbolic value. The meal commemorates the deliverance of the Jews from slavery in Egypt, and it celebrates the renewal of the year in the hopefulness of the Spring season (Gersh 1971); some dishes are symbolic.

Four cups of wine are consumed at the Passover feasts (two before the meal and two after). Each represents one of the four ways God said He would bring the Jews out of slavery. The seder is conducted by the father of the family, who speaks of the significance of the festival and who distributes special ritual foods. These foods are held on two plates that are next to the father's place. On one are three matzos (pieces of unleavened bread) representing the three kinds of Jews—priests (Kohanim), their assistants (Levites), and the rest of the Jews (regular Israelites). Early in the ceremony, the father breaks the middle matzo in two; he distributes pieces of one half to be eaten then, and he distributes the second half for consumption at the end of the seder. The second plate is the seder plate, and it holds five foods: a roast lamb bone (*zeroa*), a roasted egg (*betzah*), bitter herbs (usually horseradish [*maror*]), greens (*karpas*), and a mixture of apples, nuts, and wine (*haroset*). Only the last three are eaten. The *zeroa* and *betzah* are reminders only: the lamb bone of the special Passover sacrifice, which was a lamb, and the egg of the regular holiday offerings made in the temple. The father dips the *karpas* (often celery or a salad green) in salt water and gives each person a piece—the first act of the seder proper. The greens represent spring and renewed hope for a world at peace; the salt water stands for the tears the Jews cried in slavery. The bitter herb *maror* (standing for the bitterness of slavery) is dipped in the sweet apple-nut mixture (*haroset*) to remind participants of the mix of bitter and sweet in life. The sequence of the seder is inviolate and meaningful, but as we have seen, each ritual food is also meaningful.

The Christian Eucharist (bread-and-wine symbolizing Christ's body and blood), derived from the Jewish ritual meal, is better considered a conventional combination of signs than as a conventional ordering of signs, even though there is a simple linear order (bread first, then wine). Conventional combinations of various sorts of foods into dishes are complexes of signs (categories) which have no symbolic value in the sequence itself.

Likewise, various combinations of clothing present similar collages: headgear + garment + footgear. Natives recognize some combinations as grossly inappropriate (example: wedding veil + Scottish kilt + cowboy boots) or just slightly odd (example: tennis shoes + Bermuda shorts + coat and tie). Although such combinations of clothing are trivial examples of semiotics, a moment's reflection will convince the reader of how pervasive and important such dress combinations are in daily life. Clothing complexes may take on symbolic values: the kilt and its accouterments, a wedding trousseau, a Santa Claus outfit. Or, a clothing complex may serve as a symbol of status to some people: blue-collar worker vs. white-collar worker vs. bohemian. A clothing complex may reflect rank within a sector of a society: executive vs. mid-level manager vs. recent recruit. Any two or more basic dress codes (e.g., business suit vs. hard hat/overalls will serve to mutually define one another in a set that itself may contrast with a higher order category.

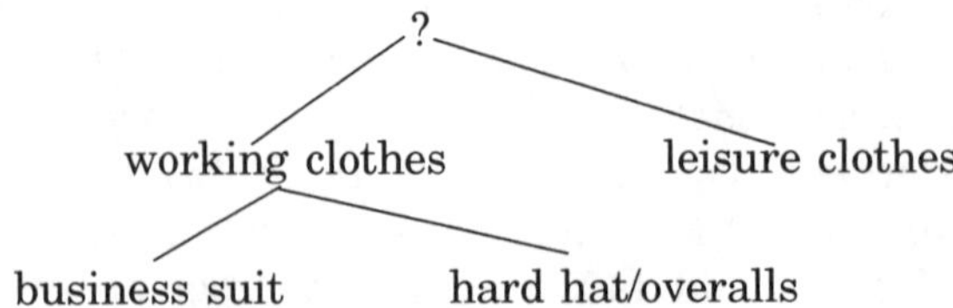

Here, we find a hierarchical organization of categories similar to the sort found in language or the folk classifications of plants and animals. The variation within each category of a clothing complex might be described as fashion. Although the term is usually not applied to the attire of construction workers, it is nonetheless true that there is fluctuation over time in what the workers wear on the job, "native" recognition of current standards, and perhaps even symbolic exploitation of any permitted variation in the current dress code. Where such variation exists, there will be named (overt) categories with which natives can discuss current fashion, even cultivate it. So, for example, the designers of chic clothing can state "This summer, dresses will be made of silk," and so shall dresses be made (Barthes 1972); a semiotic system may be manipulated to create reality.

Kroeber and Richardson (1940) examined a variety of style shifts in modern society from mid-nineteenth to mid-twentieth century. One was fashion in women's clothing. Specifically, they plotted the rise and fall of hemlines and necklines over those several generations. What they found were long oscillations from low to high to low over approximately 20-year periods. They also found that the rise and fall of hemlines and necklines were independent of one another and of other kinds of style changes. One of the "meanings" of such changes may be to signal that the wearer is sufficiently prosperous to purchase new clothing year after year. If the oscillations in height of hem or neckline were annual, one might save clothes and use them two or three years hence when they returned to fashion. With the oscillations being over such long periods, one cannot easily save garments for later use since it might be 20 years before an item returned to fashion.

From these studies, we can see that meanings of the choice of an item from a particular set (headgear, appetizer, dress with low hemline) and of arrangements or sequences of items (business suits, eggs Benedict with grits) can signal messages that convey information far beyond that of the domain in which they are cast. A choice of a fashion item can inform about financial status as well as taste in clothing. A host or hostess may convey information about travel experiences or family origins in the menu plan of a dinner party. In special instances such as the Passover feast, everything in a sequence is meaningful and the sequence itself conveys meaning which is elaborated on and explicated consciously by the father in his role of teacher and moral leader of the nuclear family.

Gesture and Social Distance

In 1946, a young anthropologist named Ray Birdwhistle, while studying the Kutenai Indians (many of whom live in the Idaho panhandle and neighboring Canada), noticed that not only did many Kutenais have two linguistic codes (Kutenai, English), they used two different sets of gestures and facial expressions, depending on which language they were using. By 1952, he had founded the study of kinesics (body movements and their meaning). Of some 250,000 possible facial movements, only certain combinations of facial movements occur in the "face work" of a given sociocultural group (Birdwhistle 1952). Some facial and body movements appear to be universal, and many have the same emotional value: stare, smile, clinched fist, curling toes, pupil dilation. Other body movements vary cross-culturally: nodding head, crossing of arms, winking. A lateral head nodding movement, for example, means 'no' to a Westerner, but means 'yes' or 'affirmative' in some parts of Asia.

The semiotics of social distance (proxemics) also varies across cultures. Edward T. Hall, in *The Silent Language* (1959), discovered that North Americans have discrete categories of interpersonal distance that vary in a short phase and a long phase (the phases have to do with the amount of space in which the interaction is taking place) (see also Hall 1963, 1974).

Interpersonal Distance

	short	**long**
intimate	0	6–18"
personal	1.5–2.5'	2.5–4'
social	4–7'	7–12'
public	12–15'	25' +

Hall also described how the typical amount of interpersonal distance in North American culture differed from the comparable parameters in Latin American culture.

> In Latin America, the interaction distance is smaller than it is in the United States. Indeed, people cannot talk comfortably with one another unless they are very close the distance that evokes either sexual or hostile feelings in the North American. The result is that when they move close, we withdraw and back away. As a consequence, they think we are distant or cold, withdrawn and unfriendly. We, on the

> other hand, are constantly accusing them of breathing down our necks, crowding us and spraying our faces. (Hall 1959:209)

The kinesic and proxemic codes of a sociocultural group may be seen as ways of marking politeness, status, role, degree of familiarity, degree of formality of the situation, intimacy, and the like. It is unusual to think of the following as signs or symbols: social relationships (senior:junior, leader:participant, spouse:spouse), contextual roles (clerk:customer, judge:accused, actor:actor), or emotional qualities (cold:reserved, informal:intimate, chatty:voluble:glib), and yet gestures, body movements, and socially acceptable use of space all serve us daily as signifiers for a multitude of social, contextual, and emotional categories that we encounter in the social environment. The meaning signaled by a signifier in a communicative event is termed the **signified**. When kinesic and proxemic signs co-occur with language usage, they are often considered to be related to **paralinguistic** signals, the tone-of-voice kinds of linguistic modifications we make to spoken language. They are all "beyond language in its normal sense" (**paralanguage**). Such a view, of course, is biased from the point of view of language.

More difficult, perhaps, is to think of habitual, everyday behavior (even by single individuals) as **ritual**. The ordinary sense of the word ritual is 'ceremony' or 'rite.' We will term any habitual sequence of behavior as a ritual: an individual's morning toilet, an exchange with the neighbor as he or she goes off to work, the procedure for starting off the day, the protocol of the coffee break, going to lunch, asking for a raise, afternoon break, happy hour, coming home, supper, and so on.

If someone's daily routines and sub-routines are disturbed, the affected individual's emotional and mental balance is at least temporarily out of order. In other words, we all, in our daily lives, create (often with others) set patterns with which we organize our day. These conventional sequences of steps (mundane rituals) that structure so much of our daily life can be analyzed as semiotic systems.

Sign systems may also take on higher-level meanings. A sport, for example, is a complex of sign systems for methods of play, organizing the players, scoring, and so on. Yet this complex of sign systems may take on a larger meaning, as when a local team becomes symbolic of their community. Sometimes the symbolism is quite overt. Home teams customarily wear white or light-colored versions of their uniforms, while visiting teams are normally clad in reversed darker versions of their uniforms, a modern expression of the old cowboy movie rule that the good guys wear white hats. The success of a professional or school team can be the success of the city or institution that it represents. Having the World Series Champion or the Superbowl Champion team gives an entire city a success that it can share; such triumphs of civic pride can even be translated into economic improvement for the community since winning teams engender positive attitudes about one's hometown that make such a location attractive, for example, to businesses looking for a new place to move.

The individuals most important in a given sport become signifiers for the public. Heroes are symbolic of the entire game process, even though they are also a single part of it. Someone like Joe DiMaggio can become known as "Mr. Baseball," representing the entire national pastime and all that is deemed noble about it. Or, a Michael Jordan can inspire a city and a nation by his graceful play and attractive character, becoming important far beyond the game of basketball at which he excels. It is thus possible to rank signs in a sign system in terms of importance. Although all the players on a team (and competing teams) can be seen as a "sign system," a limited number of player roles (perhaps only one for each team sport) will be the most prestigious. For example, the role of the quarterback holds highest prestige for the game of football; in baseball, the role of pitcher is seen as the most important by some. It is difficult to compare hockey, basketball, soccer, football, and baseball stars in terms of what they do in their respective rituals. At a higher level, the **meta-**sports level, however, they become comparable because of the manner in which they play; their individual struggles within the ongoing ritual of the game are enjoyed vicariously by the spectator.

Ritualizing behavior is also the basis of much interaction between people who regularly associate with one another. In the popular work, *Games People Play*, a psychiatrist showed that social interactions, especially family behavior, are systems of roles that are enacted over and over in context (Berne 1964). The archetypes here include 'alcoholic,' 'tyrannical husband/father,' 'shrew,' and others. Small systems of these roles (a family, office, or other clearly bounded unit) interact often in terms of role structure, like athletes in team sports. The ritual nature of interpersonal behavior as interaction in terms of archetypes is the basis for the soap operas and other popular dramatic forms, forming second-order sign systems. Our prescribed routines (idiosyncratic, interpersonal; vicarious or formal) are systems of signs which are articulated as ongoing, continuous behavior instead of as graphic or plastic art.

Narratives (fable, anecdotes, myth, legend, and so on) are easily analyzed as sets of interpersonal relations, conventional orders for action (standard plots), or as significant archetypes. A story, actually, is all of these things: linear order (sequence of events), plot (basis of the interpersonal conflict articulated by the events), and symbolic value of characters (protagonist vs. antagonist, hero vs. villain; note that a villain may be the protagonist).

Narrative form can vary across cultures. For example, in a personal narrative (a story about things that actually happened to the teller) in North American culture, there is usually an **evaluation section**, just before the end (Labov and Waletzky 1967). Better called a **validation section**, this device makes the sequence of events a bona fide narrative by use of emphatic statements ("that's the most. . . ."; "I never thought that I . . ."; etc.) that serve to underscore the significance of the reported event(s). This device is clearly exhibited in Western fiction (Pratt 1977).

In Hopi coyote stories, fables in which a trickster archetype (Coyote) is forever doomed to face the consequences of her/his own scheming and conniving, an evaluation section is most often lacking. This is because evaluative devices are used throughout the conventional structure by skilled narrators in actual performances to milk the irony of Coyote's perpetual backfires and near misses (Shaul et al. 1987).

Vladmir Propp's *Morphology of the Folktale* (1928; English translation 1968) is an essential starting point for any structural study of **folktales.** In the analysis of one hundred Russian folktales, Propp found that there were 31 elementary functions that were realized as actual events in the sequence making up a story. So, for example,

1. A sorcerer gives Ivan a boat, which carries him off to another kingdom.
2. An old man gives a horse to Susenko, which then carries Susenko to another kingdom.

In the examples above, the characters seem subordinate in importance to the plot, which clearly is the same in both stories. The plot may be of the greatest symbolic importance, with the characters serving only to modify its fundamental meaning. Plots, as configurations of relations between characters, may represent ritualized behavior of stereotypes within a given culture. There may be whole systems of character relations intermeshed at different levels within a long narrative, such as in a novel (Barthes 1970), much as sports take on larger and larger significance within a particular cultural context.

What do *Star Wars* and the fairy tale *Snow White* have in common? Both exemplify the following basic plot.

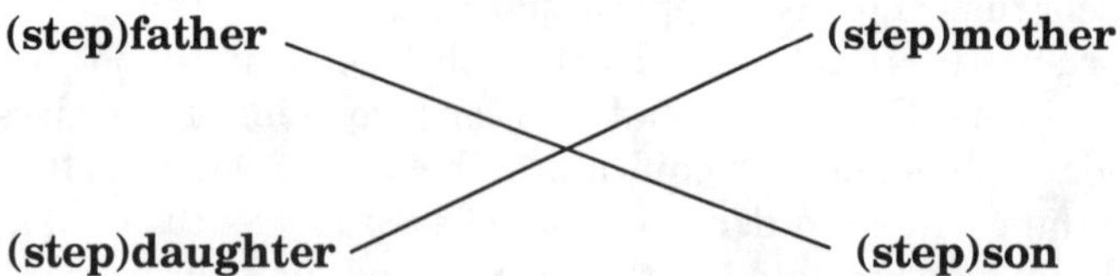

The son or daughter figure is always the protagonist and hero(ine). The relationship is usually between two members of the same sex, and the optional step-relations add sinister overtones to the conflict. In *Snow White*, the wicked stepmother is eventually overcome. In *Star Wars*, Luke Skywalker—the characters' names are archetypes—eventually overcomes his sinister father, Darth Vader (Dark Father), in a revelation scene. What we see in these two stories is the persistence over a long period of a folk story that speaks to fundamental conflicts that characterize Western culture today and have done so for many, many centuries in the past.

In **myths** (narratives about the origin of the cosmos, human nature, and human destiny, the nature of "things" in general), the characters and their relationships are articulated as a sequence of events, but the symbolic value of the archetype characters may be eclipsed by the symbolic value of the events in which they act. Which is of greater symbolic value, Huck Finn or his river? Events of mega-importance (creation, for example) outdistance most of the characters involved. Such universal themes as the Flood, confusion of tongues, virginal conception, and the miraculous birth/life of culture hero(ine)s are all more important than characters or character relations.

Claude Levi-Strauss (1963, 1966, 1969, 1973) has claimed that the type of analysis cited above for *Star Wars* and *Snow White* can be pushed even deeper, to an unconscious level. Let us briefly examine his treatment of the Oedipus myth (1963).

1. Oedipus marries his mother (Jocasta).
2. Oedipus kills his biological father (Lacus).
3. Oedipus destroys the Sphinx.
4. Oedipus means 'swollen foot' in Greek.

These themes of the myth are each deeply meaningful, and Levi-Strauss termed them **mythemes**. Mythemes (1) and (2) have to do with the valuation of kinship. In (1), kinship is overvalued, and in (2), it is undervalued. In mythemes (3) and (4), the underlying sign is **autochthony** (earthly origin). Both Oedipus (4) and the primeval monster he destroys (3) are terrestrial and not celestial persons.

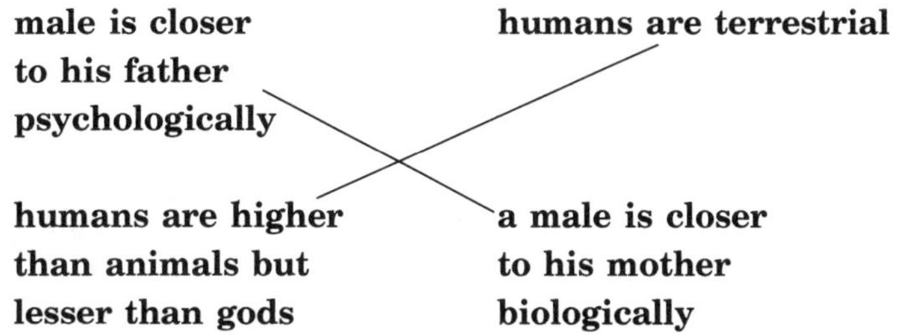
male is closer
to his father
psychologically
humans are terrestrial
humans are higher
than animals but
lesser than gods
a male is closer
to his mother
biologically

An interrelating line is a relationship of contradiction that **mediates** between the two mutual contradictions, making them both true as conditions that define reality.

It is important to understand that in myths, just as in meal sequences, the structures themselves have meaning, just as do the symbols and the **relationships** holding among the symbols. For example, in a comparison of the Indian equivalent of the cycle of the Western Oedipus myths, A. K. Ramanujan (1971) found that the structures of both were identical—and identical in meaning. The crucial **relation** holding between the protagonists and the antagonists was also identical at core; in addition, it was negative in both cases. What differed was only a single characteristic of the actors and goals—the relative age of each. Ramanujan summarized the Western Oedipus myths in the following diagram:

Western Oedipus

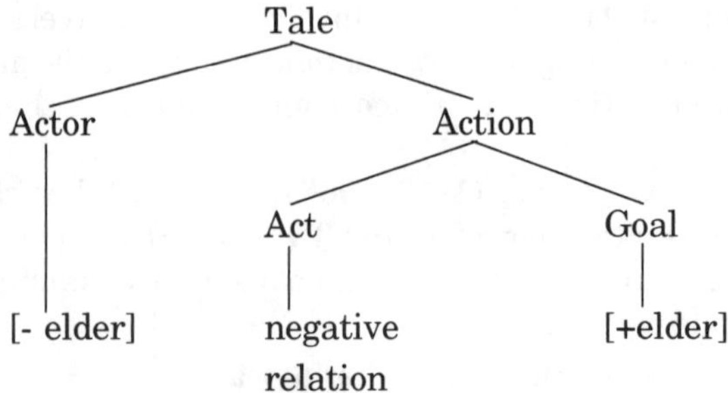

The Actor and Goal are the same sex (e.g., Oedipus and his father, Lacus), but they differ as to generation, the Actor (Oedipus) being younger and the Goal (Lacus) being older; the act (killing) is negative. In the Indian "Oedipus" tales, we see identical structure and relation, but a generational reversal of the Actor and the Goal:

Indian Oedipus

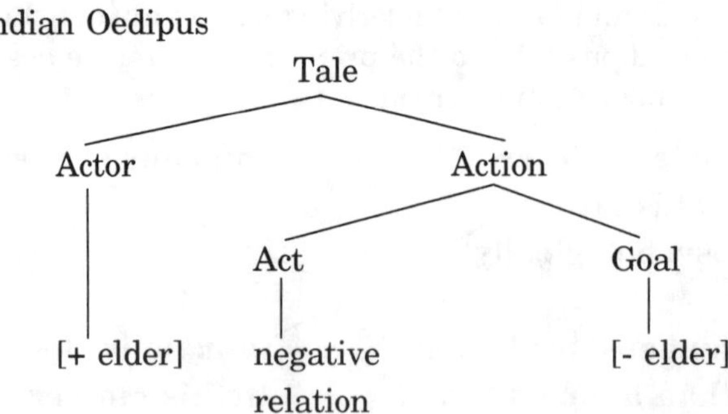

In the Indian story, an old king on the edge of senility magically trades with his son his own age for the son's youth; in exchange, the son is given eternal life, but to be lived in his father's senile state, surely a negative relation. In effect, the king lives his son's life for him. The crucial difference in the Western and Indian versions of the stories rests with the age characteristics of the actors and goals in each. In the Western version, the younger generation is acting against the older generation; in the Indian version, the older generation injures the younger one. Yet, the meanings of the structures of both are identical. Such analyses tempt one to speculate on the different tensions in relationships among generations in Europe and in India.

Stop and think about the myriad sign systems that surround us: language, language usage (think of the media), food, clothing, ritual behavior, art, narratives (one of our chief entertainments); the list goes on and on. Human culture and social organization may be now seen as a wealth of sign systems at various levels with myriad connections. Where there is meaning, structuralism claims that those meanings are a system of mutually opposing elements held by the relation of opposition.

The Return of the Native

Where there is a system of signs, there are also natives, the persons engaged in their use. By this term, we mean persons who are "native speakers" of a particular sign system, native bearers of and actors in the cultures. Natives are the folk who share folklore, the public who view shared rituals enacted in the soap operas, the members of an ethnic group who share sets of sign systems peculiar to their group (their culture). Each of us is a native to his or her language and culture. The structural method imported from linguistics into anthropology, folklore, literary criticism and **sociology** as semiotics, provides a method for analyzing human behavior. The basic assumption is that human behavior is not random, that patterns are to be perceived in behavior or its products (art, music, dance, literature, philosophy, and so on), and that these patterns are meaningful and analyzable in terms of syntagmatic and paradigmatic relationships. The culture of a definable social group may be seen as the set(s) of sign systems which the members share in common and which are peculiar to the group. In the case of many sign systems (language, belief systems, kinship patterns, economic and legal institutions), there may be variation within a group and overlapping between groups. For instance, a young speaker of a rural dialect of English might have less of the local dialect due to the influence of media, education, and travel than an older person of the same region who has never traveled outside the local community and grew up with limited contact with the national media. At the same time, the total linguistic performance of even younger speakers might have more in common with older speakers of a neighboring village than with the speech of the capital. Thus, one has in-group variation at the same time as overlap between groups and intergroup variation.

The sets of categories (sign systems) which the "natives" of a group share are described as being **emic** categories. The form **-eme** means 'fundamental (unit)' and appears in the words morpheme 'fundamental unit of meaning' and phoneme 'fundamental unit of sound.' The difference between [i] and [I] is meaningful in English because those two sounds are each separate phonemes, /i/ and /I/, of the language. For example,

bit	/bIt/	'small amount'
beet	/bit/	'red root vegetable'

Many other such pairs could be found by an English speaker. For a monolingual native speaker of Spanish, however, there is no distinction between [i] and [I]; the two would sound like two repetitions of the same sound.

From a scientific point of view, the difference between [I] and [i] is roughly one of muscle tension in the throat. The vowel [I] is lax (muscles less tense), while [i] is a tense vowel. This principled differentiation of [I] and [i] presents the two vowels as **etic** categories, that is, categories resulting from logical or scientific analysis, categories that derive their existence from considerations external to the data themselves. Etic categories are the tools of the scientist or scholar who tries to compare data from different sociocultural groups or different periods of history in order to see what the data have in common.

The etic-emic approach may be used with nonlinguistic data also. In the analysis of kinship, the **etic** categories for the biological family are as follows.

Fa	father
Mo	mother
Da	daughter
So	son
Br	brother
Si	sister

Other categories may be modeled in terms of this basic semiotic system.

FaFa	father's father
FaMo	father's mother

These etic categories or their combinations may be applied to kinship systems from all sociocultural groups.

aunt = { FaSi, MoSi }

This informally means: "the English term *aunt* consists of the set of all individuals who are female siblings of either of one's parents." In Hopi culture, the emic units are different.

kya'at	'her/his aunt'
yu'a	'her/his mother or aunt'

The etic analysis of the Hopi data is as follows.

kya-	FaSi
yu-	{ Mo, MoSi }

The category labeled by the term *yu-* consists of one's mother and her sister(s). This is because Hopi kinship is matrilineal; descent is figured from one's mother. For example, if my mother is of the Side Corn Clan, all of my brothers and sisters and I will belong to that clan, regardless of which clan my father belongs to.

The etic-emic distinction is a useful one. The scholar's tool kit of concepts (the consonants and vowels producible by the human vocal tract, biological kinship, the chemical elements, Linnean classification of flora and fauna, the Munsell color chart, etc.) are sets of etic categories. The scholar uses a set of etic categories to describe objectively the content of the emic categories of the natives, linguistic or otherwise. The importance of the etic-emic distinction for culture was first pointed out by the linguist Kenneth Pike.

> The value of emic study is, first, that it leads to an understanding of the way in which a language or culture is constructed, not as a series of miscellaneous parts, but as a working whole. Second, it helps one to appreciate not only the culture or language as an ordered whole, but it helps one to understand the individual actors in such a life drama—their attitudes, motives, interests, responses, conflicts, and personality development. In addition, it provides the only basis upon which a predictive science of behavior can be expected to make some of its greatest progress. (Pike 1967:40 41)

The etic-emic approach follows, of course, from the structural analysis of linguistic and nonlinguistic data: one must have a tool kit of concepts in order to elicit, discover, and understand native concepts.

Summary

Extralinguistic systems—such as kinesic and proxemic systems—are cultural systems that accompany language use, and may also be independent of language use. Gesture and social distance show us "silent languages" that are culture specific, existing beyond actual spoken languages. These extralinguistic systems are good examples of semiotic systems, and show how pervasive semiotic systems are in everyday life.

Many of the behaviors that we repeat every day as a matter of routine (getting up, dressing, morning toilet, eating breakfast, etc.) may be seen as rituals comprised of sequential categories, frames or scripts for automatic required behavior. Like a spoken language, our everyday rituals define ourselves, our space, and social environment, while also creating a feeling of comfortable familiarities. Such categories (rituals) may range from individual to cultural.

Other kinds of pervasive semiotic systems are myths and **folk theories** that provide conventional wisdom for much social action and acting by providing validating reasons for behavior and for conventional or situational roles. The components of these myths or folk theories are called mythemes.

The term etic—taken from the word phonetic—represents any system of terminology that attempts to do what phonetics does: provide a neutral, verifiable set of named concepts that are independent of cultural bias. An etic system tries to isolate the obvious, observable facets of a phenomenon. The emic system, on the other hand, emerges as a product of an etic description and represents the system as a particular native would recognize it. So, for example, the phonemic system of a particular language (e.g., English) would be the inventory of sounds recognized as belonging to the language by native English speakers. The emic/etic distinction can be extended to analyses of nonlinguistic cultural categories, for example, kinship terminologies.

Discussion and Activities

1. The following sentences mean 'Do you see something?' in the languages indicated.

See	ye	ocht?	(Scots)
see	you	anything	

Ya	um	hìita	tuwanta?	(Hopi)
	you	anything	be seeing	

A bheil	thu	càil	a' faicinn?	(Scottish Gaelic)
be	you	anything	at seeing	

Ser	du	någonting?	(Swedish)
see	you	anything	

The following are the statement equivalents ('You see something.').

Ye see ocht.

Um hìita tuwanta.

Tha [be] thu càil a' faicinn.

Du ser någonting.

Compare the statement and question pair for each language (English, Scots, Hopi, Scots Gaelic, Swedish). Assuming that the declarative forms (statements) are basic, for each pair make a generalization (rule) for forming questions in each language.

2. Consider the following domain. What does each term have in common? Can you make an etic description of this common property?

baroness	tigress
authoress	songstress
mistress	countess
lioness	actress
poetess	

Does this property that the terms have in common reflect more than the feature [+ female]? Are they all [+ adult] as well as [+ female]? Do these two features tell the whole story? Is there a core meaning, with core members of the domain? (Is a domain the same thing as a category?) What features or factors mediate (link) any peripheral terms/category members with the core? Describe the set in etic terms, and then try to guess what the emic features of the domain are.

3. Below are the **blurbs** of several commercial publications. Ignoring the obvious commercial purpose (to sell merchandise), what conventional wisdom informs each text? Go through the text listing each assertion made. Then figure out what assumption(s) inform each. Considering each assumption as a mytheme, express each (mytheme) in a sentence, and then figure out how each mytheme is part of the complete myth. What are the mediating factors, if any, that relate (sets) of mythemes? Take into account the layout, type design features, and relative length of each blurb. How do these factor into the total message?

(a) Text from a coffee brochure (Starbucks 1995).

Discover the Rare and the Exotic from Africa . . .

SPLENDOR

EXOTIC, **intensely**

flavorful coffees.

Out of Africa come the rare and exotic.

Africa is the birthplace of ancient civilizations. And

today, a brilliant mix of languages, dress and customs still enlivens Africa's coffee-growing regions. The land varies too, from desert to alpine snows, from acacia woodlands to open plains, from lowland forests to vast freshwater lakes. African coffee grows wild on Kikuyu farms, on the Bantu's highland plantations—it even grows on the Arabian peninsula in Yemen. Such exotic diversity is apparent in the breathtaking range of coffee drinking experiences available. African coffees also share a bright acidity and extraordinary body that are especially suited to summer . . .

(b) Text from a blurb hung around a wine bottle (Blossom Hill Collection 1995).

Pamper Yourself
Tonight . . .

HERE'S TO THE START OF A BEAUTIFUL EVENING.

Slip out of a long day with a spa bath experience at home. Set aside at least an hour, and make it known so that no phones, family member or roommates will interrupt this quiet time.

1. Change out of your work clothes, mentally shedding the responsibilities of the day
2. Put on a comfy robe
3. Select some soothing music
4. Pour a glass of your favorite Blossom Hill Wine
5. Place a group of scented candles in the bathroom; light them all
6. Turn the lights down or off
7. Start running the warm water
8. Unwrap a fresh bar of your favorite scented Yardley of London soap. Lay out your favorite, fluffiest towel
9. Sink into the bath, allowing your thoughts to wander to fields of flowers, walks in the rain, picnics in the park and dreams of the future

---

(c) Text from a brochure for ordering product-related clothing and accessories (Philip Morris Inc. 1994).

MARLBORO
GEAR

HEAD OUT, RIDE HARD, KICK BACK AND GEAR UP.
TAKING ON MARLBORO COUNTRY
TAKES A SPECIAL KIND OF GEAR.
GEAR BUILT TO GO THE DISTANCE.
GEAR THAT PLAYS AS HARD AS IT WORKS.

---

4. Another approach to the analysis of texts such as blurbs is to extract key or focal terms from each text and treat them as mythemes. Try this with the texts above. Does this approach yield a differing underlying myth?

Key Terms

autochthony
blurbs
-eme
emic
etic
evaluation section
extralinguistic
folk theories
folktales
mediates
meta-
myths
mythemes
paralanguage
paralinguistic
relation
relationships
ritual
signified
sociology
structure
validation section

7

The New Relativism

(Con)text (E)merges

> Cognitive anthropology remains closely affiliated with linguistics, both in terms of the importation of formal models and in that lexicon and verbal reports constitute the principal data. With few exceptions, anthropologists have been slow to confront the problems posed in describing systems of action and in relating cognition to action. Most have been content to pursue their inquiries into the structure of static, atemporal, semantic relations.
>
> —J. B. Gatewood

Linguistic anthropology after 1960 represents a conscious blending of semiotics (language as a model for other cultural components) and linguistic relativity (language as an influence on habitual thought), and it emerges under the influence of another linguistic movement, **generativism**. This movement looked upon linguistic knowledge as normative but seated psychologically in individuals rather than existing solely as a shared social code. At the same time, it was suggested then that this internalized linguistic knowledge was organized as a finite set of rules. Using a finite grammar (set of rules), it was thought possible to "generate" (precisely account for) an infinite number of sentences. Cultural anthropology borrowed the idea of a generative grammar as a semiotic way to infer the structure of cultural domains (**relativism**).

The Palace Revolution in Linguistics

Generative theories of language derived from the ideas of Noam Chomsky. Beginning with publication of his *Syntactic Structures* in 1957, and up until the present, it is fair to say that no linguistic theory has been proposed that did not consider those ideas in one fashion or another. The mainstream American Structuralist linguistics that dominated during the period immediately before Chomsky were largely antimentalistic; psychology was not an issue. With Chomsky's formulations, however, psychological factors assumed a central place for linguistics; in fact, Chomsky himself has repeatedly argued that the proper place of linguistics is as a part of cognitive psychology, or even biology (1965, 1981, 1986b). Under American Structuralism, semantics was also taboo because it was considered mentalistic. Although Chomsky initially skirted the study of meaning in his earliest formulations of generative grammar, he held that native speaker judgments of **grammaticality** (or acceptability) allowed one to study the psychological reality of language. Read, for example, the three sentences below as a fluent or native speaker of English.

> The boy walked the dog.
>
> *Walk the boyed the dog.
>
> *The boy elapsed the dog.

The second and third sentences are "starred"; remember that an asterisk is a convention that marks them as ungrammatical. In making such a grammaticality judgment, a person utilizes internalized (linguistic) knowledge. In the second sentence, the word order conventions of English are violated, and a verbal **inflection** (*-ed* past tense) is incorrectly attached to a noun (*boy*). In the third sentence, the meaning of *elapse* is inappropriate, both the lexical meaning (boys don't elapse) and the grammatical meaning (*elapse* is an intransitive verb and so will not accept an object). The third sentence is semantically odd.

Chomsky maintained that such internalized knowledge was best represented as a set of rules. To demonstrate this type of representation, a fragment of a generative grammar of English is presented below:

> S = NP_1 + Aux + Verb + (NP_2)
>
> NP = (Determiner) + (Quantifier) + (Adj) + Noun
>
> Aux = *-(e)s* / *-(e)d* + (Modal) + (*have*) + (*be*)
>
> Modal = *may, can, will, shall*

The simple sentence (S) in English consists of a first noun phrase (NP) that functions as a subject, and then auxiliary (Aux) that is made up of tense and the traditional "helping verbs," a verb and a second noun phrase that functions as the direct object of the verb (if the verb is transitive).

The boy takes my three red books.

The boy may have been taking my three red books.

Notice how the use of *have* as a lone helping verb requires that a past participle follow (compare *the boy may have taken . . .*). Notice also that the helping verb *be* requires *-ing* be attached to what follows.

This is an incomplete set of rules but will serve to illustrate Chomsky's method. A noun phrase is said to consist of a determiner (*the, a / an,* demonstrative pronoun, **possessive** pronoun such as *my / his / her* / etc.), a quantifier (numeral, indefinite word like *some / few / all* / etc.), adjective (*three / red / long / useful / interesting* / etc.) and a noun (*books / boy / dog / house* / etc.).

the many red books

Note that a different determiner, quantifier, or adjective may appear.

my many red books

my three red books

my three yellow books

The parentheses in the second formula above indicate that determiners, quantifiers and adjectives are optional (from a grammatical point of view).

the many red books

the red books

the books

books

The order is fixed; we cannot use a different one.

*red three my books

The order of the parts of the noun phrase represents syntagmatic relations. The relations between actual examples of each of the four classes involved (the members of the sets of "determiners," "quantifiers," "adjectives," "nouns") are paradigmatic, whereas the relation between the classes themselves (the sets) is syntagmatic. The formula (rule) for the noun phrase in English is a structuralism, as are the rules for the sentence and the auxiliary.

How, then, does a generative grammar such as that sketched here differ from one that is structural in the American Structuralist sense? The answer lies in the postulation of an underlying abstract level to which actually occurring **surface** expressions must be related. As represented in Chomsky's *Aspects of the Theory of Syntax* (1965) and related publications, that syntactic portion of a generative grammar is made up of **components.** A **base** component is comprised of rules of the sort given above that produce underlying **deep structures** (strings or complexes) upon which the rules of a **transformational** component can operate. The transformational rules specify formal links between related sentences by mapping deep structures to various **surface structure** forms of sentences. For example, consider the two surface structure sentences below.

The boy took my three red books.

My three red books were taken by the boy.

The first sentence is **active**: the **actor** (or agent) is the **subject** and the **goal** is the direct object. In the second sentence, the direct object of the first sentence has become the subject, and the old subject has been "demoted" to being the object of the preposition *by*. This construction, called a **passive**, has a specialized verb structure (*were taken* vs. *took*). Most native speakers of English judge the two sentences as somehow related, yet an American Structuralist approach can only "write" two separate rules, one for each type of sentence; it cannot specify the specialized relation between the two types. A **transformation** is an operation that derives both sentences from the underlying deep structure generated by the base; that underlying deep structure more closely resembles the active version of the sentence.

The boy *took my three red books.*

My *three red books* were *taken* by the boy.

The passive transformation inverts the subject and object, and inserts material into the string (*were, -(e)n, by*). A complete generative-transformational grammar of a language would include a structurally organized base to generate all possible basic sentences, and a set of transformations that would derive all other sentence types from the "output" of the base.

Since these first formulations, generative grammar has developed along a variety of courses, and currently practiced formal linguistic theories include a range of versions with respect to their use of transformational rules. In fact, some involve few transformations (e.g., Chomsky 1981, 1982, 1986a, 1986b), and some none at all (e.g., Gazdar et al. 1985). Perhaps the most influential of these approaches, that of the principles and parameters approach (Chomsky 1981, 1982, 1986a, 1986b, 1995; Maranz 1995; Webelhuth 1995), assumes that the universal grammar represents an innate set of principles of human mental capacity, aspects of which are modified by language-specific parameters. Movement (by transformational rule) occurs only rarely in most later models, when it is "forced" by conflicts between the principles of universal grammar and the specifics of a particular language.

Theories such as those under principles and parameters, although important in present-day theoretical linguistics and in some areas of cognitive science, nonetheless have had relatively little influence to date on that part of linguistic anthropology that adapts linguistic theory to account for nonlanguage data. **Ethnoscience**, which grew up in part as a response to the challenges of development of transformational-generative grammar in anthropological linguistics, has led to a series of cognitive anthropological formulations that continue to stimulate study in language and culture, few of which ever used the idea of transformations as an important concept with respect to cultural grammars, but most did at least recognize the possibility of an underlying, somewhat abstract representation through which variants of a belief or practice might be related. We turn now to an examination of some of these formulations as they came out of the ethnoscience of the 1960s and 1970s.

Ethnoscience, the New Ethnography, and Ethnographic Semantics

Chomsky's work did suggest the possibility of writing **cultural grammars** (Colby 1975) for various domains in a culture. Culture, as a set of systems (social organization, technology, ideology, etc., possibly united by **themes** running throughout), was seen as internalized knowledge.

> [A] society's culture consists of whatever it is one has to know or believe in order to operate in a manner acceptable to its members. . . . [C]ulture is not a material phenomenon; it does not consist of things, people, behavior or emotions. It is rather an organization of these things. It is the forms of things that people have in mind, their models for perceiving, relating, and otherwise interpreting them. (Goodenough 1957:167)

As Keesing (1972) noted, this approach treats culture as systems of knowledge. One could ethnographically study this knowledge, producing models of a specified domain (a set of terms and the rules for their appropriate combination) that could generate native-like behavior. This approach developed during the 1960s as ethnoscience (also called **ethnographic semantics** and the **New Ethnography**). The mentalistic stance and ideal of generative models of language were the main ideas taken over from linguistics by ethnoscience. Methodologically, ethnographic semantics relied primarily on an old-fashioned form of linguistic structuralism; only a few anthropologists attempted to incorporate the notion of transformations into their cultural grammars.

The ancestry of ethnoscience follows:

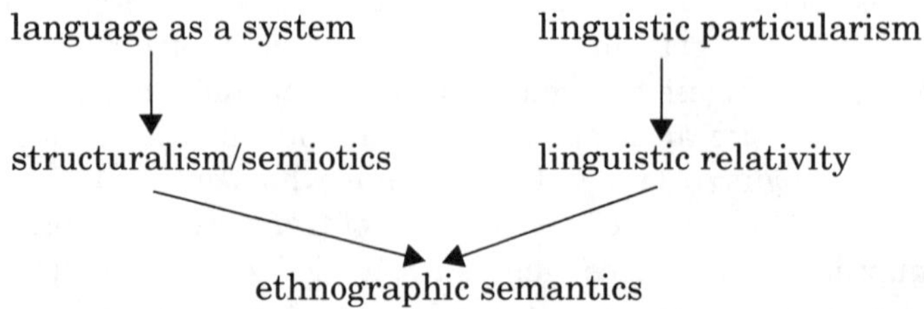

Culture-specific categories, as specified by named (overt) categories—essentially a sort of **linguistic relativism**—were to be modeled semiotically. The resulting cultural grammar (structural model of a domain) would predict ("generate") acceptable native behavior. This semiotic treatment of relativism was recycled by at least some practitioners of ethnographic semantics: Hymes (1966) notes that linguistic relativity follows from structuralism, but it did so in the context of ethnographic semantic investigation.

An example of the ethnoscience method is found in componential analysis in which the relationships of terms in a domain are defined by their shared features or components. As an example of this method of analysis, consider the following types of footgear that can be found in North American culture: moccasins, sandals, canvas ("tennis") shoes, dress shoes, boots. The analysis of the relations among these terms shown in figure 4 could be ethnographically tested on members of North American culture. There we see that we can distinguish these kinds of footwear by a series of properties inherent to some of them and not others. These properties are called semantic features; for example, the semantic feature [+ / - high tops] indicates whether or not the footwear has sides that extend beyond the ankle; the feature [+ / - enclosed] indicates whether or not the foot is exposed; [+ / - hard soles] and [+ / - casual] are self-explanatory. This model separates each term into its own cell, while showing what it has in common with the other terms. Shoe types that share the same values for several features are inherently more similar to one another than those that do not.

The appropriateness of various footgear with other domains of clothing could also be stated. For example, cowboy boots (a sub-type of boots) may or may not be appropriate footwear for a business situation. Such rules of combination would "generate" (predict) appropriate clothing behavior in North American culture, what North Americans know about their mode of dress.

Figure 4 **Componential Analysis of American Terms for Footgear**

- sides				+ sides
- enclosed	+ enclosed			
	- hard soles	+ hard soles		
		- casual	+ casual	
sandals	moccasins	dress shoes	tennis shoes	boots

The notion of transformation was used in cultural grammars to derive extended meanings of a term from a more basic sense. In Hopi, for example, two terms are used to name male adult kinsmen.

taaha = mother's brother (MoBr)

na'a = father (Fa)

What about father's brother? Since Hopi society is matrilineal, each child "belongs" to his or her mother's side of the family. Logically from the matrilineal Hopi point of view, father's brother, like father, is a male member of father's family, an extension of the basic term *na'a*.

na'a = (Fa)

(Fa) —> father's brother (FaBr)

Statements of the first kind are base rules that define the basic terms of the kinship domain, while statements of extension (marked as transformations by the arrow) are derived from the basic set of terms. This approach relies upon the universal (etic) model of the biological family in determining the emic model for the Hopi. The etic biological model of the family is useful for comparison since it is grounded in human reproduction rather than in the cultural understanding of a particular social group. The etic biological model applies equally to Hopi society and to North American Anglo society, for example. But the cultural understandings of kinship of the two groups vary considerably, and it is interesting to compare the emic models of the two. Whereas Hopis see themselves as belonging to their mothers' families, Anglos see themselves as belonging to both their mothers' and fathers' families. These facts alone help us understand why a Hopi would label the biological father's brother with the same term as the biological father, yet the Anglo would equate father's brother with mother's brother and label each with an identical term 'uncle' emically.

The notion of a base was also applied to nonlinguistic systems. For example, Colby (1973) took Propp's notion of action themes in traditional narratives (**functions** = "stable, constant elements [events] in a tale, independent of how and by whom they are fulfilled" [Propp, 1928(1968:21)]) and showed how such meta-events were ordered in Eskimo folktales. Colby found that an Eskimo folktale consisted minimally of at least three general event types:

*M*otivation

*E*njoyment

*R*esolution

Further, these elements were ordered in the following way:

$$\text{Story} = \text{M} + \text{E}^{\text{n}} + \text{R}$$

This means a string *M*otivation - *E*njoyment - *R*esolution will be found in a well-formed Eskimo tale. The superscript *n* after E indicates any number of "enjoyment" scenes may appear, but at least one must appear. So the strings

M - E - R

M - E - E - E - R

are well-formed, but the strings

*M - R - E

and

*M - E - R - R

are not. Stories with "starred" plots would be rejected by natives, even if expressed in idiomatic, grammatically correct Eskimo.

Ethnographic semantics, then, followed linguistics methodologically, and had the goal of "tapping, through linguistically expressed categories, the cognitive worlds of participants in the culture, and the thoroughgoing avoidance . . . of the imposition of alien descriptive categories on those worlds" (Hymes, 1964: 95). Ethnographic semantics relied upon named (overt) categories, ignoring for the most part the possibility of unnamed (covert) categories that are as much a part of native knowledge as conventionally named categories. Not all of the New Ethnography, however, directly relied on named categories. In dealing with situations or events such as hitchhiking, native-like decisions may be predicted more conveniently by a flow chart than by the model of a lexical domain (see figure 5). In the **flow chart**, possibilities are displayed as a **schema**, presumably stored or associated mentally with the named category 'hitchhiking.'

Even in the heyday of ethnographic semantics and the New Ethnography, there was dissent. In the famous "God's Truth or Hocus-Pocus?" article, Burling (1964) pointed out that native-like knowledge—the sort generated by the new cultural grammars—was not necessarily the same as native knowledge. Just the definition of what one thought one was capturing with the cultural grammar could be of vastly different sorts. For example, the goal might be to state all knowledge of all members of the community, or perhaps only that knowledge that was shared by all members of the community. The knowledge desired for representation might be only that of the experts for each domain since as experts they presumably had a more complete understanding than did ordinary folk. Then again, it might be that the cultural grammar represented some construct that the investigator created with experts, ordinary natives, or both. How could one demonstrate conclusively whether or not one's model was psychologically real, even if it did correctly account for all and only native behavior? It is not hard to imagine several different models being able to predict native behavior, but which one(s) could be shown to be really there in the natives' heads? The advantage of ethnographic semantics over previous investigations of linguistic relativity was that it tried to correlate linguistic expression with events in the real world, whereas many versions of the investigation of Whorf's thesis relied solely on linguistic information.

The linguistic anthropology that emerged from the busy 1960s showed a renewed interest in cross-cultural universals (etics) after disillusionment with some psychological claims for emic analyses formulated within ethnographic semantics. What remained was the mentalistic stance imported from generative grammar, and reliance upon basic terms as units of analysis which were organized in domains. Scholars also realized that interaction in context was a factor both in learning and in using cultural categories, an insight supported by linguistic studies.

Meaning and Context

As the unified vision of language and culture studies was fading in 1970, linguistics itself was undergoing another major civil war. The theory of language that Chomsky originally proposed promised to provide a single model of grammar (a single paradigm) which could be applied to any natural language, yet within a decade of the Chomskyian "revolution" that began in 1957, linguistics had become highly sectarian, with adherents rallying around their respective positions (Newmeyer 1986, Harris 1993). What was the cause of the dissent?

Figure 5 **Flow Chart Schema/Rule for Picking Up Hitchhikers**

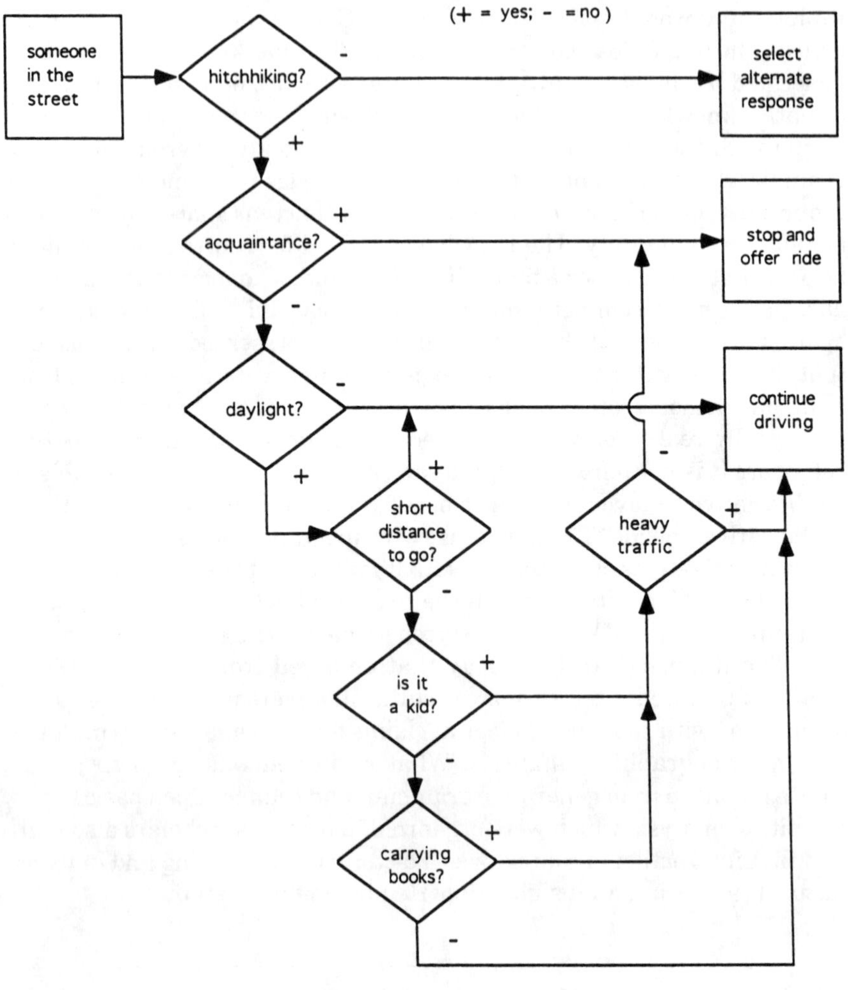

Source: J. P. Spradley, 1972b, p. 32.

Until generative grammar, the structure of sentences (syntax) had not been a central concern in mainstream linguistics. Chomsky made the **clause** (simple sentence) the basic unit of analysis in syntactic theory; this view has remained, and the semantic equivalent of the clause became a major construct in semantic theory also. The mentalistic status of linguistic and cultural knowledge persists today as well. The notion of transformation as essential (actually imported into linguistics from mathematics by Zellig Harris [1951], Chomsky's mentor), never really caught on in cultural theory, and has become less important in linguistics.

As originally proposed, syntax was independent of semantics (**autonomous syntax**). Yet it soon was realized that just as it was crucial to recognize that sentences had syntactic properties that had to be explained by any theory of language, it was also necessary to admit that meaning could affect syntax. Consider the subjects of the following classic examples.

The window broke.

The hammer broke the window.

The man broke the window.

In the first sentence, the semantic object (*window*) is the subject; in the second, the instrument (*hammer*) is the subject, and in the last, the actor (*the man*) is the subject. All things being equal, the actor will be the subject of a sentence in English; choice of another semantic role as subject depends on context.

A: What happened?

B: The window broke.

A: I thought it was because the ladder fell.

B: No, the hammer broke the window.

In each of these hypothetical interactions, the choice of grammatical subject depends on context. Some of meaning, therefore, depends on context.

Likewise in cultural grammars, context was found to be important. Laderman (1981) studied properties of foods among the Malays, a people whose culture attributes humoral properties of hot and cold to foods. She found that the same food might sometimes be classed hot and sometimes cold. Differences among individuals sometimes were attributable to varying experiences of the informants—differences in their learning about what foods were hot and what were cold. Sometimes, in such studies even the same person will class a food differently one time from another. In these instances, the hotness or coldness of a food may be being judged relative to other foods under immediate consideration. A food might be classed as hot when compared to a cold food, but the same food could be labeled cold when judged in the company of another hot food.

Similarly, Tversky (1977) studied the ways informants judged caricatures of faces as similar. He presented a set of three caricatures to each subject along with a fourth caricature. The subject was asked to group the fourth caricature with the one from the set of three that most resembled it. Tversky found that when he changed one member of the set of three—

the one not particularly like the others—a large majority of informants changed their judgments as to which caricature the fourth most resembled. This phenomenon has been seen as well in a study of similarities among different countries made by Tversky and Gati (1978). "Sweden" appears most like "Austria" to a majority of informants when the other choices are "Poland" and "Hungary." But "Hungary" is most like "Austria" when the other choices are "Sweden" and "Norway." Thus, the *linguistic context* of a question influences opinion about culturally important categories.

There are at least two other kinds of context relevant for the construction of cultural grammars. One is *social context.* A person frequently expresses different opinions depending on the setting and participants involved in conversations. An individual may even hold different opinions, and be unaware of changing opinions. That fact is the reason why social science investigators take great pains in making an experimental research setting as neutral as possible. For example, no patient should be interviewed about the quality of care he or she has received from a physician in front of that physician, or even in a hospital or medical office. Results would potentially be influenced by the social context—place and personnel—of the inquiry.

Also relevant is what has been called *internal (psychological) context.* In their study of beliefs about disease among Tojolabal Mayans, Furbee and Benfer (1983) found that a couple interviewed about diseases during a period when their infant had a serious respiratory condition gave great weight and importance in their answers to diseases of children, their seriousness, diseases associated with them, their prevention, cures, and so on. The same couple when interviewed at other times, when there was no serious medical problem in their family, gave answers that were much more neutral with respect to children's diseases.

This internal context permits studies in which the investigator sets a scenario for the informant. Suppose one asks, for example, "Let us say that you are given a million dollars, what would be the first thing you would buy?" Invited to speculate in this manner, the chances are, respondents of ordinary income will suggest priority items that they would never consider otherwise—Porsche cars, Mediterranean villas, and so on. In these instances, not only is the internal context known, it is set and controlled by the "let's pretend" scenario; of course, an unknown factor in the informant's life might still intervene—unbeknownst to the investigator, the informant might be the recent recipient of a million dollars from winning the lottery.

Looking again at language, not only lexical choice but also transformations were shown to be **context sensitive**. Let us return to the passive construction. Why are the following examples more naturally passive?

1. [*Situation:* The first sentence of a news story:]
   Mr. Steven Jones was seriously injured Thursday by a hit-and-run driver who remains at large.

2. [*Situation:* C accidentally breaks an expensive vase at the home of a friend (B); C is very close to the friend and genuinely upset by the incident. Also present at the gathering is A, who had given B the object.]

   A. Oh, what happened to the vase I gave you?

   B. I'm sorry, but it was accidentally broken earlier this evening.

In the first example, the actor is unknown; the only salient noun phrase to the hearer/reader is the object at the outset of the news story. In the second example, B (the host) knows that C is sorry for breaking the vase that was a gift from A. B does not want C, who is present, to feel any worse about the accident. Even in these manufactured examples, the point is clear: the structure of the sentence depends upon the context much as lexical choice does.

It is this sort of consideration that prompted the concept of communicative competence (Hymes 1964). Let us suppose that we have a person unfamiliar with North American culture, who nonetheless has good command of the sound pattern, syntax, and vocabulary of American English. Even though the person speaks the language well, there could still be many situations in which the specific type of vocabulary and style of speaking to be used would be unknown to such a speaker. For example, despite the fact that both females and males in recent years have come to use "four-letter" words in "mixed company," there remain some situations in which these words are still inappropriate for even younger speakers to use freely. Knowledge of appropriate use (as opposed to pure linguistic knowledge or competence) is what communicative competence refers to; it is in context(s) that we learn how to use words.

Context implies **setting** (time, place), **medium** (for example, telephone vs. written vs. face-to-face renditions of the same text), and status/**role** of participants. All these factors contribute to the shaping of instances of language use, but the most important fact about context is that language (and learning!) depends crucially on interaction: the participants work *in situ* to shape the resulting discourse or text (Friedrich 1970). In the 1960s and 1970s, linguists moved quickly to attend to meaning, and recognized two fundamental types of meaning: **linguistic meaning** (including lexical and grammatical meaning) and **cultural meaning**—an important version of the latter was cast as contextual meaning. The resulting interest in discourse/text/conversational analysis, communicative competence, and interaction was to become a major influence on linguistic anthropology in two ways. First, the contextual focus on interaction gradually bled over into **cognitive anthropology** (discussed in detail in chapter 8), the outgrowth of ethnographic semantics and ethnoscience (with the new etic emphasis). Secondly, interactional conceptions of culture arose. In the early 1960s, it looked as if the two disparate traditions of linguistic anthropology (language-as-culture [semiotics], and language-is-culture [relativism]) were finally joined. The result of the decade was the continuation of this union, a semantically cast relativistic quest for universals and the arrival of a new linguistic anthropology: the conception of culture as (con)text. Each enterprise will be considered in turn, after a short review of linguistic anthropology as it developed during the 1970s.

The study of ethnographic semantics borrowed linguistic methods (elicitation of **key terms**) to name culturally important objects, events, activities; structuring domains of key words hierarchically or schematically to study cultural categories. These methods helped anthropologists to see things from the native's point of view. The issue of connotation vs. denotation and of verifying categories persisted, while novel issues arose (the effect of context in learning and maintaining cultural categories, the perennial problem of norms [variable meaning of categories, degrees to which categories are shared by individuals]). The progressive impact of linguistic models and methodology was documented by Roger Keesing. Originally, ethnographic semantics was based on the following four premises (Keesing 1972):

1. Culture is a conceptual code (like language).
2. Every cultural code has its own distinctive, idiosyncratic, emic categorization (Boas' particularism).
3. The emic categories of each cultural code are discoverable by systematic inductive procedures (structuralism).
4. The primary data of ethnographic analysis come from statements of the natives themselves (they are linguistic).

But the application of structural and occasionally generative models to cultural domains ignored context and the shared, interactional nature of culture. Such types of applications were "unable to move beyond the analysis of artificially simplified and delineated (and usually trivial) semantic domains" (Keesing 1972:307). The use of key terms as a metalanguage to describe cultural domains was to persist and be transformed into studies of basic terms. Also persistent was the idea of a cultural code underlying actual behavior. As anthropologists came to confront the learning and use of categories in actual contexts, so linguists came more and more to appeal to context. The emphasis on methods (a lack of substantive theory), lack of interest in universal principles governing cultural category systems, and nonverifiability of results were both the downfall of the New Ethnography as originally conceived as well as the impetus for a program to revise the approach. The central notion of cultural grammar survived. Major domains were seen as cultural grammars in their own right: "the cognitive component of a culture [may be viewed] as an information-processing system based on the principle of assimilation to a system of learned schemata" (Rice 1980:168). This modular approach produced an atomistic view of culture: "Culture is not a well integrated, holistic system but rather an orchestrated constellation of many small systems" (Colby 1975:187). Each domain (kinship, food preparation, etc.) interacts with others as distinct modules to generate contextually appropriate cultural behavior. Cultural knowledge came to be seen as dynamic, not as something that is mechanically applied to contexts but rather as something that participates in a context. In each instance in which cultural knowledge from different domains (which may be differentially shared) is applied in contexts, the activity occurs through a conversation-like interaction (Agar 1981).

Let us look at two studies that deal with the same subject. One study (Brown et al. 1976) represents an outgrowth of ethnoscience: it classifies hand tools along the lines of the universals of lexical classification suggested by the folk biological studies of Berlin, Breedlove, and Raven (1973). The second study (Dougherty and Keller 1982) focuses on actual contextual use of hand tools.

Recall the following levels distinguished by Berlin, Breedlove, and Raven (1973:215) in a study of the classification of plant life:

Level	**Example**
unique beginner (UB)	plant
life form (LF)	tree
generic (G)	oak
species (S)	coast live oak
varietal (V)	Thompson's coast live oak

Brown et al. (1976) applied this to a taxonomy of hand tools.

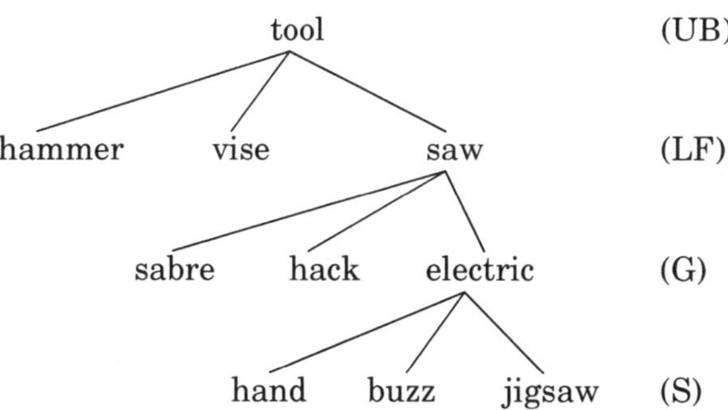

Brown and his colleagues suggested that the taxonomy borrowed from folk biological classification was adequate to model the domain of hand tools.

Dougherty and Keller (1982) were able to show in a given context (blacksmithing) that tool use never depends upon the ability to name and classify the tools: indeed, they found that linguistic classification by type and function played no part in the use of tools in context. Their study draws on the importance of context by showing that named categories (and classification of the same) may be irrelevant to some contexts. On the other hand, the model derived from the folk biological classification suggests that there are some universals in the way lexical categories are arranged and possibly constructed. Moreover, there are many contexts (for example, playing cards, trading in a stock exchange, doing jump rope, etc.) where linguistic categories are used to facilitate interaction, and it seems plausible to seek qualitative and organizational universals in each domain.

Summary

The idea of abstracting behavior in the form of grammars was imported from linguistics into anthropology in the 1960s. Essentially a structuralist model of a language, a grammar in linguistics is a set of rules or conditions that allows one to judge linguistic behavior as native. Seen as a predictive model, a grammar was said to "generate" correct sentences (and only correct sentences), by mapping output to an **underlying form** of some abstractness.

Anthropologists who engaged in the New Ethnography were trying to extend the linguistic model. They attempted to enter the culture-bearer's head. They made cultural grammars that mirrored what natives know. The important issue was grammaticality, or acceptability of the behavior. Did the model (of whatever domain) "generate" (predict, find acceptable) certain behavior or term usage as native (in the case of named categories)?

The transformational model was early abandoned by most scholars building cultural grammars. Instead, componential analysis (with its matrices of semantic features), structural diagrams (also known as schemata, plural of schema), flow charts, decision-trees, prototypes, and scripts (or frames) for modeling procedures were used to capture native knowledge. These models were built on key terms that were used in some sort of context. They were primarily models of ideal behavior rather than of the full range of behavior.

The dependence on context also separated cultural grammars from their equivalent in linguistics. Instead of seeking autonomous description, anthropologists saw meaning as coming from context.

Because written material takes on a life of its own—the speaker (author) is potentially removed from the hearer (reader)—written texts provide their own context. The study of texts, especially of short ones, is a way of systematically controlling context, and maximizing cultural analysis of key terms.

Discussion and Activities

1. Chomsky claimed that at their most fundamental level, all languages have a genetic basis, hence a foundational identity. This means that the underlying structures of each human language should be the same, no matter how the surface structure of each actual human language varied. Looking back at the data in activity 1 in chapter 6 (on word orders), how might you account for the variety of the superficial forms in terms congruent with Chomsky's suggestion about fundamental, underlying identity?
2. In another previous activity in chapter 6, we analyzed commercial blurbs. Below are two additional blurbs. One is from the same brochure as a previous blurb, and the other is an updated version of a previous blurb. Because they are similar in content and purpose, we could say that they are examples of the same **genre**. Choose one of the blurbs, and decide how to present it to a consultant (you can use key term analysis, for example) to elicit the deeper meaning of the text. The class can then pool the results. Do your consultants read the same deeper meaning from these texts as the class did?

   (a) Additional blurb attached to a wine bottle (Blossom Hill Collection 1995).

INGREDIENTS FOR A
soothing experience

You don't have to go to the department store and spend a lot of money for effective beauty aids. Try these tips using items found right here in your grocery store.

Problem	Solution
Tired, puffy eyes	Cucumber slices or tea bags soaked in cold water
Impurities in facial skin	Egg whites applied as a mask
Dull, dry hair	Condition with mayonnaise, olive oil and egg yolks or beer
Dull skin	Oatmeal and water paste—let dry, then scrub off
Rough elbows	Avocado skins with avocado scooped out

(b) Updated blurb for product-related clothing and accessories (Philip Morris Inc. 1995).

MARLBORO
UNLIMITED

GEAR

GEAR WITHOUT LIMITS

THE MARLBORO UNLIMITED [*motorcycle caravan trip*].
A THIRD OF A MILE OF SLEEK
RED STEEL READY TO ROLL WEST.
AND NOW THERE'S MARLBORO
UNLIMITED GEAR. IT'S GEAR
WITHOUT LIMITS, MADE TO TAKE
ON A LAND THAT KNOWS NO LIMITS.
30 NEW ITEMS TO CHOOSE FROM,

. . .

YOU DON'T HAVE TO WIN
THE TRIP TO GET THE GEAR.
JUST GET THE MILES.

Key Terms

active
actor
autonomous syntax
base
clause
cognitive anthropology
components
context sensitive
cultural grammars
cultural meaning
deep structures
ethnographic semantics
ethnoscience
flow chart
functions
generativism
genre
goal
grammaticality
inflection
key terms
linguistic meaning
linguistic relativism
medium
New Ethnography
passive
possessive
relativism
schema (pl. schemata)
setting
subject
surface
surface structure
themes
transformation
transformational
underlying form

8

Cognitive Anthropology

> [I]f we penetrate to the true inwardness of a concept, we find that it tells us nothing of the thing itself, but only sums up what one can do with it, or what it can do to one.
>
> —José Ortega y Gasset

The premature copying of the linguistic method in vogue in the 1960s by linguistic anthropologists shaped the successor of ethnographic semantics, cognitive anthropology. A good review of cognitive anthropology is given in D'Andrade (1990).

Consider the following points in light of chapter 7's discussion of context.

1. The individual is the locus of linguistic and cultural knowledge.
2. Culturally appropriate behavior can be accounted for solely by use of a set of finite rules.
3. Meaning is the sum of the constituent parts that make up the message.
4. The context of linguistic and cultural elicitation is equivalent to naturally occurring linguistic and cultural usage.

Clearly, neatness of the analysis was threatened by context. **Formal elegance** and **economy of explanation** are two of the key folk terms traditional among linguists for describing the maximal reduction of social phenomena in the manner of the hard sciences. Such reduction is prized by social scientists trying hard to emulate the natural sciences, and is often labeled somewhat pejoratively as **reductionism**. Ironically, an important buzz word in the earlier Chomskyian enterprise was *creativity*. Basically, Chomsky pointed out that speakers of a language produce novel sentences and use varying ways of casting the same thought. He did not stop to ask why they do this, an activity that occurs every time they speak (!), but was content to make a formal account of the structures they produce.

The **taxonomy** as a model was often taken as the *only* psychological model of domains (culture as a stored mental template) that generate behavior, yet when empirically tested, the idea was not supported. Speakers of O'odham (a Uto-Aztecan language spoken in southern Arizona) used a variety of models, including taxonomy, in making folk classifications. Casagrande and Hale (1967:168) found no less than thirteen ways in which O'odham speakers defined words in their language as the need arose.

1. attributive (distinctive characteristics)
2. contingency (necessary prior conditions)
3. function
4. spatial orientation
5. operational (characteristic goal or recipient)
6. comparison (similarity or contrast)
7. exemplification
8. class inclusion (membership in a hierarchy)
9. synonymy
10. antonymy
11. provenience
12. grading (placement on a continuum or in a series)
13. circularity (item defined in terms of itself)

The need for a variety of models for categories is further bolstered by the fact that some cultures apparently make little or no use at all of hierarchical classification, the favorite of Western thought. Blackfoot Indians consider their culture to be made up of domains whose members are listable; either an item is in the domain or it is not (Nettl 1989), but there is little organization of those items in the domain by hierarchies. The Melpa people of highland New Guinea are also not prone to taxonomy, preferring a pairing strategy; they do poorly at hierarchical sorting (Lancy and Strathern 1981).

Gestalt Models

Nonetheless, the obvious need to acquire and modify categories through learning or analytical thought prompted an interest in models that were more like global, gestalt representations than were the componential analysis ones (the hierarchical definition by features). Further, the gestalt models were interactive. Among the prominent gestalt models proposed were fuzzy sets (Zadeh 1965), as adapted by Kempton (1978, 1981) and others, prototypes (Rosch 1973, 1981; Lakoff 1987:12–57), scripts (frames, schemata) (Sacks 1967, Schank and Abelson 1977, Holland and Quinn 1987), and expert systems (Benfer 1989, Furbee 1989, Read and Behrens 1989). These four models may be considered along with the flow charts of decision theory illustrated in chapter 7 in the hitchhiking example (Spradley 1972b). Work within the first two has been predominantly on lexical items; that within the latter two has more typically attempted to represent larger, less linguistic entities, although in principle any of these approaches can model the whole range of phenomena under discussion. Here we will first describe them, and then consider their possible interactive properties.

According to set theory, an item is either a member of a set (category) or not. **Fuzzy set** theory (Zadeh 1965) holds that an item can have a probability of belonging to two or more different sets through overlapping (intersection of the sets) or composition (union of the sets). Recall the *grue* category that grew out of classic color studies (Berlin and Kay 1969): some languages have a named *grue* category in which the ranges of two primary colors (*green*, *blue*) are named by a single term. Kay and McDaniel (1978) theorized that color categories like *grue* were fuzzy sets.

Tarahumara (a Uto-Aztecan language spoken in northern Mexico) offered a chance to test the Kay and McDaniel hypothesis about the existence of fuzzy sets in color categories. In Tarahumara, color terms obligatorily indicate relative intensity (Burgess, Kempton, and MacLaury 1983:137).

$$\text{stem-} + \left\{ \begin{array}{l} \textit{-ka}\ \text{`augmentative'} \\ \\ \textit{-na}\ \text{`diminutive'} \end{array} \right\} + \textit{-(e)me/n} + \textit{-ti}$$

The suffix *-me* (*-me* has the form *-n* before *-ti*) is a nominalizer and *-ti* marks a word as an approximate, something close to the central sense but not exactly that. Three degrees of color intensity are grammaticalized in Tarahumara.

sitá - ka - me	'very red'
sitá - na - me	'somewhat red'
sitá - na - n - ti	'only slightly red'

Thus, with Tarahumara speakers, one could test the possibility of gradient rather than absolute membership in a category. And indeed, it was found that Tarahumara *siyó* ('grue') was a category of clearly graded membership: It is the union of blue and green, skewed towards green. Note that context had to be taken into account. Not only does a word have meaning (semantics), but a word's user must take stock of the word's meaning in context (**pragmatics**). Besides the importance of context, the experiment demonstrated the use of language in cognition.

A related experiment (Kay and Kempton 1984) was designed to show a *Whorfian effect* in English use of *blue* and *green*. The experiment had two tasks: one (given to both English-speaking and Tarahumara-speaking subjects) was designed so that the English speaker had an advantage (the concepts 'blue' and 'green' have distinct names in English—they are overt categories). Sets of three color chips from the *grue* range were presented; the subjects were asked which chip was the most different on each trial. English speakers used the words 'blue' and 'green' to name examples, while Tarahumara monolinguals had only the single term *siyó*. Colors near the boundary of *blue* and *green* on the spectrum were subjectively pushed apart by English speakers; the intermediate example was judged as *blue* rather than *green* by 29 out of 30 subjects. The control Tarahumara group sorted the intermediate examples as more *green* than *blue* 50 percent of the time and more *blue* than *green* 50 percent of the time—that is the Tarahumara speakers with the *grue* category performed the task at a chance level.

A second task given only to the English subjects was designed to neutralize the Whorfian effect. Similar in design to the first task, on each trial a subject was asked to label the intensity of the intermediate chip that he or she had just named. The subject was asked which of the three chips was the most green (is the first chip greener than the intermediate and the third chip bluer than the intermediate chip?). The subjects, who saw only two chips at a time, had to tell whether the difference in 'blueness' was greater than the difference in 'greenness.' The result was that about half the judgments fell to the *blue* side and half to the *green* side. Cognition can clearly be guided by language, and a mild sort of linguistic relativity attends language-driven cognition, *but only in some contexts*. Again, the relevance of context—even in a laboratory situation—is clear.

It is the importance of context that MacLaury (1987a, 1987b) notes for **co-extensive semantics**, where the same category has more than one possible lexicalization. MacLaury, interested in the semantic range of basic color terms, used an adaptation of a methodology developed for a survey of basic color terms and categories throughout the world. Whereas the original color studies (Berlin and Kay 1969) had used only naming tasks, MacLaury also had informants map the semantic ranges of basic terms in stages. Different types of semantic relations emerged from his study of Meso-American languages: **near-synonymy** (categories with overlapping ranges but with different foci [best examples] outside the areas of overlap) and **co-extensivity** (occurrence of at least one category focus in the range of another category), for example. In cases of near-synonymy or co-extensivity, speakers have to choose between one or the other focus when encountering a color in the overlapping area. MacLaury proposes that speakers focus from different **vantages**. Those vantages can be motivated by context in focusing on different coordinates (in the case of color terms, degrees of similarity or difference between contrasting named foci).

The notion of **prototype** (an abstract set of criteria/attributes that may be ranked, may be only partially applicable, or both, in any given instance) ultimately derives from the insight of Wittgenstein (1958) that concepts (categories) have no field boundaries or fixed reference. Rather than having examples either belong to a category or not, Wittgenstein argued that examples exhibited **family resemblances**; the examples of a concept resembled each other, much as a human family does. The examples have features in common that overlap. Certain examples may show a particular feature more intensely than others. Both prototype theory and fuzzy set logic follow the tradition of Wittgenstein in rejecting the classic notion of independent categories in favor of a notion of gradient categories defined by features (criteria) that could vary in intensity or application.

The notion of prototype may be conveniently illustrated by the example of English *bird*. Imagine asking city-dwellers which of the following words is the best example of 'bird.'

canary	chicken
penguin	ostrich
robin	

Certain features in common (beak, feathers, wings) define the category of birds, but the issue of whether (and how much) the example can fly and whether or not it is domesticated are important factors in determining goodness-of-fit for 'bird.' The cultural value of songbirds (small, wild birds that sing) is another important factor. The types of birds listed have family resemblance, but some types are not as "bird-like" as others: the robin is the best "example" of 'bird' in the list (beak, feathers, wings and can fly, wild, sort of a songbird). A list of features defines goodness-of-fit, but each feature is not necessarily applicable; feathers may apply in degree, and some features may be more important than others. An example is a potential member of a category if it displays some of the attributes. This combination of attributes is considered a logic that cannot be validated by truth or falsity. Category membership is defined in degrees by reference to a prototype.

Not only does the problem of gradient members arise, but also the issue of membership of examples in more than one category must be considered. Take the classic example of *cheap*, *stingy*, and *thrifty*. All three have to do with frugality. *Thrifty* implies a wisely directed frugality; *stingy* implies a selfish frugality, while *cheap* connotes frugality motivated by lack of taste or dignity. All three words might be reasonably applied to the same individual, and it would be difficult to show, one way or another, that an individual so characterized was 100 percent cheap, thrifty, or stingy. Moreover, one individual can be even momentarily a better example of cheapness, thriftiness, or stinginess, than someone else who is also frugal.

Complex concepts present additional problems for the true-or-false semantics inherent in Aristotelian categorization.

Before he joined the CIA, he was a *good narcotics dealer.*

The Milky Way is a *small galaxy.*

Well, here comes Ms. *Wonderful*!

In the case of *good narcotic dealer*, the concept 'good' is extended. The concept 'small' is relative and stretchable by nature, and 'wonderful' is used sarcastically in the last example. Concepts such as modals ('perhaps,' 'in general,' 'maybe,' 'probably,' etc.), which modify the truth values of sentences, and **deictics** (Greek for 'pointers')—pronouns, locatives, demonstratives—that situate sentences in time and space, are impossible to analyze in a natural way in the true/false logic of classical categorization. There can be no prototype for them in the ordinary sense, no "I" is a better "I" than some other referent. The meaning of modals and deictics derives totally from context; for example, the pronoun 'I' has a different referent depending on whoever utters it. The study of such elements that shift reference by context is labeled **deixis**, and it assumes an important role in present-day formulations of language and culture theory.

Coleman and Kay (1981) applied prototype theory to characterize the English word/concept *lie* ('prevaricate'). The following prototype specifies a context in which a speaker (S) asserts a proposition (P) to an addressee (A) (Coleman and Kay 1981:28):

P is false.

S believes P to be false.

In uttering P, S intends to deceive A.

This definition excludes honest mistakes and unintended misrepresentations, sarcasm, hyperbole, tall tales, fibs, "pulling someone's leg," and figurative speech. "White lies"—those intended to spare the addressee embarrassment or emotional harm—and "social lies"—like *come by anytime* told to be civil or minimally sociable—do not fit the criteria above exactly. Coleman and Kay's subjects equivocated in considering social lies and white lies to be bona fide lies. In fact, the falsity of the uttered statement was the least important of the three factors given above when subjects rated the "liehood" of brief stories intended to simulate actual contexts. Yet the same subjects rated falsity of the uttered statement as the most important defining characteristic of *lie*. This is because, most prototypically, *lie* means 'tell a falsehood,' and it is falsehood that implies intent to deceive. Falsity is the most conscious and general defining attribute of *lie*—one assumes relative truthfulness and cooperation in ordinary conversation (Sweetzer 1987). Thus falsehood was the factor most consciously rated by subjects, but a speaker's *intent* to deceive was the important weighted factor when those same subjects performed actual ratings of Coleman and Kay's pseudo-falsehoods for reprehensibleness.

The idea behind a script is equally situational in orientation: a **script** is a stored mental recipe for how a particular event or procedure usually or ideally occurs. The "directions" for a gamut of everyday actions (morning toilet, getting to work, banking, answering the phone, etc.) are mentally stored in terms of a flow chart of routines and perhaps subroutines. Such idealized conceptions of conventional action may have conventional names that are contextually based (*I have to go to the bank / john / *forest*), or they may not (example: typical procedure and protocol in a restaurant as an array corresponds to no conventional vocabulary item in English). It would be possible to consider scripts to be a kind of prototype. Scripts are a system of events that are likely to happen, and most of them do, but not all of them have to occur.

The server brings the check.

The server bugs you (subtly) to have a drink.

The server presents water/bread/flatware.

You flirt with the server.

The four possibilities above focus on the participants in the script "going to a restaurant." Only one of these (the first statement) is likely to occur most of the time (you may rarely have a poor server—or no server—and hence no check). The others are all characteristic of restaurant behavior, but they depend on actual contexts.

Like scripts, expert systems extend the idea of a cultural grammar rather directly by employing linguistic principles, especially those of functional grammar (Weigand 1990). **Expert systems** (also called knowledge based systems) are computer programs (or "programming environments"—high-level programming languages) that permit one to model belief or behavior for specific domains with results that mimic the performance of experts in these areas of expertise (Benfer, Brent, and Furbee 1991). They require extensive knowledge from specific domains (Colby 1985). Although they can be written in any programming language, they are most often constructed using **expert system shells**, which resemble theories of grammar in that they constrain the representation of knowledge, are modular, provide specific modes of logical operation and inference (the "inference engine"), and make assumptions about the appropriate representations from which inferences can be drawn; they also offer a user interface. An example of a simple expert system is given below. It predicts when a woman will first present herself for prenatal care and is based on interviews with 25 pregnant women (Fisher et al. 1991). The model was constructed from a training set of 17 of the 25 cases studied (Benfer, Brent, and Furbee 1991:75).

Rule 1	**IF**	Encouraged by Influential Other = Yes,
	THEN	*present early.*
Rule 2	**IF**	Encouraged by Influential Other = No,
	THEN	*present late.*
Rule 3	**IF**	Encouraged by Influential Other = Indeterminent (from interviews),
	AND	Early symptoms = Yes,
	THEN	*present early,*
	ELSE	*present late.*

This model correctly predicted the time of presentation for prenatal care for 7 of the 8 cases that were reserved from the 25 original ones for testing the model. The single error was for a woman who presented at 22 weeks (the cut-off was somewhat arbitrarily set at 20 weeks).

There are strong parallels between expert system representations and decision-theory flow-chart ones, such as the hitchhiking example given in chapter 7; however, it should be noted that decision-theory flow-chart models are likely to do best as models of understandings that are ideal (or at least broadly held), whereas expert systems are often designed to capture the range of variation in judgments and performance. This feat is accomplished most directly through use of a frequently featured capability of expert systems not illustrated above, namely the assignment of **confidence factors** to the application of rules in an expert system. Confidence factors are rather like probabilities of occurrence of the firing of a rule; however, there is some difference. If, for example, a rule of an expert system is assigned a confidence factor of .8, it could mean either that 100 percent of the informants consulted thought that the rule should fire 80 percent of the time, or that 80 percent of the informants consulted thought that the rule should fire 100 percent of the time. In addition, the ways in which confidence factors that have been assigned to different rules may be combined can also vary; these present interesting possibilities requiring sophisticated treatment. Some expert system shells combine the "probabilities" assigned by confidence factors by using fuzzy logic; some average them; some treat them as independent, or dependent probabilities; some offer several of these alternatives. Choice of the appropriate method requires considerable testing with the data so the best representation for a particular set of phenomena can be selected.

Originally, expert systems were used to model the decision making of a single expert, for example, an expert medical diagnostician. Recently, their use has been extended to modeling the cognition (Furbee 1989) or behavior (Guillet 1989, Read and Behrens 1989, Ryan 1991) of ordinary people, for example informants in anthropological studies, thereby creating "folk expert systems." Because expert systems permit employment of powerful heuristic devices, they can be used to model an individual's thinking, or that person's behavior, in a real-world, commonsense manner that accords well with the intuitions of informants. One can then evaluate how well the folk expert system predicts correct decision making or behavior by testing it with new cases and consulting with additional informants (Furbee and Benfer 1989). One may relate these multiple models or pathways into a coherent cultural statement, using the expert system, or with some other formalism. Expert systems can also be used as modeling tools for developing general theories (Behrens 1987, Read 1987).

Multiple pathways theory as a representation of the cultural whole derived from the variety of cultural opinions may be contrasted with **consensus theory** (Romney, Weller, and Batcheider 1987). The latter represents what is agreed upon in a community as the "consensus," the truly cultural, and eliminates variation as error. Multiple pathways claims that variation (and knowledge of how to manage and translate it) is a part of culture, and seeks to represent and relate differing cultural conceptions and plans. In relating such differing conceptions and plans, each of which is thought of as a legitimate pathway, the investigator especially privileges patterns of variations that are organized according to some universal schema; for example, in implicational hierarchies.

Table 4 gives a fragment of a multiple pathways model of the simple task of classifying soils in the Andean community of Lari in Southern Peru. As can be seen, consultants differed as to a the importance of several critical characteristics of kinds of soils, yet every farmer in an Andean village is in some sense an expert who has been farming land that has been in continuous production for more than 1,000 years. Nonetheless, Andean farmers have different sets of fields with nonidentical repertoires of soils; each also has had unique experiences. Differences included whether they classified a soft, white soil that was one of the best as sandy (two consultants) or not (one consultant). Variation among consultants is not usually error in this view but more likely represents alternative strategies for arriving at the same solution; in a way, we might think of it as the range of variation that exists in the system. As described above, each rule may also be assigned a "confidence factor," which roughly equates to probability.

Table 4. A Fragment of a Multiple Pathways Model: Classifying Soils in the Quechua-speaking Community of Lari in Southern Peru

Is the soil **soft**?
- yes: **white?**
  - yes: **one of the best?**
    - yes: **sandy**?
      - yes: then the soil is **usp'a hallp'a** (2 consultants)
      - no: then the soil is **usp'a hallp'a** (1 consultant) or **qhilli** or **lamosa**
    - no: **silty**?
      - yes: **grows maize**?
        - yes: then the soils is **qhilli**
        - no: **sandy**?
          - yes: then the soil is **hallp'a**
          - no: then the soil is **kuntayu**
      - no: **sandy**?
        - yes: then the soil is **qhilli**
        - no: **clayey**?
          - yes: then the soil is **yuraq hallp'a**
          - no: then the soil is **qhilli**
  - no: **needs fertilizer**?
    - yes: **sandy**?
      - yes: **grows maize**?
        - yes: then the soil is **ñut'u akku**
        - no: **stony**?
          - yes: then the soil is **ñut'u akku** or **akku**
      - no: **stony**?
        - yes: then the soil is **akku** (2 consultants)
        - no: then the soil is **akku** (1 consultant) or **ñut'u akku**
  - no: **one of the best**?
    - yes: then the soil is **hallp'a** (3 consultants)
    - no: **silty**?
      - yes: then the soil is **ñut'u akku**
      - no: **grows maize**?
        - yes: then the soil is **usp'a hallp'a**
        - no: then the soil is **akku**

Source: Benfer, Brent, and Furbee 1991, p. 49.

It is clear that these analyses have come a long way from "checklist" semantics in which the meaning of something is characterized as a list of attributes it possesses. The word schema is often used in cognitive anthropology to designate fuzzy set models, prototype models, and script-frames. **Script-frames** go beyond the mere act of naming and anticipate **discourse** (interactive use of language—for a detailed discussion on discourse, see chapter 10) and text (the resultant used language). Fuzzy set theory and prototype theory are concerned with single terms, whereas script-frames are concerned with procedures (which may or may not have names, and even potentially, combinations of names), yet to the cognitive anthropologist, they are all schemata. The single, integrated approach to date (Lakoff 1987) is based on prototype theory. Yet borderline cases—fence-straddlers, examples of multiple class membership, and co-extensivity (all of which imply a relation between at least two categories) will undoubtedly increase in importance as research progresses. Schema(ta) will take on a more global, interactive denotation in light of these developments. As mentioned previously, both script-frames and expert systems extend the idea of a cultural grammar. In doing so, however, a script more closely resembles a discourse theory, whereas an expert system may be thought of as more derivative of formal, rule-based theories of grammar. The expert system's use of confidence factors with rules can also be seen as related to the **variation theory** (Labov 1969; D. Sankoff and G. Sankoff 1973; G. Sankoff 1971, 1973) of sociolinguistics, which will be discussed further in the following section. To give a familiar example of the kind of variation modeled under multiple pathways theory, some North Americans use the term "first cousin once removed" for the same relative that others would call a "second cousin." The first term is motivated by generation; the second by laterality (Rose and Romney 1979). The two systems produce similar maps of kinsmen, except for this one relative, and both are valid. Indeed, one may say that knowing that such variation exists and how to equate one term with the other is part of the cultural knowledge that North Americans have. The question of the range, character, and integration of variation in a domain is more directly treated by expert systems than by scripts, but the phenomena modeled by expert systems are typically more restricted than some attempted by script models.

Metaphor and Metonymy

The vexing question of how to relate lexical cognitive anthropology to contextual cognitive anthropology within the tradition of semiotics blended with semantics has been answered by the anthropological interest in metaphor and metonymy (Friedrich 1986). Context demands that single categories (words, if the categories are overt) be related to a lot of other concepts/words; metaphor and metonymy are quick to supply such a vehicle.

A **metaphor** is a comparison of like ('a is like b'), while a **metonym** is a relationship of association (generalized association, part-for-whole—the latter restrictively known as **synecdoche**). Metaphor corresponds to the intersection of two domains, while a metonym is a selective focus within a single domain (J. D. Sapir 1977). Let us consider a simple example which may be variously analyzed.

All hands on deck!

The noun *hands* can be seen as a metaphor ('people are hands') or a metonym focusing on a part (hands) of a whole (person). Both readings depend on discrete entities ('person = hands'; 'hands of a person') abstracted to the plural. This saying also represents a script in which discrete entities interact: the setting is a ship; the situation is imminent danger which requires the attention of the entire crew. This script interpretation may also have both a metaphoric and metonymic reading. Discrete parts of the ship complex (crew, deck area) are focal in a metonymic reading, while the classic **image** of a sinking ship may stand for any threatening situation requiring coordinated group efforts to combat. This single example illustrates the terms metaphor and metonym, their interrelationship (metaphor is approximate to overlapping of fuzzy sets, metonym approximate to prototype), and their consequent interchangeability (union/intersection of two domains or combination of two examples into a larger whole). The concept of metaphor allows the linking of two domains in reference to context, and the concept of metonym allows one to establish a higher level of abstraction or analysis of a metaphoric linking by creating a **frame**.

The rich use of metaphor in everyday North American English is illustrated in Lakoff and Johnson (1980). They argue that all concepts are based in concrete experience (1980:117) but are defined by their inherent characteristics and their roles in context (1980:125) mediated by metaphor and **hedges** (qualifiers like *in general* and *sort of*). Consider the following example:

Smith attacked Jones' theory,

but his reasoning had so many holes in it, it went nowhere,

and so his own reputation went down the tubes.

In this example, three metaphors are exploited: 'argument is war,' 'argument is a container,' 'argument is a journey.' A hybrid metaphor ('war is a container') is present through the bridging of 'journey.'

argument = war

argument = container

argument = journey

((argument = war) = container) = journey

The expression *his own reputation* refers to, of course, the war-like quality that may attend rivalry in any theater of human life. Note how the hybrid *relies on context* to make any sense. Each of the constituting metaphors (the first three lines of the analysis) may be independently verified with data from English.

argument = war	Susan and Jim declared a truce before they ended up in court.
journey = container	The journey held many surprises.
argument = journey	It was a long bitter road, but I finally convinced him.

The metaphoric-symbolic nature of language (actually, language use in context) has a long-standing importance in cultural anthropology. One influential source holds that all **speech acts** are symbolic, even the simplest such as "here is the cat," because the act of naming invites or intends a response (Burke 1957). The metaphoric/metonymic use of categories as **shifters**, deictic elements that link an utterance with the context in which it occurs (previous examples include pronouns and modals), gives insight into how new categories might be found or old ones modified; the importance of context is again evident (see Jakobson 1957 [1971], J. D. Sapir 1977, Crocker 1977, Silverstein 1976).

The use of metaphors as ways of organizing categories may differ from language to language. In English, for example, heat is most commonly metaphorical of anger.

blow one's cool

one's blood is boiling

hot under the collar

The basic metaphor "anger is heat" in English usage is actually more complicated (see Lakoff 1987:380 and following).

It should be noted, also, that in English, heat can be metaphorical of pleasure, especially sexual pleasure or popular entertainments.

a hot momma

the temperature's rising

a hot jazz singer

right now, it's hot

This usage of heat as a metaphor has a sense of immediacy or currency.

In Sotho, a Bantu language of South Africa, the metaphor that involves heat is "hot is bad" (Hammond-Tooke 1981). As in English, 'hot' may refer to anger (and consequent agitation or impatience) in Sotho, yet it may also refer to

pain or any illness

grief

fatigue

insanity

events connected with pregnancy

These latter abnormal or unpleasant conditions cannot be marked by a heat metaphor in English and still make any sense.

*My flu is really hot.

*I'm so sad, I'm about to boil.

*He's so tired, he could cook

*S/he's real hot (crazy).

*Gus' wife got hot.

The cross-linguistic exploration of metaphoric usage, even for such obvious concepts as 'hot,' has only begun.

Lakoff (1987) proposes the following types of schemata: frame (set of related things); script (procedure); **scene** (typical time and place); taxonomy (componential analysis); image (iconic relations). He calls these *base* models. Metaphors connect different base models, while metonyms connect peripheral members. Both of these operations and the schemata generate prototype effects and Whorfian effects. Schemata related by metaphor or metonymy involve the effects of goodness-of-fit because of the nature of relating abstraction to the ongoing context of usage. At the same time, the dependence of contextual applications on linguistically specified concepts is evident; the idiosyncrasy of the schema(ta) may color the understanding of context, though this is a matter of degree. By taking focus into account, it is possible to do away with peripheral members (examples): a speaker uses schema(ta) from the vantage point of context. Context dictates what he or she will focus on. This proposal, vantage theory, was developed independently by Morrow (1986) and MacLaury (1987a, 1987b, 1997).

Systems and Sharing of Knowledge

The cognitive anthropology that emerged from ethnographic semantics sees culture as systems of knowledge, with representation of knowledge and its relation to context being central concerns. In method, an ethnographic approach is taken: one listens for **key words** in conversation or other discourse and then analyzes the key words as a domain with relations to contextual meaning using schema(ta). The resulting model must have sufficient interrelationship to interpret novel discourse. "[K]nowledge about the world in process is systematically stored and subsequently reapplied as it is appropriate to emerging experience" (Dougherty 1985:243).

As an example of the newer sort of modeling in cognitive anthropology, let us return to the folk biological classification. Despite the earlier success of the taxonomic hierarchy model in suggesting neurological constraints on the organization of categories, a componential analysis of the way folk classify the life forms around them is deficient in and of itself in that it can ignore the relation of the folk to the environment. Brown (1977, 1979) and Berlin and associates (Berlin 1972; Berlin, Breedlove and Raven 1968, 1973) originally concentrated exclusively on the organization of plants named, excluding data on habitat and use. Yet, Hunn (1982) would argue that cultural knowledge is adaptive and that such knowledge shows how factors of use and potential danger pertain to the naming of flora and fauna. Instead of a simple feature or set of related features imposed on reality, Hunn suggests the use of intersecting sets of features (use, structure, habitat, danger) to investigate folk biological classification in order to ground the results in context, in biological reality as the folk see it.

The position that folk classification is utilitarian in design has been called "pragmatic" (Hunn 1982). The opposing view—that folk classification reflects a uniform, fundamental human ability to categorize—is called "intellectualist" (Atran 1990). Some work has tended to support the intellectualist position. Berlin (1990) reported that four Jivaroan groups (Peru) mirrored the scientific classification in the naming of invertebrate animals in their natural context in Jivaro. Brown (1992) found that natives of Great Britain applied British bird names to pictures of those North American species closest in the scientific classification to the British species.

The more purely taxonomic approaches to the understanding of folk knowledge associated with earlier ethnographic semantics are structuralist in orientation (Benfer 1989). The goals of such investigations are to discover the organization of knowledge and to achieve understanding of that organization in terms of universal principles, evolutionary trends, or patterns of historical change. The organization may be an end in itself.

On the other hand, much recent work in cognitive anthropology is **functionalist**. As we have seen in the critiques of studies on color and folk biological classification, the goals of these investigators center on how knowledge is applied. Hunn (1982) urges that the function of systems of knowledge ought to be seen in terms of ecological factors. Others (J. D. Sapir 1977, Crocker 1977, Holland and Quinn 1987) center the investigation in social interaction, seeking understanding in terms of the social use of knowledge.

Folk biological classification also illustrates the degree to which information and categories are shared by members of a given society. Gatewood (1983) found that Aguaruna Indians (western Amazon River Basin) have a 90–100 percent recognition rate of tree species in their environment, while college students at institutions in the eastern United States had an approximate 50 percent recognition rate of tree species in their local environment. In small, face-to-face societies, where nearly everyone is engaged in similar activities, knowledge tends to be more shared, and certain kinds of information important to the members will be both extensively known and extensively shared (tree species names among the Aguaruna). In complex societies with labor specialization, Gatewood argues, knowledge (and corresponding categories) tends to be shared less. This fact has implications for the ways in which we study culture, and possibly the corresponding linguistic categories as well.

As we have seen, semiotics advanced in the 1970s predominantly in the direction of extending linguistic models beyond language per se. Recently, a second line of research has extended semiotic analysis of linguistic events toward creating formal accounts of language use; it is especially concerned with the role of the native speaker's awareness of linguistic forms and their use in his or her language. This line of investigation concerns itself almost exclusively with linguistic phenomena, rather than those that lie within the nonlinguistic cultural realm, although it gives equivalent importance to the use of language in context as to language itself. The major formulator of this approach (Silverstein 1976, 1979) has identified it as a development out of Whorf's insight that native speakers are differentially aware of various aspects of language. Silverstein has sought to demonstrate that this relative variation in consciousness of linguistic categories and linguistic forms can be used to account formally for the interrelationship of language structure, function, and ideology (1981). Silverstein seeks the set of universal constraints on the awareness that native speakers have about their own language and its functioning. He hypothesizes that native speakers will more readily apprehend and speak about certain kinds of metapragmatic events than others and that these events will provide direction in identifying the set of universal constraints.

Silverstein distinguishes referential and indexical forms in language. **Referential** forms are those that often stand unchanged and independent of context; they form the basis of most work in formal linguistic theory and in the philosophy of language, and they are relatively easy for native speakers to identify. Basic terms (color names, folk biological nomenclature, and so on) are good examples of referential forms. **Indexical** forms, on the other hand, cannot be interpreted apart from context; classic examples of indexical forms are shifters (also called deictics) like personal pronouns and verb tenses (Jakobson 1971, Silverstein 1976). These categories "point" to elements that change within a **speech event** according to the actors and issues spoken of and that have no fixed referent: to persons with a role within the speech act (*I*, *you*, *we*, etc.) or outside it (*they*, *she*, etc.), to the times the events spoken about occurred (present, past, future tense) or situations surrounding of those event (aspects such as progressive, habitual, durative, momentary), places (*here*, *there*, *over yonder*, etc.), and so on. Language is uniquely reflexive in that it is used to speak about itself, and this characteristic has great potential for studying and understanding how speech functions as a social action, how meaning (and potentially reality) is created in social interaction.

(Con)text

Interest in language use and the ethnography of communication had engendered another branch of linguistic anthropology, sociolinguistics, which is concerned with the relation of language to specifiable social groups and settings. Sometimes these accounts are cast in the form of statistical-based analyses of the distribution of socially marked forms. Labov's (1966) study of the social stratification of English in New York City is a classic of this type. In it, he related variable linguistic traits of New York English to the social class of the speaker, the style of the speech, and the context of the conversation. The linguistic traits—or variables—were occurrence of /r/ after vowels as in the word *car*); use of 'd' for *th* in *then* and 't' for the *th* in *three*; centralization of vowel sounds such as those of the word *floor*. These investigations of sociolinguistic variables lend themselves to statement by rules that incorporate aspects of context and probabilities of their occurrence depending on factors of context and speaker, an approach that has come to be called variation theory (Labov 1969; D. Sankoff and G. Sankoff 1973; G. Sankoff 1971, 1973).

In other cases, the study of the interaction of speakers in actual contexts led in turn to development of **discourse analysis**, the study of how different kinds of discourse are structured and used in a culturally appropriate way, including **conversational analysis** as study of a type of discourse. The concepts of text (a discourse as artifact) and genre (discourse type) emerged as important for these investigations.

The field of sociolinguistics has a large and active life in its own right, and there are excellent introductions to its study, such as Saville-Troike (1982) and Trudgill (1974). Here we can do no more than select some of the more obvious aspects of sociolinguistics that have particular relevance for the study of discourse in language and culture studies.

Structuralism provided the impetus for the development of discourse analysis as one increases in *levels* of complexity (clause, sentence, paragraph, verse, section), a larger and larger structure is built up. A convenient example is the traditional song "The Twelve Days of Christmas."

On the first day of Christmas,

my true love gave to me ____________ .

There are twelve gifts in all ("a partridge in a pear tree, two turtle doves, three French hens, four calling birds," etc.) that fit in the blank. Before the text gets to a new gift, the previous gifts must be mentioned. Not only does this song cogently illustrate the structural aspects of a text, but also it points out that some texts take on a life of their own; they have an individual existence being shared as a part of a given culture. The meaning of the text of "The Twelve Days of Christmas" is negligible; the verses are formulaic in the same way that an inquiry like *How are you?* is. The meaning of the latter is customarily only a greeting, not an inquiry about health. In fact the context of the inquiry defines whether the question has any literal meaning or not: passing on the street, it does not, but in a hospital, it might. Although historically the "The Twelve Days of Christmas" song referred to the twelve-day Christmas festival during which the Yule log burned and servants were given a holiday, today such customs are no longer practiced, and knowledge of them is limited. Thus, the meaning of "The Twelve Days of Christmas" is similarly nonliteral, even nonlexical; for the most part the singing of such a verse today only has meaning as a celebration of the holiday season. Imparting information about particular gifts received on particular days is not really a function of the performance. In both instances, we find much structure but little informational meaning.

Now consider the following two short texts, both graffiti:

Meat is murder.

Make my murder medium rare.

In graffiti, there is a minimum of structure, and the meaning is maximized. The first statement was presumably left by a vegetarian (on a university restroom wall); the second was penciled below it in response. Only knowledge about vegetarians and the preparation of steaks allows interpretation of these texts. The first statement makes sense by itself; it is its own context. The second depends on the first for its meaning. The reader of both graffiti must work actively with the transmitter who has left the folklore on the wall. In both cases, culture-specific knowledge that is external to the text must be known. It is not enough to discern the structure of a discourse/text; an instant cultural analysis must be performed in order truly to *decode* the text.

Specialized language (technical terms, words never used outside a particular context, and the like) help to cement a context and its interactants into a "text" that would have to be videotaped to record it in all its dimensions. Here, an example that comes to mind is a religious service where the speech or singing (language use) is restricted to technical terms and formulas largely exclusive to the context. However, such ritualized language use may also be found in the workplace. A good example is "McLanguage," the specialized jargon of workers for the McDonald's restaurant chain. The most important goal of McDonald's is to prepare a food product of uniform quality in the shortest possible time. The language use of McDonald's workers reflects this. They employ a technical language (type of product, cooking technique, rate, roles of personnel) that actually structures interaction. For example,

> "Give me a fast turn by series on Macs and regulars"

means to cook the patties for deluxe and regular hamburgers so that new meat is added to the grill every time a batch is turned over. Such expressions as

> "Slow five on quarters"

means that a supply of five quarter-pound sandwiches is needed, but it is not necessary to rush them. These expressions were current in the late 1970s. A survey of current usage will reveal innovation and change in McLanguage, which shows the importance of the historical study of categories, even in specialized argots such as this one. There can be no doubt that the crews involved in McDonald's production share a ritualizing vocabulary that creates a tightly bonded "text" at their worksite.

Another aspect of text is the potential **dialogic** (multivoiced, as opposed to **monologic** or single-voiced) nature of any text. The Russian scholar Bakhtin (1981) pointed out that a written text has at least the voice of the speaker/author. Conversations, on the other hand, are entirely dialogic: at least two different voices structure the discourse together as a cooperative venture. Yet it is possible for a written text to be dialogic also. Although the classic example of this is the novel, especially when the psychology of characters is developed (the voice of the narrator, characters' voices, etc.), the notion of the dialogic nature of discourse may also apply to spoken text. A good example of this is code-switching (Gumperz

1982[1970], J. Hill 1986a, J. Hill and K. Hill 1986). **Code-switching** refers to the shifting of dialects or languages (codes) by a single speaker during the course of conversation. Following are several examples taken from the work of J. Hill and K. Hill (1986), where the speakers code-switch between Mexicano (also called Nahuatl, a primary Indian language of central Mexico) and Spanish (written in italics), achieving various effects:

> In nona:ntzi:n, *podoroso.*
>
> As for my mother, *she is powerful.* (1986:353)

In the example, the speaker both demonstrates that the code switch can occur at an intonation contour and picks up on the power of the dominant Spanish language to illustrate the power of the mother. Again,

> *Pero Dios eterno.* A:mo tlen nicte:hui:quilia, o:mpa ma chica:hui ma quincua, *bendito sea al* (sic) *Senyor.*
>
> *But God is eternal.* I do not owe anyone, there let him grow strong, let him prosper, *blessed be the Lord.* (1986:360)

In this example, Spanish is quoted from the Catholic liturgy as a sign of sincerity. Finally,

> In te:lpocameh den nica:n, ¿cox oc ihqui:n tlahtoah de mexicano?
>
> A:mo, a:cmo, a:macah. *Verdád tú Leobardo, nadien sabe mexicano, aquí puro castellano.*
>
> As for the young people here, do they still speak thus in Mexicano?
>
> No, no longer, nobody. *Isn't that true, you, Leobardo, nobody knows Mexicano, here it's nothing but Spanish.* (1986:367)

In the example above, the shift is ironic.

Consider the following excerpt from a radio commercial in Hopi; in it there is both Hopi and English, but the English is restricted to place names and addresses only.

> Pay it piw yan màatsiwqat engem *McDonald's*—
> me pam hapi pan màatsiwqa yep *Winslow* ep
> *North Park Plaza* epeq
> sinmuy amungem noovalawu.
>
> Well, that one called McDonald's,
> that one here in Winslow
> at North Park Plaza
> makes food for people. (Shaul 1988:97, 100)

There are two voices in the speaker's monologue: a Hopi voice, which uses Hopi language in persuasive conventions, and an Anglo voice, which anchors McDonald's (an alien thing) in Anglo space. It is a dialogic monologue.

Texts, whether written or spoken, whether tending toward monologic or dialogic postures, whether full of multilayered meaning and symbolism or simple in structure and rhetoric, depend upon an interaction of topic, speaker/author, hearer/reader with reference to appropriate cultural conventions they share. The French scholar Barthes devoted much of his efforts to showing that texts structure reality; for example, to list a person's name with those of other persons tends to class that person with those in the same list; the extreme case of name dropping associates the speaker with the persons mentioned in his or her own narrative. Moreover, written texts viewed in isolation stand as their own entire context and *are* reality. This ideographic, relativistic aspect of all texts suggests a tenet of North American symbolic anthropology: culture in this view is not inside peoples' heads, but resides in publicly held symbols, the meaning of which is learned, re-affirmed, and modified through interaction and ritual (Turner 1969; Geertz 1973, 1985; Schneider 1976). Texts are cultural artifacts made of language. Discourse is an intersection of linguistic and cultural knowledge (Sherzer 1987), especially in specialized genres. Both spoken and written texts may be considered to be the location of linguistic relativity (Barthes 1970, 1972).

Discourse may be seen, then, as intermediate between culture (models, beliefs, and the world in symbolic terms) and society (individuals organized into various groups who share rules for the use of symbol-oriented behavior). The idea of discourse (language use) as a link between culture and society is not novel. What is new is the emphasis on texts as artifacts of a culture or cultural practice, because texts may be actual instances of lexical items and grammatical devices being used symbolically in addition to referring to entities outside the discourse. This characteristic is true of the gamut of discourse, from specialized genres (auctions, novels, prayers, etc.), where specialized contexts yield specialized discourse types (Sherzer 1983, 1987), all the way to such highly individualistic uses of language as poetry (Friedrich 1986), where novel symbols or combinations of symbols are preferred. The problems of interpreting discourse, then, one can easily see, are legion. It is no surprise that those in the field of linguistic anthropology in the 1980s increasingly became interested in the problem of interpretation itself.

Summary

Cognitive anthropology presents different ways of analyzing and representing lexical domains as cultural grammars: fuzzy sets, prototypes, feature matrices (discussed in chapter 4), taxonomies, schemata, structuralisms such as diagrams, frames, scripts, scenes, expert systems, flow charts, metaphors, and metonyms. The type of model sometimes reflects the type of domain analyzed (process or procedure, sets of things or concepts, continua, inherent hierarchies); they have in common that they are all more-or-less formal treatments.

These various ways tend toward reductionism, as a consequence of the practitioners' goal of "scientific" formal elegance and economy of explanation and a need to account for the wide variety of behaviors in terms of some agreed-upon ideal. This desire is reflected in the names of the enterprise of making cultural grammars: ethnoscience and cognitive anthropology.

In trying to analyze and model native knowledge, cognitive anthropologists stressed using an ethnographic approach. This means that data should be elicited from native consultants or recorded by observation of their normal behavior. The resulting analysis is tested further by consulting with native culture-bearers. Cognitive anthropology depends on context (or rather, transcriptions or texts based on actual contexts).

The reliance on key words in context (especially in written texts or transcripts) as the raw data for cognitive anthropology does present limitations. Although written texts are convenient, since a text is both limited in size and can constitute its own context, it can lead the observer to underestimate his or her influence on the enterprise. Further, as the influence of context became more evident to investigators, it also became evident that there is a problem inherent in determining core meanings in a vastness of meaning-influencing contexts. We will turn to these issues in the next chapter.

Discussion and Activities

1. The following blurb is for gourmet salsas. It represents a kind of food item that is fashionable. Analyze this text as its own context, as in the exercises with advertising blurbs in the previous two chapters. Is there an overlap in key terms or underlying assumptions?

CAHILL

Desert [*Outline of Mission-style building in sky blue and mauve.*] **Products**

Cactus Salsa

Medium Hot

[*Blurb on left of main label:*] Cahill Desert Products is pleased to present the Cactus Salsa line. We have concocted three temperature settings; one will truly satisfy everyone's palate. If you are adventurous and don't mind riding the wild side try the Scorching Hot. We do recommend that you have an adequate supply of chilled margaritas on hand. For those who wish to enjoy the unique blending and remain seated, try the Medium Hot or Mild.

2. One of the ways that natives use to create new terms for innovations in their culture is by use of metaphors and metonyms. Such innovation is present, for example, in children's language. Consider the following pair of terms (Carlos Alonso Nugent, personal communication).

   clear milk

   wet milk

   Both terms were used by a three-year-old boy for milk. *Clear milk* is a term he used for a sweet yoghurt and juice mixture that comes in a clear glass bottle that was not refrigerated. *Wet milk* is what he calls milk that must be refrigerated and that comes in a carton. The concept of 'wet milk' was disgusting to the child who coined these terms, while 'clear milk' was greatly esteemed by him. The essential semantic features coded in these two concepts are: taste (sweet or not), container (clear or not), and temperature (refrigerated or not). Yet neither modifier *clear* or *wet* directly code any of these critical semantic features. The use of *wet* comes from wet diapers; therefore, an uncomfortable and nasty condition is coded by the word *wet*, a metaphor for 'disgusting.'

The use of *clear* is a metonym. Something associated with the referent 'milk' (the glass bottle) is used as the name for the referent. If clear were extended as a word for 'good' or 'sweet,' the extension would be a metaphor if the referent didn't come in a glass bottle.

Each class member can elicit a similar, small lexical domain from his or her own children or the children of acquaintances. Make an analysis of the set that you elicit. Class members can then compare the results of their fieldwork.

3. Consider the following sentences in English. Each contains a hedge. Identify the hedge in each sentence. What is the function of each hedge with respect to category membership?

    A dolphin is not a fish as such.

    Strictly speaking, a computer is not furniture.

    Loosely speaking, a computer is a kind of furniture.

    A dolphin is not a fish per se, but is like one.

    A dolphin is a "fish" in that it is adapted to a marine environment.

    Technically, an octopus is not a fish.

    Loosely speaking, an octopus is a fish.

   Refer back to the section "Classical Semantics" in chapter 4, to review the basic claims of the classical theory of categorization. What do the hedges show about categorization? What is the effect of context on categorization? In trying to identify the function of these hedges, try to think of contexts in which a speaker might use them. Another way to think about them is to make up a scenario in which the hedge might be appropriate: to take the first example, "A dolphin is not a fish as such.", perhaps one is thinking of characteristics that define *fish* [+ fins], [+ swims], [+ lives in the sea], for example, all of which apply also to *dolphin*. To say, "A dolphin is not a fish as such" might lead one to identify features that would distinguish *fish* from *dolphin* (e.g., [+ scales]). Thus *dolphin* can been seen to share many characteristics of *fish* but be distinguishable according to different values on one or a few features—[- scales].

Key Terms

code-switching
co-extensive semantics
co-extensivity
confidence factors

consensus theory
conversational analysis
deictics
deixis
dialogic
discourse
discourse analysis
economy of explanation
expert systems
expert system shells
family resemblances
formal elegance
frame
functionalist
fuzzy set
hedges
image
indexical
key words
metaphor
metonym
monologic
multiple pathways theory
near synonymy
pragmatics
prototype
reductionism
referential
scene
script
script-frames
shifters
speech acts
speech event
synecdoche
taxonomy
vantages
variation theory

9

Interpretivism

> And the great gap here [in language and culture studies] is the comparative study of meaning: we know almost nothing new, save in a few domains, about lexical semantics from a systematic cross-linguistic point of view, very little about indexical systems, almost nothing empirical about cross-linguistic tendencies in pragmatics.
>
> — J. J. Gumperz and S. C. Levinson

Cultural anthropology and linguistic anthropology have been influenced by a group of overlapping philosophical positions collectively known as **postmodernism**. The postmodern positions represent a continuation of reaction to structuralism, and they tend to share common themes.

The key tenet of postmodernism is the difficulty (or even possibility) of arriving at universals of the human condition; this denial or near denial of any **nomothetic** (general, universal) goals of the social sciences results from heightened appreciation of the fact that an observer has an effect on the observed or observation. The very presence of an outsider-observer of an event or activity can change the character of that action as performed by insider participants. Postmodernists question whether science truly accumulates knowledge, building new knowledge upon the accomplishments of past discovery (Kuhn 1970). Further, human existence is extremely complex, so much so that one can hardly hold a part of an activity constant to observe the alternation in some part of the whole. Instead, one appears to be recording an endlessly shifting ground. Additionally, postmodernism has brought heightened awareness that knowledge is power (conventional signs or sign systems privilege one position while suppressing others), thus biasing observations.

Postmodernism also challenges the idea that a text (literary or cultural) can be analyzed independently of its social and historical context; indeed, it holds that important aspects of belief and behavior are the consequences of prior actions and thus reflect a historical order. In this view, for example, we can see present-day North American racial conflict as a consequence of sixteenth and seventeenth century British attitudes toward foreign resources and peoples. Despite its pessimism, postmodern ideas contribute positively to the enterprise of linguistic anthropology by requiring a serious examination of the assumption that a nomothetic explanation is possible.

Best known in physics, nomothetic explanations have enjoyed great success and have seldom been questioned in that field. Yet, as early as 1929, P. W. Bridgeman pointed out that at the most fundamental level of investigation, the investigator is always influencing the "objective" measurements desired. In order to know the velocity of a particle, we must affect its mass, and if we try to know the mass of a particle, then we must change its velocity. Physics has not suffered unduly for this problem, nor should linguistic ethnography be paralyzed by it. Ethnographic events resemble quanta in that as long as they are unmeasured, they can be anywhere, have any polarity, any meaning, but once measured, they must collapse to a point and seize a polarity.

We will examine the major proponents of the postmodern movement, stopping at convenient points to reflect on particularly influential developments. The heart of postmodernism is epistemology: "How do we know what we know?"

Philosophical Background: How We Know

This concern with epistemology is the central issue of **antirationalism**, a label that ought not be construed as irrationalism. Antirationalism rejects received or established classifications and questions both the notion of language as a mirror of cognition and the idea of history as an orderly chronology. Actual reality is too detailed, it is argued, and actual contexts too rich to permit ease of definition, classification, and explanation. Further, language fails to represent a complete picture of the complexity of the real world (chaotic reality), since its use reduces that complexity by way of habitual categories (reductionism). The history of things is neither orderly nor progressive. Rather, history is held to be as diversely rich and chaotic as is synchrony.

Any attempt to impose order on reality, whether it be a folk theory, a natural language, or a deliberately constructed theory, is deemed to fail as an adequate presentation of that reality because the participants in a given "reality" have potentially competing goals, and inevitably differing views of the same events or projects. Knowledge can only be a discussion that arises within the confines of a given practice, a discussion limited to those experiencing the contexts that make up the reality. The conventional facets of human existence (like history, society, nature, and self-image) are to be taken as processes that are negotiated and experienced. Any approach to knowledge must be **experiential** (reality is experienced, not independent or secondhand), dialogic (a reality consists of contexts in which people interact), and must abandon the prospects of arriving at objective truth (either independently standing or motivated, or existing as a set of generalizations from an averaging out of reality). Instead knowledge is **ontological** (related to being or existence). These dicta constitute a radical departure from the intellectual enterprise set in motion by structuralists such as Saussure. Examining the history of these ideas can aid in our understanding of the challenge they bring to language and culture studies.

The philosophical background of antirationalism is important for a consideration of its influence on the anthropology of language. René Descartes, in his famous statement (*Cogito ergo sum*: 'I think, therefore I am.'), posited each thinking individual as the locus of the only reality he or she could know or experience. Definition and classification must be accepted with doubt: reason or knowledge as self-awareness ultimately has political consequences, as noted by the philosopher Immanuel Kant. This perception of the individual as potentially political eventually came to figure prominently in antirationalism.

> Enlightenment is man's release from his self-incurred tutelage. Tutelage is man's inability to make use of his understanding without direction from another. Self-incurred is this tutelage when its cause lies not in lack of reason, but in lack of resolution and courage to use it without direction from another. (Kant 1965:3)

It is this position on knowledge that is inherent in the opposition of individual vs. normative (collectively held) theories of knowledge. Hegel expanded upon this idea, by describing the way in which a person arrived at individually held truth. According to Hegel, there are hypothesis formation (**thesis**), consideration of opposing ideas (**antithesis**), and conclusion (**synthesis**) in which the details of thesis and antithesis are reconciled. One may see the basis of the scientific method in this schema (assuming objective truth is possible), but to Hegel, truth appeared static because, although it is abstracted from the details of reality, it is still the property of an individual. Knowledge, according to Hegel, is an interaction of identity and difference. Knowledge (truth) is reached by a gradual, conscious process of exploring and reconciling subjectivity (self) and objectivity (otherness, ideas alien to the self). Absolute knowledge (complete self-recognition), if possible, comes only through an awareness of everything the self is not.

Saussure, although he recognized the arbitrariness of signs, still held that language and other sign systems were sufficiently shared and conventional to permit abstraction of meaning. Accepting that there are sign systems that have a certain stateable value because of social contract, the problem remains that commonly held sign systems may obscure reality by not encouraging individual evaluation of it. Wittgenstein (1958), who initially agreed with Saussure that some conventional aspects of language may be described, eventually concluded that the meaning of any term is its use in a particular "language game" (context), and that the variety of linguistic contexts cannot be synthesized into a whole. What is left unthought (because it is unsaid) is thus crucial to definition of what constitutes reality. "In contrast to Hegel, this is not a traditional problem, already posed, but what has always remained unasked throughout this history of thinking" (Heidegger 1969:50). It is the unasked, the unstated that constitutes **otherness**. Any attempt to offer a general definition leads us back to Hegel, Kant, and Descartes, and away from Saussure, because general definitions inherently exclude context. Jacques Derrida seized this philosophical quandary (can a single self ever acquire enough information about otherness?) and extended it (can a self ever achieve otherness?). Meaning depends on context; contexts are dialogic and fleeting, and so the plausibility of the self bridging otherness is slight. Meaning is momentary. A written text is its own context in which author(s) and reader(s) cannot negotiate or provide feedback. This fact points up the hopelessness of arriving at objective truth (Derrida 1976). This position falls short of nihilism, but its skeptical stance provides the philosophical foundation for antirationalism.

It should be noted that the philosophical basis of antirationalism must be taken individually. It must also be taken in varying degrees. Those who adopt an extreme reading may be considered to be antirationalists. Those who think that enough may be abstracted from contexts to permit limited understanding of the usage of language may be considered to be, in a general sense, adherents of some sort of hermeneutics, which is concerned with achieving careful readings of and explications of texts, including cultural texts. Labeling both ends of this continuum is the term **interpretivism**, the consideration of individuals' constructions of reality and their affectual responses to them as they interact in contexts by using sign systems.

Foundations of Interpretivism

It will be helpful to look at the work of two antirationalists before considering hermeneutics, and afterward, to examine interpretation in linguistic anthropology. Two major figures in the antirationalist camp are Michel Foucault and Jacques Derrida. Both exemplify distrust in received knowledge about ways of knowing, and both abandon the goal of seeking objective truth to some extent. Both challenge the main themes of language and culture studies, the question of the relation between linguistic relativism and language universals (including, of course, the study of categorization) and the development of semiotic theory.

Two different concerns derive from the rejection of rationality; one is textual, and the other, political (Felperin 1985:28–29). These positions are exemplified by the work of both Foucault and Derrida. On the one hand, postmodernism centers its concern on texts, especially written texts. This work is the deconstructive textualism of Derrida. On the other hand, postmodernism takes the position that "all texts are political" (Felperin 1985:29). As Felperin has noted, both these seemingly disparate foci have in common an attack upon traditional ideas of authorship, authority, and the authorial self, and "if the author himself is only an intersection of texts or discourses, the concept of author becomes meaningless" (1985:29). Since stories that are culturally important must in some way have collective authorship, the more culturally centered an author's text may be, the less claim that author has upon it as an original work. Michel Foucault typifies this intellectual and political stance of postmodernism.

Foucault developed the idea, stated above by Kant (and others), that a relation exists between knowledge (which is equivalent to conventionalized sign systems) and power: knowledge is a way of naming and ordering the world that favors a group in power and serves to maintain some status quo. Expertise licenses power; judges, teachers, physicians, social workers, lawyers—only licensed experts—exercise authority because of their specialized knowledge in institutionalized settings. *Madness and Civilization* (Foucault 1973a), for example, charts the development of the concept of 'insanity' in Western culture. Prior to the late 1700s, madness was defined by the divine; unreason was of supernatural origin. The mad person was accommodated socially, even welcomed as "God's fool." In the modern era, as technology and science developed, insanity came to be defined in terms of human beings. The mad became strangers to themselves, sciences arose to deal with them (psychology, psychiatry), and the insane were socially isolated. The rise of science had **decentered** the divine in Western culture, that is, it had removed the role of God from its previous position of being relevant to all aspects of life and thought, not just for an individual but for all society.

In a similar vein, prior to the decentering of the divine in Western culture, death was the great leveler of all: in the Medieval mind, for instance, reward or torments after death were universally believed to be meted out on an egalitarian basis, without regard to social rank or wealth acquired during the course of life. Foucault, in *The Birth of the Clinic* (1975), again points out that in earlier eras the divine was considered the source of illness; consequently, prior to modern times, Western culture sustained a long discourse about death which is a major theme in many of the writings and artifacts left to us. With the development of science in the modern era, a new rationalized discourse (modern medicine) arose in an attempt to combat death. So, the cause of illness and death came to be regarded as physical or mental and not divine: discussion of death became cast in euphemisms, as is so obvious in North American culture.

Foucault differs from other kinds of interpretivism—phenomenology and hermeneutics—for example. **Phenomenology** is a philosophical position which sees human beings as meaning-creating and values especially their subjectivity in the process of meaning creation. Hermeneutics locates meaning in sociocultural practices and texts (context) from which truth may ultimately be extracted on a limited basis. For Foucault, subjectivity is not autonomous, but rather it is linked to context (the locus of meaning), with no truth being possible.

The Sign Variously Regarded

An even more skeptical position is **deconstruction**, the project of Jacques Derrida (1976), another major figure in postmodernism. Deconstruction is probably the most important ingredient of the postmodern movement. Derrida proceeds from Saussure: he accepts the arbitrariness of the sign; he agrees that sign systems are mutually defining and that sign systems are autonomous (only reflecting reality, not actually linked to it). However, Derrida extends the arbitrariness of the sign considerably. Deconstruction, like structuralism, requires the tenet that binary opposition is basic in meaning systems; however, deconstruction tends to concern itself more with "intersections" of meanings in the web or network of a text, rather than with the links between signifier and signified that to structuralists identify meanings through opposition.

For Derrida, all associations of referent and sign are chance; only some of all possible associations are conventionalized as categories. Saussure's notions of an association among referents themselves and among signs themselves are ignored (Ellis 1989:45–60). Those chance associations among referents and signs that have become conventionalized as categories in a cultural or linguistic system are a microcosm of the power inherent in the institutions of human groups. Where there is a named concept, it gives a particular referent-sign relationship a favored (conventionalized) status, thereby suppressing opposite meaning(s). For example, the concept of literacy brings to mind not only the ability to read, but associated conventions and attitudes of being able to read. Semiotics can become a moral or ethical problem; we can inquire into what is left untold or unacknowledged. The opposite of literacy, for example, might be illiteracy, preliteracy, oral tradition, perhaps even collective consciousness, or maybe some unnamed or invented concept. Whatever opposition is chosen, a deconstruction of literacy would try to show how that particular opposite is less favored by social convention in a given culture or situation than is the concept of literacy. Deconstruction is essentially a celebration of the arbitrariness of the sign, with political implications. Although this may appear trivial in some of its illustrations (for instance, a deconstruction of table), deconstruction serves to remind the analyst of the real dangers inherent in labeling, concept formation and sign manipulation. Even more important, it illustrates the power of omission or failure to label. Called **erasure**, this practice often identifies politically important categories and activities. For example, undermention of the contributions of women to an enterprise in Western society constitutes erasure and points up the economic and political privilege enjoyed by men in that society.

The use of binary or polar opposites is the most clear illustration of the concept of deconstruction, and so Derrida and others have concentrated on conventional, received cultural assumptions. Western culture has a notion that language is an absolute, that it resembles an ultimate truth (this idea Derrida calls **logocentricism**). Yet, even the very semantic atoms of a language (morphemes) may be seen to be infinitely polysemous: for each use of a given morpheme, there is a potentially endless array of occasions and contexts in which it could be employed. Thus, a definitive account of its absolute meaning is impossible, particularly if one admits poetic, extended or other novel uses.

Feminism offers another classic example for deconstruction; in addition to the erasure mentioned above, the concept of "woman" brings to mind, in addition to a literal female reference, many emotional and social meanings. Lacking here are notions of power, public authority, and the like being ascribed to the concept of woman. A good candidate for a feminist deconstruction is the myth in Wyoming of the state's being the first polity in the world to give women suffrage; the state nickname is the "Equality State." In fact, in 1868, women were given the right to vote in the new Territory of Wyoming not out of noble sentiments of equality of the sexes, but because there were too few people in the territory to organize it unless women and men were both counted, and because all of the neighboring lands had become states or territories (leaving an embarrassingly large square of unorganized real estate). Underscoring this deconstruction is the fact that the second territorial legislature tried in 1871 to revoke women's voting rights (the appointed governor vetoed the measure) (Larson 1965:85–87; Gould 1988:35–36).

Deconstruction can be applied to single concepts, sets of related ideas, or to whole texts. Deconstruction not only points out an ignored possibility. The ignored possibility under erasure is usually a political inequity. So,

eschew obfuscation

advises the reader to be clear; it will take, however, a sophisticated reader to get the message. The deconstruction of this little text is not the fact that it does not do what it advises, but that only linguistic snobs will get its message. Indeed, the style of deconstructionists is often deliberately difficult and opaque, to point up not only the arbitrariness of the sign, but also the idea that knowledge is power, and only a privileged few have access to it.

Deconstruction attempts to make plain the assumptions and ulterior motives of a discourse. A convenient example can be found in the following piece of photocopy lore, the kind of folklore perpetuated at the copy machine:

Dial 1-800-PSY-HELP.

If you are obsessive-compulsive, press 1 repeatedly.

If you are co-dependent, get someone to press 2 for you.

If you have multiple personality disorder, press 3-4-5-6-7-8.

If you are paranoid-delusional, don't press anything; we know who you are and what you want.

If you are depressed, it doesn't matter which button you press; no one will answer.

If you are schizophrenic, just wait; a little voice will tell you which button to push.

When viewed closely and with a deconstructionist perspective, this somewhat goofy text actually reveals much of a serious nature about how emotional illness is viewed in North America. Perhaps most important is the fact that the very existence of the text indicates that it is acceptable to trivialize serious emotional illness in a "joke" format such as this one, whereas one cannot image serious physical illness being treated in a similar manner. Constructing a similar "joke" about leukemia, diabetes, or ebola would not only be in unacceptably bad taste, it would not be funny. It is unthinkable. There is an unrecognized assumption underlying this photocopy joke, which is that mental illness is both funny and not really very important.

Of course, mental illness *is* important to all who know it firsthand—to its victims, to their families and friends, to professionals who treat the mentally ill. But the fact that this joke is a widely circulated piece of folklore suggests that most people think they are immune from emotional illness; furthermore, the emotionally ill are too weak an interest group to establish themselves as a category of persons about whom jokes ought not to be made. Again, imagine the political incorrectness of a "joke" such as this circulating about a racial or religious minority. Sharing such a "joke" would brand the distributor as hopelessly insensitive and gauche.

Another interesting aspect of this text is that it is given in the form of a call to an 800 number. North Americans not only shop via impersonal 800 numbers, they also seek information and help of an extremely personal nature with such calls. Through the anonymity of an 800 number call, we face some of our most difficult crises—even seeking help for rape counseling and AIDS information. This text tells us that we prefer to obtain some of the most embarrassing and personal information about ourselves alone and anonymously, that we often do not want to share a difficult moment of revelation with someone we know and care about.

This sort of analysis of texts, laying bare their motivations and unstated assumptions, is not novel. An excellent example is the dramatic literature of Euripides. More of his plays survived than did those of any other ancient Greek playwright because he treated his traditional, mythic material in everyday contexts, explored the psychology of the characters, and addressed contemporary issues (some of which are still relevant). Ironically, Euripides' body of deconstructionist writings became part of the Western literary canon, becoming politically privileged texts.

At this point, we will take stock of the value of deconstruction for linguistic anthropology. Taken deterministically, deconstruction claims that ultimately such things as definitions, classifications and theories are impossible. Any definition or theory undermines itself by excluding potentially relevant factors or data. Yet note that Derrida relies on a structuralist apparatus to perform the deconstruction: even if one is divorced from direct relations with reality, one can still expect members of the same culture to tend to cohere in their use of shared signs. Deconstruction must be more of a cautionary measure. Further, it makes central the examination of political and economic factors which are the products of history and which are not necessarily in the awareness of individuals by freeing study of the sign from the immediate structures that embody it.

A musical analogy may help to contrast the search for meaning within deconstruction from that in other interpretive approaches. Suppose a composer took innovative, highly unfamiliar musical motifs (melodic fragments) and strung them in sequences according to a familiar frame (for example, the rondo, divertimento, fugue, or scherzo). To do so would yield a radically modern piece of music, but one that would be readily accessible to the concert goer in terms of the frame itself (a musical form already known). Any meaning assigned to the innovative motifs will be constrained by the "meaning" of the structure into which they are set, which will itself direct interpretation. On the other hand, those same motifs released from a familiar structure, either placed by the composer into an unfamiliar frame or set out free of structure (perhaps randomly), will force the listener to consider them individually, each in its own terms, not as dependents of some larger (familiar structural) entity. In a sense, deconstruction seeks to treat such small (often word-level) meanings freed from larger structures.

Thus, it is possible to see deconstruction as the foundation for a linguistic relativity that is not based on structuralism. Language use, in varying degrees, is driven by individual selection and imagination. A natural language has an infinite capacity for creating novel categories and for novel uses of old ones (Friedrich 1986). Much as Derrida points to an infinite number of possible contexts for the use of a single word, Friedrich argues that while linguistic norms exist (otherwise translation and language use itself would be impossible), language use of these norms is inherently variable, ever creating a contextually derived linguistic relativism within a single language. It may be noted that this linguistic relativity may be put to normative use; linguistic creativity is not incompatible with normative behavior. The field of advertising attests to this poetic linguistic relativism. One industry leader advises that the strongest trademarks are "neologisms . . . new words coined for your [exclusive] use" (Bachrach 1983:72), while noting that the more original a trade name is, the more successful it will be (some of Bachrach's examples: Ben-Gay, Exxon, Kotex, Mylar, Yuban). Linguistic creativity is put to normative use in advertising and elsewhere; linguistic relativity (in the form of creative use of lexical material) can be exploited to create normative behavior.

The issues of comparability, the potentially poetic role of the individual in actual language use, and the narrow line between thought and linguistic encoding of thought all highlight the problems of any study of language and culture, in or out of context. Clearly, there is some comparability of knowledge among the speakers of a particular language, and it is possible to extract and study such knowledge. Although polysemy "emerges as a natural, indeed necessary consequence of the human ability to think flexibly" (Deane 1988:325), it is not beyond study. One may examine it by considering actual use of linguistic categories as shifting attention to poles of category identity and category distinctness (Deane 1988; compare with MacLaury 1987a, 1987b). Context of usage is crucial to any answers that Derrida might put to the linguistic anthropologist. Indeed, plausible arguments can be made that linguistic science could exist without the assumption of differential linguistic coding of the same reality (Grace 1987).

In fact, Derrida's notion of text provides a way of doing linguistic anthropology by taking account of normative behavior. A "text" for deconstructionist purposes is a collection of signs, be it a person, a social group, a written text, or a videotape. Agreement between texts (communication) depends on how many signs and conventions are shared. This **intertextuality** is a functional analogue to semantics, but is situational and not absolute. The contextual impact on semantics also demands that the linguistic anthropologist examine Derrida's tacit assumption (with Saussure) about autonomous sign systems; contexts imply interaction, and it is the emergent, cooperative nature of text-making that separates Derrida's from many other varieties of postmodernism. If one takes a text to be "any configuration of signs that is coherently interpretable by some community of [sign] users" (Hanks 1989:95) and assumes that any complex of signs can never be completely self-consistent (i.e., any text contradicts itself because of fine semantic differences between constituent signs, or because of what the text omits and leaves unsaid—the erasures), at least a mild form of deconstruction is inevitable in the interpretation. Interpretation must therefore be sought in context, whether it be a conversation, the performance of a narrative, or the more difficult interaction of author, text, and reader (recall that a written text takes on a life of its own; the author and reader are removed and may not negotiate the interaction or clarify meaning). One possible solution is to use genres (discursive practices) as a way of uniting the formal (structural) and interactive aspects of interpretation (Hanks 1989). It is this approach which leads us from deconstruction to phenomenology and hermeneutics.

The Phenomenological Critique

A possible reading of the philosophical position known as phenomenology is that social and cultural phenomena are the products of the consciousness of interacting individuals, however similar they may be. What is observed of sociocultural interaction is not an independent object or entity, but a process in which individuals who partially share symbols use these symbols to interpret and reinterpret each other. In this view, scientific observation of a sociocultural milieu is intentional and involved, not detached and objective as empiricist and positivist philosophies would claim. Phenomenology thus rejects **empiricism** and **positivism** not only because these approaches fail to explicate the assumptions and rhetoric of the interactions, but because they also fail to state completely the biases and rhetoric they bring to the process of observation. Under phenomenology, the act of observation becomes part of the observation itself, part of the phenomenon being studied.

The inescapable position of this reading of phenomenology is that it is impossible to study sociocultural phenomena in a completely objective manner or to subtract the effects of deliberate observation. People must interpret one another in order to interact; we interpret our fellows and anticipate how they will interpret us. Culture is thus dialogic, a discursive undertaking. The assumptions upon which a kind of anthropology (say, linguistic anthropology) and some native system to be observed both rest can be expected to guide the interaction. Ultimately, what humans have in common with respect to a particular topic (for example: the way kinship or faunal terms are structured and used) should be able to be derived. Phenomenology urges slow, careful, ideographically based induction as the only course for a truly accurate human science.

Some theoreticians influenced by these ideas (e.g., Taylor 1979) take a more pessimistic view. For them, the phenomenological critique of social science appears complete and incapacitating, and they have abandoned the goal of developing a science of human behavior as inappropriate, in favor of encouraging an interpretive enterprise more closely resembling the textual criticism of the humanities. Nonetheless, for others, the concern with objectivity is taken as a caution against premature theorizing (especially about universals of language or culture), rather than as a devastating critique, since phenomenology clearly permits the derivation of ideographic typologies. Can the comparison of such typologies ultimately produce a theory? For a phenomenologist, there are many problems with such an attempt for they caution that what is compared may not be truly comparable, the assumptions of the observer and the observed may not be understood, and the degree of reductionism allowed is undetermined. They note that many unobserved, abstract constructs may be used in theorizing if they facilitate efficient, economical, neat accounts of a phenomenon, but wonder whether this inventory can be justified. What part of observable reality should be classified or used as a theoretical construct (the reification problem)?

These dilemmas exemplify a fundamental difference between humanistic and scientific inquiry into knowledge and our ways of knowing about our world. Scientific approaches see multiple interpretations as an interesting problem to be investigated and attempt to select the best of the candidates by application of scientific methods and by relying on the language of mathematics or logic for representation. Further, an explanation is always tentative and subject to refutation within scientific theories. No understanding is accepted as immutable truth.

On the other hand, a search for universal truth constitutes the goal of the humanities. Humanistic approaches ordinarily do not consider alternative explanations, at least not as the major activity of their enterprise, or in relation to some test case or prediction. Thus, the goals of the humanistic and scientific perspectives speak to different frames of reference. Whereas validation proves the essential test of all scientific approaches, humanistic theories deny its relevance, involving instead chains of natural logic (Gardín 1988).

Phenomenology moves on a ground intermediate between an extreme scientific and an extreme humanistic position and seeks to establish a mediation between the two. If, as phenomenology claims, social phenomena surely exist in the consciousness of each separate but interacting individual, then it should be possible to rehabilitate empirical observation and theory construction in light of the phenomenological critique. First of all, one must ask what the basis of the interpretation is. Clearly, categories and models exist in the minds of natives and are amenable to systematic description. Otherwise, it would be impossible to learn even one's native language or culture. Experimental bias, the **Heisenberg uncertainty principle**, and the dangers of participant observation have long been known. Science has its own "deconstructionists," as evidenced by the suggestion that a scientific hypothesis or theory can never be verified, although a simple prediction can be falsified (Popper 1965).

As pointed out at the beginning of this chapter, nomothetic explanations are best known in physics, even though the physical sciences were among the first to recognize the effect of investigator on the phenomenon under study. The pursuit of the advance of knowledge of our physical world has not been halted by this insight; rather, it is possible to construct what appears to be an increasingly accurate model by systematic experimentation. (For additional comment on phenomenology as a critique of social science, see Husserl (1927), Strasser (1963), Natanson (1973), Roche (1973), and Kultgen (1975).)

Viewed phenomenologically as a set of underlying assumptions and interpretive conventions, a text is composed of sentences. This constellation of sentences requires contextual interpretation, and there may be cultural conventions (including genres) for interpretation of given structures. A universal device, such as paired concepts, may have varying uses in different cultural practices. The principle of paired concepts, for example, in the Genesis account of creation, is used to indicate polar opposites, things diametrically opposed.

God vs. World

Light vs. Dark

Male vs. Female

This type of rhetoric is a familiar tactic in much of European(-derived) culture. The versions of the creation given in the Mayan Popol Vuh use paired duality also, but the pairs form continua rather than opposites (Tedlock 1983):

> The World and Divinity
>
> Light and Darkness together
>
> Sky and Sea.

Paired continuities do occur in English (sand and surf, sage and sand, for example, often used as names of motels) but have a trivial force when compared with paired opposites.

We can see that one response to the phenomenological critique is hermeneutic analysis, textual interpretation within a given tradition. As a kind of scholarship, hermeneutics originally referred to the interpretation of sacred texts, particularly Biblical ones. In a more general sense, it refers to interpretation of a (lexical) domain (type of context) as a **practice** (series of contexts with common themes, motivations, or both) in which the individual participant is as important for understanding as is the observer-interpreter. Hermeneutics may also refer to the "reading" of whole cultures as texts according to established conventions (genres, styles), though some scholars might object to even wholesale interpretations of even single cultures. In summary, any approach to knowledge that is experiential, dialogic, and ontological may be called hermeneutic (writ large). Let us consider two well-known hermeneutic positions.

The first (Gadamer 1976) stresses that agents and actions are not mechanical; agents have prejudices and differing interests. Consequently, an interpreter tries to understand self, the environment, and situational demands. (Understanding is limited: interpretation is a gradual process of reflecting on data that enters and is stored in the brain. The collective efforts of a group of people who share a similar understanding of data constitute a tradition). Discursive practices (traditions), then, must cluster around a set of signs which are understandable and describable to a point. On the other hand, a second view (Ricoeur 1967) accepts the systemic nature of signs, but stresses that the meaning attached to signs is dynamic; signs are used in contexts that are socially defined and constructed, mutually negotiated events (cf. Bourdieu 1977). Interpretation involves uncovering possibly competing forces and factors.

A major figure in anthropological hermeneutics is Clifford Geertz (1973, 1985). In his view, insight, empathy, and imagination are the tools of hermeneutics and are to be preferred over testable principles or theories. At least two things are necessary, however: (1) culture or language must be seen as a unified entity (not exactly Derrida's position) that exists (2) without reference to change. In addition, the reading of cultural texts involves two sets of relations: (a) the reader's relation to the text, and (b) the interpretive practices of the parties to the original dialogue.

Consider the following abbreviated text, which serves as an introduction to a short book:

> While recipes of the Pueblo tribes are unique, delicious and attractive, the need for Nature to provide us with the basic needs are: Rain to make the seed turn in the ground, the sun to break the earth, the air to freshen the crop and the tender care of the farmer to provide the crop. . . .
>
> Our Great Spirit also gave us the knowledge to know the different wild greens we eat in the spring, summer and fall. The wild berries, nuts and seeds too. We know exactly where to look for all these things. Our thanks to Mother Nature for all the good food we get from our fields and the wild places. (Priscilla Vigil, in Hughes 1977:5)

This text only indirectly introduces the *Pueblo Indian Cookbook*; it refers only to the kinds of food (personally cultivated or gathered) that make up the cuisine being introduced to the public. The theme of nature, personified as the creator (Nature, Rain, Great Spirit, Mother Nature) illuminates the attitudes about food traditional among the Pueblo Indians. From this example, one might also conclude that Pueblo rhetoric values indirection, and that Pueblo texts are often organized around four repetitions of the same referent (four is the important symbolic number among the Pueblos, just as three is for European cultures). The external knowledge that a reader needs to "unpack" this text is of two kinds: (a) Pueblo rhetorical devices (why, for example, the juxtaposition of Pueblo recipes and Nature at the start?), and (b) the conception of all-encompassing Nature as the creator of the world in the middle of which the Pueblo people live.

Written discourse stands on its own. Unlike conversation, it is neither directly dialogic, nor potentially self-clarifying. A written text constitutes its own context. Writing is a way of freezing the moment, and offers a model for the study of culture. Culture exists in context, and contexts may be filmed, videotaped, or otherwise "written," thus making it possible to study a cultural context like a text. Ricoeur (1967) has described a delineated pattern that results from a "reading" of a cultural "text." That pattern may be compared to similar instances or situations from the same culture, and an outline of the practices of a given culture can be made.

The results of hermeneutic analysis are not unlike a structural analysis. The components of a text interact with each other; the meaning of the elements derive at least partially from their relationships to each other. Furthermore, hermeneutics insists on a holistic treatment of cultural texts.

> The text must be treated as a whole; only then can the parts make sense. Of course, one must begin by guessing or approximating what that whole might be. This initial guess is highly fallible and is open to

> error and recasting, to reinterpretation. There is a dialectic of guessing and validation. . . . (Rabinow and Sullivan 1979b:11–12)

A cultural text, however, may have more than one reading. A notable example of this is the Japanese film classic *Rashomon*, in which the same series of incidents is viewed very differently by a husband, his wife, a robber who accosts them, and a passing woodcutter. In the film, there is a sexual encounter between the wife and the bandit (rape or seduction or something in-between), and there is the death of the samurai husband (either suicide or murder). Each of the four testifies, and the testimony of each justifies his or her own position and assumptions as a witness. In fact, the film has served as a critique for the way ethnographers go about studying and then describing another culture (Heider 1988). Pluralistic readings of the same cultural text suggest that individuals may have different texts of the same observed reality. The role of cultural interpreter (performer of a text [Bauman 1977, Tedlock 1983], ethnographer, reader, etc.) is a crucial one: how can a non-native experience an alien form or genre? How can an outsider convey cultural meaning? Ideally, the design (structure) of the "text" will allow meaning to be sensed, even more so with access to relevant native theory. Such a position as one that proclaims, in effect, that there are as many versions of North American culture as there are Americans, as many versions of Hopi culture as there are Hopis, and so on, may be tolerable within purist hermeneutics, but it would prescribe endless reinterpretation of the human condition. Many hermeneutically oriented anthropologists temper this stand and consider themselves able to deal with the observable, normative nature of culture through texts. Individuals who share the same culture have some similar behaviors; the symbols used obviously have enough in common to serve as a basis for the social interpretation and a social construction of reality.

The hermeneutic project accords well with the notion of intertextuality. Texts are interconnected in much the same way as Derrida suggests, except that the holistic concept of culture is retained. It may be dangerous to compare different cultures, but it is possible to interpret a single culture, at least through one's own responses to a different culture. Scientific projects present the difficulty of categorizing for comparative linguistic or ethnographic purposes, which invites a deconstructionist criticism, as in the following statement (Tyler 1986:123–124).

> [The success of science] depended . . . on the descriptive adequacy of language as a representation of the world, but in order to move from individual percept to agreed-upon perception, it also needed a language of communicative adequacy that could enable consensus in the community of scientists. In the end, science failed because it could not reconcile the competing demands of representation and communication. . . . The more language became its own object, the less it had to

> say about anything else. So, the language of science had become the object of science, and what had begun as perception unmediated by concepts became conception unmediated by percepts.

The cultural anthropologist can question the validity of scientific ethnography; ethnography should be a qualitative, descriptive, perhaps even meditative enterprise that allows for a dialogue between the ethnographer and the Others who appear in her or his pages. Given this pessimistic stance, the status of universals is held in check.

Summary

It is impossible to study sociocultural phenomena such as languages from a completely objective view, or to subtract the effects of deliberate observation from analysis. Languages themselves are not absolutes; they are not neat self-consistent systems frozen in time for the linguistic anthropologist to view at leisure. Language use by meaning-creating humans is potentially symbolic interaction in which people can (re)interpret each other and the language(s) they use.

What is not said by using a linguistically coded category or what is deliberately left unsaid (erasure) may be deconstructed, and this may be fed back into analysis. Also, because languages and cultures have to have some commonly understood content (as well as conventional means of imparting meaning), structuralism is still a viable means of locating cultural and linguistic saliency (Shaul 1992). It is at least possible to construct ideographic categorizations and theories, by taking text (or context) into account. The scholar can foster localized, hermeneutic studies of cultural categories.

This approach is especially possible with the use of genres (as a model of discursive traditions) as a unit of analysis. Intrusion and biases of the observers may be part of a dialogic analysis that takes stock of the political economy of doing language and culture studies. This sort of enterprise resembles humanistic scholarship, with its focus on introspective observation, some or no reductionism, and little or no need for validation via replication by other scholars. Empirical observation (taking stock of the factors pointed up by interpretivism) is possible for the purposes of ideographic description (and perhaps even theorizing).

The search for universals (with the concomitant nomothetic theorizing) is impossible under some readings of interpretivism given phenomenological considerations. It is reasonable that at least some generalizations about the human condition may be made apart from biological considerations, however, by examining parameters common to all cultures. Major parameters in all cultures include: social organization, the economic and political impact of state-level organization, the organization of biological kinship, jokes, some sort of music and dance, beliefs about the afterlife, and so on. It remains to be seen how comparable such similarities are, and if symbolic values of even such commonplace things as food, clothing, and shelter are comparable between cultures.

Discussion and Activities

1. The following are **loaded terms**. The literal meaning of these terms, while readily recognizable, is subordinate to the associated beliefs and assumptions that each term implies. Racial and ethnic slurs are the most common type of loaded terms, but there are many others as well. Some loaded terms are positive rather than negative in affect. Consider the following:

svelte	jerk
fib	broad
schmooze	nerd
fag	dyke
mensch	twit

   Arrange the terms into groups, making as many groups as you wish. Clearly state what each group has in common. A term may belong to more than one group. Try to deconstruct each group of loaded terms. Ordinarily, the kind of associated beliefs and assumptions that come readily to mind with loaded terms are the sorts of things that are left "unsaid," assumptions to be deconstructed. What, then are the deconstructions of these loaded terms?

2. **Surface deconstruction** is a term or expression that explicitly directs the reader's or hearer's attention to assumptions and/or **affective meanings**. Manipulations of conventional spelling is kind of surface deconstruction. The associated beliefs of respellings are perhaps less obvious than those of loaded terms. Read the list along with the referent which is given in parentheses.

   Fonecard (long distance calling card)
   Ye Olde Shoppe (curio or antique shop)
   Xmas (for "Christmas")
   Clinique (women's cosmetics)
   Brooke (girl's name)
   xtra (short for "extra")
   klub (part of the name of a nightclub)

thru (for "through")
TV (and many other acronyms)

Sometimes respellings imply casualness. Others connote ease and efficiency, and yet others signal stylishness. Such **respelling** implies things the ordinary spelling does not. Can a unified theory of respellings in English be made, even though the actual implications may differ?

3. Another kind of surface deconstruction is the **collocation** (literally, 'noticeable arrangement'). The following are names of actual sporting goods stores in a major U.S. metropolitan area:

   Sports Chalet
   Chivalry Sports
   Soccer Locker
   Ken's Klubs
   Big 5 Sporting Goods
   Pro Image
   Famous Footwear
   Play It Again Sports
   All Star Sports
   Greg Willis Golfe Shoppe

   Some of the collocations use **alliteration** or respelling as **modifiers** to a collocation. Group these names according to the type of product or audience implied by each surface deconstruction. Is there any correlation between the deliberately manipulated forms and the implied message complex?

4. Below are two puns that were used in public discourse.

   We're going Baroque, because we have no Monet.
   (art museum exhibit slogan)

   Johnny on the Spot (name of a portable toilet firm)

   In the previous three activities, the intertextuality was based on similarity of signs and referents. Intertextuality may also be based on shared conventions of interpretation and delivery (performance factors), as well as shared conventional forms (genres). Most puns require a (feigned) negative reaction, but puns in the public arena are common as headlines, campaign slogans, and business names. Why are these less "offensive" than puns delivered in private? How can you account for the interpretation of public puns as "acceptable" puns which don't elicit a groan?

Key Terms

affective meanings
alliteration
antithesis
antirationalism
collocation
decentered
deconstruction
empiricism
erasure
experiential
Heisenberg uncertainty principle
interpretivism
intertextuality
loaded terms
logocentrism
modifiers
nomothetic
ontological
otherness
phenomenology
postmodernism
positivism
practice
respelling
surface deconstruction
synthesis
thesis

10

An Interpretive Version of Language and Culture Studies

> Much of [the] world is ontologically real, in the sense that an outsider from a different culture can see and document it in a fashion that other observers can verify. But much of it lies hidden in the minds of the observed natives, whose cultural traditions, interpretations, and assumptions infuse it with spirits, project into it meanings, and view it in a way that the outsider can discover only by learning the language and, through the language, the intellectual dimensions of the culture.
>
> —Napoleon Chagnon

At the end of chapter 9, we discussed the development of an interpretivist school in linguistic anthropology, a school that emphasizes the uniqueness of each event within its own context. Interpretivism is an expression of a movement widespread throughout the social sciences and the humanities, a movement more grounded in humanistic thought and method than in scientific approaches to knowing. Its stress on uniqueness, however, controverts the conventional starting position of the humanities in investigations. Traditionally, humanistic study begins with an assumption of there being certain universal themes, expressions of the psychic unity of humankind, to which all human expressions relate. Acceptance of a strong version of **cultural relativity** inverts this conventional understanding and imbues the unique variant with greater force.

Interpretivism presents a profound challenge to conventional sociocultural theory and practice, one that has led to the formation of new professional societies within which the more scientific and the more interpretivist cultural anthropologists have grouped. Yet, we see no equivalent convulsion apparent in language and culture studies, which has incorporated a great deal of interpretivist thinking into its structural-semiotic tradition. Why might this difference be? To arrive at an answer to that question, we must begin by examining interpretivism within sociocultural anthropology. We do so by reviewing a prominent critique of the movement in terms of its relation to concepts of cultural relativity.

Spiro (1986) positions the intellectual and historical antecedents of the interpretivist movement with respect to sociocultural anthropology in a manner that has general applicability. Briefly, he identifies three kinds of cultural relativism: *descriptive*, *normative*, and *epistemological*. According to Spiro, the first, **descriptive cultural relativism**, is grounded in a theory of cultural determinism. It states that if social and psychological characteristics are produced by culture then, given cultural variability, descriptive relativism is a corollary of the fact that cultures vary. **Normative cultural relativism** pertains to a position that one cannot make value judgments about the merits of individual cultures because all standards are culturally constituted. There are no transcultural standards available by which we can make such judgments. This position holds for comparisons between cultures as to their value or level of accomplishment (e.g., Hopi culture is as good as German culture), between systems of culture (Western science is not qualitatively different from folk science), and between moral propositions. Further, since there are no acceptable standards for evaluation among cultures, any judgment about a social group, its behavior or emotions, must be relative to the variable standards of the culture that produces them. **Epistemological cultural relativism** derives from a form of descriptive relativism that accepts the strong claim that all knowledge comes to the individual from culture, that we are each a product of our culture and our unique experiences within it. Spiro quotes M. Rosaldo (n.d.) as having a clear statement of the strong form of cultural relativism:

> Thus, if "culture patterns provide the template for *all* human action, growth and understanding (M. Rosaldo n.d., emphasis [Spiro's])," and if moreover "culture does not dictate simply *what* we think but how we feel about and live our lives" (M. Rosaldo n.d., emphasis in original), then virtually [all human social and psychological characteristics are culturally determined.] (Spiro 1986:261)

Interpretivism in sociocultural anthropology emerges from this conclusion of cultural determination, in Spiro's view. It is a position with which he disagrees, and much of the remainder of his paper is devoted to answering the interpretivist critique. He especially strongly attacks the product of linking what he calls "wholesale" cultural determinism with an all but limitless view of cultural diversity. In the case of particularistic cultural determinism, the version held by strong descriptive relativists in his view, the tenet exists that since cultures are radically different from each other, each culture produces a set of culturally particular human characteristics. Spiro sees epistemological relativism as drawing two conclusions from strong descriptive relativism: First, that panhuman generalizations about culture, human nature, and the human mind are likely to be either false or vacuous, and only when generalizations are confined to a single group do they offer the hope of being both true and nonvacuous (Geertz 1973:25–26, cited in Spiro 1986:262). Second, "Since cultures are incommensurable [lacking a basis for comparison] and all science is ethnoscience [in the interpretivist view], the very notion of cultural explanation is misplaced" (Spiro 1986:263). For Spiro, the acceptance of human evolution alone establishes that there are many nontrivial cultural universals, and he stresses that universals can refer not just to the *content* of culture (equivalent to the *substantive universals*—of linguistics), but also to cultural *function*. Spiro also argues that if it is the case that cultures are incommensurable and science is just folk typology, then the very notion of cultural explanation is misplaced; thus, interpretivists would be equivalently paralyzed in their goal of generalizing about individual cultures as they would claim they are in generalizing about human nature.

The latter goal is perhaps best stated by Geertz in, for example, his essay on "The Impact of the Concept of Culture on the Concept of Man" (1973: 33–54). There he states that his "point is not . . . [that] there are no generalizations that can be made about man as man, save that he is a most various animal, or that the study of culture has nothing to contribute toward the uncovering of such generalizations. . . . [Only] that such generalizations are not to be discovered through a . . . search for cultural universals" (1973:40).

The substance that might make up a cultural universal in those cases turns out to be so general or insubstantial as to be impossible to relate to particular biological, psychological, or sociological processes. The necessity instead is "to look for systematic relationships among diverse phenomena, not for substantive identities among similar ones" (1973:44), to seek what the linguist would call *formal universals*, the universals of form or organization. Herein lies a key to the question with which we opened this chapter: Why does the interpretive movement present such a crisis to cultural anthropology and less so to linguistic anthropology?

First, all linguistic anthropology takes its orientation from formal, theoretical linguistics through its role of providing knowledge about unfamiliar languages to theoreticians. Even for those who participate in the theoretical enterprise only by accumulating examples of the diversity of human languages, there is a sense of engagement in a scientific activity, the equivalent in terms of linguistic relativity, perhaps, of the strong version of descriptive cultural relativity discussed above. Regardless of the motives of the investigator-collector of such variety, the fact is that the accumulated examples serve as resources for theoretical linguists. They provide the counterexamples to proposed theories, while often indicating the direction of revision in the theory needed. Notwithstanding Pullum's (1989a) fear for the viability of theoretical linguistics, it remains true that the discipline of linguistics as a whole, and certainly one would include anthropological linguistics and linguistic anthropology here, has been guided by the formulations of theoretical linguistics, formulations that are the products of an undeniably scientific pursuit. However, linguistics has a long history of integration of humanistic and scientific endeavors. Sometimes one finds a linguistics department classed as a humanities discipline in a particular university or college, sometimes as a social or behavioral science. The recent reliance upon linguistics as providing key models and methods for psychology and computer science within cognitive science speaks to the conversant nature of the discipline with scientific pursuits.

Practitioners within formal linguistics agree on two important issues: First, there is little doubt about what constitutes a datum or a proper entity for analysis, regardless of the particular theoretical framework. So strong is this understanding, that several years ago when a conference was held to compare various syntactic theories (Moravcsik and Wirth 1980), the same set of data were submitted to each conference participant for the exposition of the version of a theory of syntax that he or she was charged with presenting. Second, as a corollary of the agreement about the nature of data, there is a long history of easy translatability among theoretical frameworks in linguistics, a translatability that is not so easily made among theories of culture.

Finally, although most linguists—especially those concerned with linguistic anthropology—accept some form of linguistic relativity, none would espouse a version so strong that it would preclude there being an underlying similarity among all languages, something one might say is characteristic of the human capacity of language. To test this assertion, let us rephrase the quotation from M. Rosaldo given by Spiro that we have cited above as a statement about language rather than culture:

> Thus, if language patterns provide the template for all human action, growth and understanding, and if moreover language does not dictate simply what we think but how we feel about and live our lives, then virtually all human social and psychological characteristics are linguistically determined.

Although such a version of linguistic relativity might have been entertained by some linguists thirty years ago, and although it has currency today among some nonlinguists, this statement is unacceptably strong to linguists because it precludes there being any commonality among languages. Linguists customarily approach that commonality through study of universal properties of language by examining similarities of both form and content, the latter being of the same nature as the substance of which Geertz (1973) speaks for culture. The difference lies in the fact that formal linguistics does more than catalogue putative similarities; it seeks "systematic relationships among diverse [cultural] phenomena, not [only] . . . substantive identities among similar ones" (Geertz 1973:44). It identifies characteristics as similar or related, if not identical, as long as they participate in implicational relationships, often leading to typologies; for example, the establishing of word order universals (Greenberg 1966, Comrie 1981). Although some linguists might hold a fairly "wholesale" view of linguistic determinism, none would adopt a limitless view of linguistic diversity because universal properties of language constrain the variability among languages.

Nonetheless, postmodern ideas have affected language and culture studies significantly, and they continue to do so. Among the formulations of special importance, the preeminent are those that privilege the sociocultural effects of the economic expression of power in language. In all instances, these studies are **ideographic** in that they value especially what is unique about a culture or language. Let us turn to some of these approaches for examples.

Practice Theory

One solution to the dilemma of the social scientist intruding as observer into the observed context is offered by **practice theory** (Bourdieu 1977 [1972]). Under this view, the mélange of symbols of everyday life regulates the interaction and negotiation of social life, while imbuing it with a rich fabric of meaning, some of which is emotive. This view relies on the notion of context as a sort of text, but it adopts the rhetoric (underlying concepts and model) of the physical sciences. The physical sciences rely on hypothesis testing to formulate rules, out of which theories are built. The scientific method does not include all available factors (despite the cautions of deconstruction) but it systematically tries different combinations of factors in experiments as a means of seeking to explicate observation.

Pierre Bourdieu modifies the scientific metaparadigm to make the primary frames of practice theory by introducing context and affect into the underlying rhetoric. He begins by noting that people feel uncomfortable in unfamiliar surroundings, especially in different cultures. As soon as one steps out of one's own cultural milieu into another culture or a context where the "rules" are suspended (examples: victims of high-pitch sales or proselytization, neophytes in a ritual situation), one experiences cultural discomfort. Viewed more positively, when one is nested in a culture, one "knows" that culture, one feels at ease. Two phrases that describe this are:

have a feeling for

feel at home/ease

Bourdieu calls this sense of ease habitus. **Habitus** is a cultural version of the linguistic notion of *Sprachgefühl* (German for 'feeling for a particular language'); it is a disposition that generates and structures practices, an affective tendency to think and act in certain ways. This tendency leads to a collective feeling of **communitas** (Turner 1969): a mental image of society as homogenous and consequent feelings of "belonging" to the given group. The term habitus partakes of the emotional value of the usual, but the habitus of some cultural forms (rituals, confrontation, and the like) may involve specific and intense emotion. A careful series of reinterpretations of a cultural tradition may produce a description that approaches adequacy and takes the act of observation into account, but Bourdieu does not cast description as rules. Rules, in the social science sense of the term, are formulations of objective regularities or models derived from these regularities; this sense of rule defines some behavior as acceptable and some as not. Instead of rules, Bourdieu speaks of strategies, bringing to mind cultural texts: scenarios of activity and interactive symbol manipulation, slices of life in process, not static photographs or still lifes. Seen as a game, culture may be used only after one has mastered it and feels comfortable playing. Viewed this way, culture appears to be systems of strategies that produce habitus. The approach recognizes the importance of incorporating emotion and affect into the view of culture as a system of strategies for using rules, schemata, and symbols interactively in real life. At the same time, Bourdieu shares the concern of Derrida for the link between power in a social group and knowledge.

Bourdieu seeks an interactional basis for culture; for him, categories are a convenient notation for interaction. His work fits the notion of texts by seeing cultural interaction as dialogue. Bourdieu is a phenomenologist, stressing the experience people personally have of the world. Geertz may also be construed as a phenomenologist, because he too backs away from an objectivist point of view (outsider's experience, view, or knowledge). Both Geertz and Bourdieu are concerned with relations between social actors and the ideas that they utilize, and both are concerned with the degree of objectivity (if any) that is possible in social analysis. Thus, they are both interpretivist in orientation (deconstructionist critiques, texts and intertextuality, Rashomon effect, and, for Bourdieu, knowledge as power). Yet the projects of both Geertz and Bourdieu cannot deal with two important aspects of social systems: (1) the potential for change in linguistic or cultural systems over time, or (2) the possible coexistence of contradictory voices in the same text or dialogue. For an interpretivist account of history, one looks to the work of Michel Foucault. For the impact of divergent voices in a dialogue (or monologue, for that matter), one turns to the work of Mikhail Bakhtin. Both Foucault and Bakhtin share Derrida's and Bourdieu's concern about the link of knowledge and power.

Discourse and Voices

For Foucault (1973a, 1973b, 1975, 1980; Foucault and Gordon 1980), discourse is a set of conventions for making statements about a given domain of culture and a set of assumptions that underlie them. Important also are the social relations in which a particular discourse is embedded. The history of a domain may be seen as a metadialogue continuing over time, preserving conventions, vocabulary, and power structures intact. Where there is a set of signs, there is a power structure. Eventually, however, the axiomatic assumption-convention(s) of a tradition of discourse (a discursive practice) may be called into question, causing the power structure associated with the discourse to collapse, and a new one to arise in its place, much as occurred with the astronomical revolution of Copernicus. Recall Foucault's example of the treatment of the insane in Western culture. During the Medieval period, when all of Europe's eyes were turned toward Heaven and cathedral spires dominated the urban skylines, the insane were God's fools. When Humanism and the Renaissance ushered in the Age of Reason, which was man-centered instead of God-oriented, the insane were seen as unfit to live in rational society, and they were chained up. Then, as the Age of Science and the Industrial Revolution produced specialists, the insane were consigned to the medical industry for treatment. In each case, the means of "understanding" and "talking" about the insane changed due to changes in Western discursive practice; as each major cultural premise expired, the insane were recast in the light of the new agenda that paid particular attention to the maintenance of power throughout the changing intellectual landscape. Foucault provides for a **diachronic** interpretivism.

> (1) Truth is to be understood as a system of ordered procedures for the production, regulation, distribution, circulation and operation of statements.
>
> (2) Truth is linked in a circular relation with systems of power which produce and sustain it, and to effects of power which it induces and which extend it. A 'régime' of truth.

> (3) This régime is not merely ideological or superstructural; it was a condition of the formation and development of capitalism. (Foucault and Gordon 1980:133)

Foucault agrees that a single cultural system may be studied, and that it may be studied over time. The synchronic vs. diachronic opposition of Saussure persists in his thought.

The work of Mikhail Bakhtin (1981) stems from a consideration of the novel in Western culture. In this genre, and especially in long novels, the possibility of many characters having their say or thinking their piece creates a patchwork of **voices**. Then there is the narrator's voice, which may or may not be the same as or different from the author's voice. Also, there is the possibility of a single party to the discourse (character, author, narrator) having several emotional views of the same situation, creating the possibility of several voices in one single party to the discourse. This approach is technically known as **heteroglossia** ("diverse tongues") or **polyphony** ("many voices"). A classic comparison here is one contrasting Flaubert (who exercises careful control over his characters to achieve a monolithic tone) and Dickens (who allows his characters' Victorian idiosyncrasies to run riot). The potential and actual conflict that Bakhtin sees in novels reflects the differing goals of dialogue participants in everyday life. Culture is not only a text, but a fabric of differing voices, each trying to get its own way; it is helpful to reflect on the central principle of Western acting: what does my character want? In novels, ethnographies, or scientific writings, the writer chooses which voices may speak, and how much of each to include. In this function, the writer behaves like an orchestrator or conductor. This authorial voice is Bakhtin's analogue of the institutionalized power of Derrida, Bourdieu, and Foucault. But in the gaze of deconstruction, even the authorial voice may be diffused or recognized; indeed, from the point of view of conducting the ethnographic enterprise, it should be elucidated in order to create a responsible ethnography.

The shared assumptions, traditions, and formats of a group of persons that produce similar cultural texts over time (memos, letters, pornography, novels, conversation filled with shop talk) will tend to create a style that reflects a single ideology. Bakhtin refers to this as **canonization**. On the other hand, the individual text producer/interpreter is at least in part the locus of language, and since there are as many viewpoints as there are individuals, it follows that individual language usage in actual contexts will be varied, possibly conflicting. Given that linguistic communication is interactive, and that there is a fluid relation between context and literal meaning, even "texts" of the same "genre" (tradition of discourse) may exhibit heteroglossia (multiple voices with conflicting views). Bakhtin saw the opposition of canonization to heteroglossia as representing two kinds of forces he termed centripetal (canonization) and centrifugal (heteroglossia). **Centripetal** forces drive discourse toward common themes or modes of expression, whereas **centrifugal** forces pull them apart, expand them, and give voice to varied meaningful expressive forms within a discourse.

A good illustration of this phenomenon can be found in political writing, especially newspaper editorials. Such writing practices become symbolic of a speech community, and such canonization is thus an index of the **political economy** of a language-using community. Laitin and Rodriguez Gomez (1992) examined Spanish language and Catalan language editorials of newspapers of Barcelona. Catalan is the native language of the region; it has great symbolic value; it is not dying out. Laitin and Rodriguez Gomez examined editorials in two papers published in each language; of each pair, one paper was liberal and one conservative. They found that to underscore their ideological points "the Castilian [Spanish] language newspapers' editorials have a more exaggerated discourse style than that of the Catalan press. Both Castilian papers emphasize their points by using colloquialisms, sarcasm and irony" (Laitin and Rodriguez Gomez 1992:22). It is thus not a language, but the way a language is used that is the critical factor; presumably Catalan may also be used ironically and sarcastically, but their newspapers do not employ these devices. Both Catalan papers "use a more matter-of-fact style and usually underline their points by overtly stating their political position" (1992:25).

Indeed, the primary use of language may be culturally relative. Whorf spoke of "fashions of speaking" (1956:158), meaning styles and genres that transcended vocabulary, pronunciation, and grammar. The example of the Catalan press is a good illustration. Moreover, speakers of any language may be aware of how they use their language and have informed opinions about the ways they use it (**linguistic ideology**; Silverstein 1979). Rumsey (1992) documented such a situation when he examined reported speech in English and in an Australian aboriginal language, Ungarinyin. The dramatic value of direct quotation in English (*He said, "The toaster is broken. I'll fix it."*) is lessened with indirect quotation (*He said he would fix the toaster.*). In Ungarinyin (northwestern Australia), there is no equivalent of indirect discourse, a finding Rumsey attributed the Western ideology of language—that language is somehow separate from its use (*table* has meaning, and therefore an existence, out of context) does not hold for the speakers of Ungarinyin. For them, language structure is language use; language has no separate existence. This emphasis on language as a form of action has also been documented for the Kunas of Panama (Sherzer 1983), Mexicano speakers of central Mexico (J. Hill and K. Hill 1986), and the Huli of Papua New Guinea (Goldman 1983).

Determinacy and Meaning

If one accepts that one can study a single cultural tradition solely by examining texts in which language and culture merge, the possibility of a science of sociocultural behavior for linguistic anthropology becomes less crucial, and the quest for universals of human language or culture questionable. **Indeterminacy** claims that the relation, causal or otherwise, between language structure and language understanding cannot be **determined**. Just as there are stronger and weaker versions of the Whorfian hypothesis that drive various approaches in scientifically oriented semiotic studies, there are corresponding strong and weak versions of indeterminacy that motivate different interpretivist approaches. One end of the continuum—deconstruction—is anchored by a strong formulation of the indeterminacy view about the nature of language. That view states that nothing in language is consequent on special cognitive givens about the linguistic human capacity but rather that there is near total arbitrariness in language resulting from the fact that linguistic "meaning" is negotiated in sociocultural context. Both this strong indeterminacy viewpoint and the strongest versions of the Whorfian hypothesis avoid the possibility of finding linguistic universals. On the other hand, more constrained versions of the Whorfian hypothesis correlate with a weaker formulation of indeterminacy in language. Such a position could be assigned to Bourdieu, for example. It does not rule out the possibility of there being discernible linguistic universals, although it constrains the search and the possible nature of such universals in certain ways, most especially through the priority given to the social construction of reality. Some of the same tensions as those that have traditionally driven linguistic anthropological investigation persist in interpretivism, for example, the problem of the universal versus the particular.

One of the ways in which a weak version of indeterminacy may be used in hermeneutic linguistic anthropology is to reject language as homogenous, and assume instead that the multifunctional nature of language precludes homogeneity. Language is seen as context-bound and interactive, not monolithic: its true description should be multivocal. One of the ways of approaching a hermeneutic analysis is to use voice as the unit of analysis (Bakhtin 1981, 1986). Each speaker has many potential voices (examples: Ms. Smith's power code, the solidarity code of Ms. Smith, etc.). Voices are clearest in conversation, but may be detected in monologues and written materials by shifts in vocabulary, style, code-switching, and the like.

Once a discursive practice (such as language and culture studies) begins, its conventions become strictures that are politically or volitionally motivated. Foucault (1975, 1980; Foucault and Gordon 1980) argues that establishing a given discursive practice actually leads to less meaning (and freedom of expression) because of institutionalization. Language can be symbolic capital (Bourdieu 1977), used to keep subordinate groups in line and to maintain the status quo. Moreover, "[c]ontrol of the representations of reality is not only a source of social power but therefore also a likely a locus of conflict and struggle" (Gal 1989:348). Knowledge is power, as reiterated by Kant in the quote relating to the role of Enlightenment in the release of one from self-incurred tutelage.

The suspicion of a homogenous description of language as being a distortion has led to renewed interest in linguistic relativism. Institutionalized settings provide convenient examples of speakers in the same context, speaking the same language but often not using the same rules of language use. The classroom is a good example. In a celebrated program of research of this sort, Bernstein (1975) theorized that working-class students in Britain faced difficulties in the classroom partly because they came from a tradition of language use that stressed face-to-face linguistic interaction, tending toward simple sentences tied to immediate context, and that rarely made the logic of the interaction explicit. This system of language use contrasts with the autonomous style, explicit logic, and complex syntax of the classroom which is tied to literacy and to the speech of the middle and upper classes. Acquisition of the "educated" sort of language use, along with Received Pronunciation, is the ticket to advancement in class-conscious Britain.

The linking of language use to political economy (how resources or access to resources is controlled) constrains the amount and degree of hermeneutic interpretation, as well as any renewed interest in linguistic and cultural relativism. A culture or discursive tradition may be taken as a total of interactive contexts with intentional participants. Moreover, the participants are possible combatants. A hermeneutic method, cast in this mold, must aim

> to develop a principle of intentionality—action responsive to and directed at mental objects or representations—by which culturally constituted realities (intentional worlds) and reality-constituting psyches (intentional persons) continually and continuously make each other up, perturbing and disturbing each other, interpenetrating each other's identity, reciprocally conditioning each other's existence. (Shweder 1990:26–27)

Instead of taking categories or sets of categories as primes that are examined relativistically (thus uniting relativism and semiotics), contexts are taken as basic units out of which both voices and (sets of) categories emerge (Friedrich 1989). Consider, for example, the meaningful nature of context for the insult of public figures. Public insult of a politician or celebrity through ordinary channels of the print or broadcast media can swiftly lead to charges of libel. Yet the gossip column and the tabloids are contexts where outrageous claims about public figures appear regularly. The contexts of these media permit attack, but generally the insult is cast in an extremely indirect form. Otherwise, the act could be one of libel. Consider also the celebrity or political "roast." This context also negates the libelous nature of character defamation. A "roast" of a political figure recognizes the importance of the person, renders affection for him or her, and must be regarded as complimentary, even though the event consists wholly of having one's friends and admirers make insulting verbal attacks upon the character and image of the honoree. The "insults" cast in that context carry certain didactic suggestions; they may inform someone about his or her shortcomings, who otherwise would be too powerful and imposing for most associates to criticize openly. The roast context is a ritual involving role-reversal; it provides a rostrum for criticism, even as it is a means of expressing admiration and affection. The celebrity roast offers us a meaning-rich context, one that we can think of as strongly determining the meaning of any verbal message conveyed within it.

The idea of the **determinacy** of a linguistic and sociocultural expression (especially underdeterminacy) derives from work in philosophy; it incorporates context in a principled way. A fully determined sentence, for example, is one of a type that has been regarded as requiring almost no outside information (i.e., contextual information) for interpretation:

A cat is on a mat.

The sentence above can be said to contain within itself virtually all the meaning necessary for understanding it. An **underdetermined** sentence, on the other hand, is one which cannot be understood without supplying larger or smaller amounts of contextual meaning. For example, the following sentence out of context is meaningless:

I think I'll go.

Who intends to go (Who is the 'I'?)? Where are they going? Just anywhere? When?

Underdetermined sentences require that there be more information conveyed in the context, and some of that context may be built up through spoken discourse, but the differences between linguistic context and sociocultural context are not easy to separate. Culture will always supply context, whereas it is possible that linguistically produced context is also a cultural matter, since ways of building up context vary more by culture than by language, as is shown by the fact that two native speakers of the same language representing different cultures often find themselves establishing contradictory contextual frameworks in their communication with each other (Gumperz 1982). One might say, then, that an underdetermined sentence will require a context that is heavy with meaning, one we could call an **overdetermined** context.

Occasionally, a context is so overdetermining that it will be given an interpretation regardless of what the actual utterance is. A nice example of this extreme and its consequent effect on interpretation is an apocryphal story about the linguist R. M. W. Dixon who is a leading authority on aboriginal Australian languages. According to the story (the truth of which, incidentally, Dixon denies [K. Maynard, personal communication, 1995]), Dixon stood a good part of a day on a street corner of Edinburgh, Scotland, saying to each passerby, "The kangaroo is crossing the road," in Dyirbal, a language spoken by an Australian aboriginal group, but probably not understood by any other resident of the British Isles except Dixon at that time. At the end of the day, when he tallied up the sorts of replies he had received, Dixon learned that about 80 percent of the people had interpreted his Dyirbal utterance as a request for matches, the time, or directions (only 20 percent displayed any suspicion or confusion). We have all had versions of this sort of misunderstanding, when the contextual meaning overwhelmed or overconstrained the attempted linguistic message. When an underdetermined sentence is made meaningful by an overdetermined context, one might consign the source of meaning (or the mediation of a meaning) to the sociocultural realm. In the earlier example of the celebrity roast, we saw that context can completely reverse the polarity of a comment: an insult must be interpreted as affectionate recognition of the recipient's reputation and accomplishments. When a sentence is fully determined, one might say that all (or almost all) the meaning is in language, specifically in that single sentence.

There are also cases in which a sociocultural expression is overdetermined and requires no linguistic interpretation or expansion, as well as instances in which a sociocultural expression is underdetermined and requires linguistic explication if it is to be understandable. The former has to do with what might be called fully determined sociocultural symbols or expressions. Any recognizable cultural symbol that conveys meaning without benefit of linguistic explication could be said to be fully determined. Such a symbol might be regarded as supplying all the context necessary for its own interpretation, the cultural equivalent of the linguistic "A cat is on a mat." An enormous amount of anthropological research deals with such fully determined cultural situations: a whole range of social actions, taboos, and customary behaviors (even everyday ones, such as table manners) that resist explication and for which anthropological efforts have devised ingenious means of investigation, perhaps just exactly because they defy facile identification and explanation. Underdetermined cultural symbols, on the other hand, are less obvious. These would be cultural expressions that are ambiguous depending upon the linguistic environment in which they are placed, or not just ambiguous, but uninterpretable in the absence of linguistic context. A possible example would be the close interpersonal distance of approximately 8 inches (Hall 1959, 1963, 1974), which in the United States can be used when delivering two opposite kinds of expressions—words of love or words of rage. The linguistic context in this instance (along with facial expression at least) disambiguates the meaning of the use of close interpersonal distance.

In the case that the linguistic context (i.e., environment) is so meaningful that the cultural symbols cease to function, one might say that the linguistic environment is overdetermined in the presence of extremely underdetermined cultural symbols. A. L. Davis tells an anecdote from his years directing a program in Izmir, Turkey, to teach English to native speakers of Turkish. This example illustrates the possibility as well as the danger of overdependence of recorded language-laboratory drills. One of Davis' students, a life-long resident of Izmir, practiced so diligently with the tape-recorded dialogues that when he was stopped on the street by an American tourist who asked in English, "Where is the railroad station?", he responded automatically with a reply from his lesson: "I'm sorry, I don't know. I'm a stranger here myself." The language learner had clearly been overwhelmed by a meaningful linguistic context in a language he did not fully control.

Whereas much of interpretive anthropology concentrates on what things mean, *how things come to have meaning for individuals* is equivalently important and forms a central issue for language and culture studies, especially those that concern themselves with the relation of linguistic expression to historical and economic influences (e.g., Foucault 1973a, 1975; Friedrich 1989; Gal 1989). This effort directs language and culture studies to examine the social world of participants not only as meaningful contexts in which knowledge may be obtained and communication may take place, but also as the community whose histories, collective and individual, offer its members acceptable interpretations of symbols and conventional manners of symbol creation.

In an attempt to provide this kind of synthesis between symbolic and cognitive anthropology, Shore (1991) identified two kinds of meaning: the first kind is objective and semiotic (often equivalent to scientific); the second is the subjective, "processes of meaning construction through which cultural symbols become available to consciousness as 'experience.'" Shore attempts to relate the two in a principled fashion through considering how each is grounded in sensory experience. He begins from perception, and uses the idea of **cultural schemata**; one may think of cultural schemata as conventional plans for understanding or meaning creation that are appropriate to a culture. They resemble the previously described strategies, or the idea of scripts (Schank and Abelson 1977). Shore, however, proposes cultural schemata as essential constituents of perception because they alone provide the basis for intersubjective meaning constructions. In his view, each cultural symbol is created in a kind of public and private dialogue in which the public, conventional form is perceived by the individual, who integrates it into his or her own cognition, thus reinventing it in the process. The critical factor for Shore is the perceptual apparatus and the nature of the constraints it places upon these processes.

If interpretation is largely a perceptual operation, it nonetheless proceeds according to a cognitive plan, a plan which it updates and revises to accord with experience. One proposed means of building concepts is **generalization**, an idea that developed out of the work of Cassirer and Vygotsky. Cassirer (1946) proposed that the prime intellectual capacity of human beings is conception, a process that always ends in symbolic expression. Conception and symbolic expression are both embodied in myth and language and are the only characteristics of thought in myth according to Cassirer. Further, to Cassirer, conception and symbolic expression precede logical reasoning, which he argued is a unique human accomplishment. Thus, we would then add that the human ability to reason is modeled from conception and symbolic expression. That is, language, unlike myth, is not bounded but is expansive because it has developed a new mode—reasoning—via the intellectual mechanisms given to human beings. Cassirer's idea came out of his discussion of metaphor, in which he defined two sorts of metaphor: metaphor in the *narrow* sense is conscious denotation, a genuine translation where one fixed concept is made to stand for another fixed concept via the process of metaphor. This sort of metaphor can result from word taboos. *Radical* metaphor, on the other hand, is a condition of the formulation of mythic and verbal conceptions. It is not only a translation from one category to another but actually the creation of a category itself. Cassirer was unable to describe a mechanism by which such categories might be created. How one forms concepts, as opposed to how one manipulates them, remained an unanswered question.

In the work of Vygotsky (1962), we find a possible method for creating categories. He wrote that for a concept to be characterized, it must be placed within two continua, which he likened to the longitude and latitude lines on a globe. One of these represents objective content; the other, acts of thought-apprehending content. Their intersection determines all relationships of a concept to others (coordinate, superordinate, subordinate). The emphasis on intersections of meaning—in this instance between objective content and acts of apprehension—is a precursor to a similar privileging of intersections of meanings in deconstruction, as discussed in chapter 9. In the deconstruction case, the intersections of interest are those involved in the meanings in the web or network of a text. Vygotsky called this placement of a concept its "measure of generality." Every new stage in the development of generalizations is built on generalizations of the preceding level. Products of earlier phases are not lost, but higher concepts transform meaning of lower ones, so for example, one's view of arithmetic changes when one has learned some algebra. Productive thinking is contingent on transferring a problem from the structure in which it is first apprehended to a different structure or context. This transfer can be accomplished only by shifting to a plane of generality, to a concept that subsumes both the original and the new structure. There are correlations between Cassirer's idea of mythic thought and what Vygotsky calls spontaneous concepts (which are a child's initial sort of thinking) in that both lack logical reasoning, a consequence of underdeveloped relations of generality. Only scientific concepts have logical reasoning: for a child to be disturbed by a contradiction, according to Vygotsky, he or she must be able to view a contradictory statement in light of some general principle, which is in turn part of a system.

Language and culture are variables of the same universe that are realized at the same time, much as the sound pattern and meaning patterns of a language are simultaneously realized. This duality of patterning of a higher order must allow for inventive individuals as well as dynamic norms.

Summary

Interpretivism stresses the uniqueness of each event in its own context, but since the structure and meanings of languages and cultures have to be normative to some extent, it is necessary to reject a strong reading of the interpretivist critique. At the least, language and culture specific description and theorizing are possible.

The notion of genre as a discursive tradition is a good model for interpreting categories, domains, schemata, and so on. A genre has a name within a given culture, along with a recognizable form and interpretive conventions. It is a recognized way of using language (linguistic ideology) to foster the comfortable feeling of the usual (habitus) and cultural solidarity (communitas). An actual instance of a genre (performance), when recorded, becomes a snapshot from which the analyst and the analyst's consultants may engage in interpretive conversation where the bias of observation, other biases, political consequences of doing research, and excluded facts are all overtly acknowledged. It is actually possible to make the act of observation and the act of analysis a genre that is dialogic and experiential. Taking stock of the interpretivist bugaboos, a genre approach to doing language and culture studies is a way of realizing the plausible ideographic studies referred to above.

This prescription also controls for determination, the relative importance of context on interpretation, because the discursive practice (genre) of "language and culture studies consultation" is neither overdetermined nor underdetermined. It is a self-admitted heterogeneous dialogue about data being considered.

It is the job of cultures to be peculiar and idiosyncratic. Cultures are a collective reductionist project. When we study a culture or part of one, we study a reduced way of looking at chaotic reality. The culture has already done reduction for us. We are not studying reality, but a reflection of reality; we are studying linguistically coded categories as they are used in context. Language and culture studies, using a genre approach to data collection and analysis, can let a culture speak for itself through its discourse. By realizing that culture is reductionist, and that we are not focusing on reality as such when we study culture, we can provide culture-specific description and interpretation while not losing sight of the prospects of cross-cultural comparisons.

Discussion and Activities

1. Thinking back over your own experiences, identify an instance in which you participated in a conversation or cultural communicative event in which the context overdetermined the understanding. Think next of one in which the context was underdetermined. Compare your examples with those identified by other members of the class. Make of list of the examples by (1) whether they involved (a) cultural communication or (b) linguistic communication, and (2) whether they involved (a) overdetermined context or (b) underdetermined context. Is there any difference in numbers of examples of each type? If so, speculate on the reasons for these differences.
2. Select a number of well-known novels. Copy the first paragraphs of each onto a paper or card. Ask a number of persons you know, preferably of different backgrounds (your consultants), to summarize the story of each novel for you after reading just the opening paragraph of each text. How well can they do in gauging the whole story from just the introduction? It is often claimed by writers that there is a finite number of plots and character types, at least it is said to be the case for Western fiction. Try to characterize the basis of your consultants' intuitions. Do they share schemata of all the typical plots that stories may take in our culture? To what extent do they need details or information from a given opening paragraph?

   A way of refining this activity is to have teams investigate different types of novels (horror, gothic romance, mystery, etc.). See if your consultants can outline the essentials of each genre. Teams could take different genres and then compare generalizations. It is possible to check your analyses with some of the texts that teach aspiring writers to produce commercially saleable fiction.

Another way of looking at genres is to study subgenres. For example, there are many different kinds of romance novels. Can readers of one kind tell or summarize the story of subgenres that they don't read? Can persons who typically don't read romance novels predict the plots of each different sub-genre, and how well?

One goal of this activity is to fashion a kind of intertext for each of these novels or genres. (An **intertext** is the product of an analysis using the concept of intertextuality, an intermediate form to which the variant texts may be related.) Another is to see how well culture bearers can use the category of "story," and to what extent they can use terms like *plot* or *character development* in their recounting. The category of story (or fiction, or novel) is internally complex; most North Americans will know the meanings of at least some of the technical terms used in analyzing fiction. How much interest in the internal complexity of the category fiction/story/novel does the lay public (nonwriters) have? Is this knowledge equally shared?

3. There are a large number of verbs in English that name the action they perform: *promise, command, threaten, declare,* etc. Make a list of as many of these **linguistic action verbs** as you can. Then sort them into related groups. Characterize each group with a schema, frame, prose description, etc. What do linguistic action verbs tell you about the linguistic ideology of the users of American English?

Key Terms

canonization
centripetal
centrifugal
communitas
cultural relativity
cultural schemata
descriptive cultural relativism
determined
determinacy
diachronic
epistemological cultural relativism
generalization
habitus
heteroglossia
ideographic
indeterminacy
intertext
linguistic action verbs
linguistic ideology
normative cultural relativism
overdetermined
political economy
polyphony
practice theory
voices
underdetermined

11

Integrations

> [L]anguage does not exist apart from culture, that is, from the socially inherited assemblage of practices and beliefs that determines the texture of our lives.
>
> —Edward Sapir

In the face of the postmodern challenge, one cannot help but be struck by the persistence of the central concerns of language and culture studies—the enduring preoccupations of scholars with the creative tension between linguistic relativity and language universals, and the effort to enrich cultural studies by borrowing aspects of a developed semiotics from linguistic study. The influence of the latter appears the more comfortable, even the more natural development, since influential postmodern formulations, such as those of Derrida and Foucault, themselves derive in a quite direct intellectual pedigree from the semiotics of Saussure. Although frequently the dialogue takes the character of challenging some presumed dictate of Saussureanism, it is nonetheless the case that Saussure's ideas set an agenda still pursued under the postmodern paradigm. The enterprise of extending methods, models, and concepts from linguistics into cultural analysis proceeds unabated. Of course, it is also true that the postmodern critique has informed a changing linguistic anthropology; the road has not been one-way. In some ways we can see postmodern influences most strongly in revised formulations treating the first theme of language and culture studies, the concern with the balance between adherence to some version of linguistic relativity while pursuing efforts to identify commonalities among the world's languages. As we have seen, scholars have adopted (and debated) stronger versions of cultural relativity recently, an exercise critiqued by Spiro (1986). These concerns are even more evident in Shore's (1991) effort to marry cognitive and interpretive approaches through grounding them in perception, an exercise that argues for a common psychophysiological foundation underlying the variety of both languages and cultures in the world.

Perhaps anthropological linguistics profits from the florescence of interpretivism exactly because it retains its reference to theoretical linguistics, its concern with mutual translatability among theories, and its acceptance of universal constraints on variability among languages. For language and culture studies specifically, interpretivism has returned texts to a central position in linguistic description, overtaking the role elicitation held two decades ago (for example, see Hanks 1986, 1987, 1989) when much linguistic theory was built upon data that had been elicited directly from native speakers and that was seldom more than a sentence in length and nearly devoid of rich context. We have been reminded that we must keep epistemology ever in mind. Indeed, the interpretive movement has provided us with alternative views. We have also witnessed an enrichment of analysis through adoption of **functional** perspectives, and a concomitant rise in the relevance of context.

Throughout the intellectual development of the field of linguistic anthropology, one can discern two major traditions in the United States: the **neo-Boasian tradition** and the **linguistic metaphorist tradition**. Both are outgrowths of historical particularism, and both have developed two approaches—scientific and **interpretivist**, but one can be more closely identified with the historical and particularist concerns of Franz Boas and his students than the other. For that reason, it is convenient to think of this first group of studies as falling within a neo-Boasian tradition. Such studies have been concerned principally with the languages and histories of anthropological populations, especially those of American Indian groups, and with the exploration of linguistic relativity among grammatical categories and contexts. The second major tradition may be called the linguistic metaphorist tradition. Studies that are linguistic metaphorist have been less concerned with the description and classification of specific languages than with the linguistic interpretation of nonlanguage behavior, with sociolinguistic issues, and with the testing of linguistic relativity hypotheses that pertain especially to lexical domains. Through investigation of topics that at first seemed contradictory—relativism and the universals of human cognition—the linguistic metaphorist tradition developed two kinds of theories, a scientific semiotic one and a context-based interpretivist one. Studies within context-based interpretive approaches have led recently back to a close examination of specific languages and their unique properties, making the concerns of linguistic anthropologists appear to have come full circle from ideographic to nomothetic and back to a concern for unique characterizations of individual languages, as well as making general statements about universal properties of languages and human cognition.

In the remainder of this chapter, we first describe these two traditions, developing a typology of approaches to studies of language and culture by which we may conveniently refer to different types of investigations. Next, we take up two kinds of integrations within anthropological linguistics, one having to do with integration within linguistic anthropology and the other pertaining to the integration of linguistic and other areas of anthropology. The former concerns the two themes deriving from Boasian historical particularism that have been the focus of this book (linguistic relativity and extensions of linguistic models to nonlinguistic data—semiotics). In relating the two traditions to the two intellectual themes of anthropological linguistics, we discuss examples of particular research efforts. We also review ways in which language and culture studies intermesh with investigations in the whole of the field of anthropology. In this latter instance, we present several examples in which linguistic and sociocultural, archaeological, and biological anthropological investigations have complemented one another. Finally in this chapter, we take up some of the lines along which the field of language and culture studies seems to be developing and attempt to identify major trends in the discipline that are outgrowths of the themes discussed here, trends that can be expected to drive investigations for some time to come.

Two Traditions

The historical particularist neo-Boasian tradition in linguistic anthropology represents the "normal science" (Kuhn 1970) tradition throughout the development of the discipline; that is, its conduct has been regarded as noncontroversial and steadily productive of data and readily useable analyses. Neo-Boasian work is language-centered and oriented to linguistics proper in terms of its theoretical relevance. Over the years, such studies have provided access to rare examples needed by linguistic theoreticians and have tested, and in several instances developed aspects of, newly proposed theoretical frameworks. Still neo-Boasian research tends to be more descriptive than theoretical, even though two of the most important leaders in the development of the tradition—Edward Sapir and Leonard Bloomfield—were pioneering linguistic theoreticians. Sapir, as we have noted in chapters 2 and 3, had strong interest in the relationship of language to culture and, especially through his association with Whorf, some involvement with work that took language as a primary influence on culture and psychology, although he did not adhere to the linguistic causal metaphor that characterized the strong version of the Whorf hypothesis.

Some neo-Boasian studies are predominantly areal in orientation. Among the efforts of area experts, the work of Leonard Bloomfield stands out as especially worthy, not only because it presents outstanding examples of linguistic analysis, but also because Bloomfield's book, *Language* (1933), codified many tenets of the methods and theory employed in such studies, synchronic and diachronic, and served as a basic text for a generation of linguistic anthropologists. Bloomfield's approach in *Language* was not mentalistic like that of Sapir (1931, 1933, 1936), but was much more influenced by behavioral psychology. Those attitudes predominated virtually until the rise of generativism in the early 1960s.

So what do area experts do? They write the traditional triad of descriptive studies for unfamiliar languages (a grammar, an edited volume of texts in the language, and a dictionary). They recently have turned attention to the study of language endangerment and death as linguistic diversity has been threatened through the loss of a majority of the indigenous languages of the Americas and of the languages of many other small-scale societies throughout the world (Dorian 1981; Eastman 1979a, 1979b; Palmer 1988). Even today they still do a considerable amount of "salvage" linguistics, but they are relying more on written documents now that many indigenous languages have lost their last speakers. Area experts concern themselves with the influence of living languages on one another, the genetic classification of languages, with matters of linguistic prehistory, including trying to determine the paths of migration taken by groups prehistorically, editing maps of language distributions, and deciding on probable influences from outside an area on the language or region under study.

Other neo-Boasian studies are comparative and center on cross-cultural comparisons and typologies rather than on the past and present of an area. Among this second group of neo-Boasian works we find the ethnography of communication and many studies concerned with sociolinguistic issues, including recent developments that bridge to linguistic metaphorist concerns such as performance theory and practice theory.

In general, the neo-Boasian linguistic tradition today articulates with concerns of other anthropologists through cooperation in integrative studies of a people or region, for example: studies of the Yanomamö Indians of the Amazon Basin; of California Indians (see Hinton 1994); or of various African groups and regions. In such instances, the linguist is customarily an expert in the language(s) of an area, often collaborating with sociocultural, archaeological, and physical anthropologists, as well as native experts, toward solving some problem of common interest, for example, determining the likely prehistoric homeland of a particular group or toward providing a general description of a culture area such as the Great Basin.

The linguistic metaphorist tradition, on the other hand, centers on use of linguistic ideas in analysis of nonlinguistic data and, like linguistics itself, shows considerable influence from cognitive psychology; nonetheless, its theoretical relevance and orientation is to sociocultural anthropology rather than to the discipline of linguistics. This is the part of language and culture studies most influenced by interpretation. Our discussion in chapters 7 through 10 presented the development of ideas in linguistic metaphorist tradition. Linguistic metaphorist work is often issue-oriented; the tradition embraces many studies of universals of language and culture, especially evolutionist ones, most semiotic formulations for cultural analysis, color and taxonomy studies, several sorts of decision studies, discourse text and context studies, and a host of symbolic and structuralist accounts. Recently, studies of gender have provided a focus for integrative linguistic and cultural accounts within this tradition. Like the neo-Boasian tradition, there are two versions of the linguistic metaphorist tradition: the scientific and the interpretivist.

The *scientific* subtradition (cognitive anthropology, ethnoscience, strict semiotics) is generally structural and leans toward the behavioral and social science forms of explanation. Within it, primacy is given to meanings of structures as revealed by study of the symbols within them and of contexts in which they appear. Direct parallels with language are easily accommodated, especially since many efforts here have been concerned with properties of semantic domains. The concepts of emic and etic retain currency within this subtradition.

The *interpretivist* version of the linguistic metaphorist tradition draws strongly upon the humanities, including postmodern frameworks. It incorporates directly many influences from literary, symbolic, cultural text, folklore, and poetics traditions. As discussed in chapters 9 and 10, the work of literary critics and philosophers such as Derrida has become influential among the interpretivists, as much as that of Levi-Strauss has been, among members of the scientific subtradition. One may see the interpretivist approach as generally symbolic, giving primacy to the meanings of symbols in structures and contexts. It is via this approach to the study of language, as either a model for culture or as an avenue to the understanding of sociocultural differences, that linguistic anthropology has come back to a concern with differences among languages. The entire important field of discourse analysis has grown markedly through these studies. Discourse analysis now offers to linguistic theory a method which systematically takes context into account and has proven important for functional grammar.

Recently, **functional theories of grammar** have found support within theoretical linguistics, a development that heralds a return to the significance of linguistic anthropological studies for linguistic theory. For example, Hopper and Thompson (1984) motivated the establishment of noun and verb as categories by examining the range of syntactic constructions in which various elements participate. The shift in the linguistic orientation of linguistic anthropology, from descriptive to theoretical, may be among the most consequential for the discipline since its acceptance of generativism. In parallel, such functional approaches have also begun to appear in other anthropological endeavors.

Using this typology, let us now look at a series of studies as models of integration. The first of these are concerned with the interaction between the themes of linguistic relativity and the extensions of linguistic models to other anthropological concerns.

Integration of Traditions

How exactly might we discern the twin themes of linguistic relativity and semiotics (in its most general sense) in work conducted within the neo-Boasian and the linguistic metaphorist traditions? Let us consider the kinds of studies under each that seem to exemplify these traditions. Table 5 gives some examples of the kinds of topics studied under the scientific and interpretive rubrics of the neo-Boasian and linguistic metaphorist traditions. Each of the four sets of topics favored by these investigators includes some studies that are expressly synchronic investigations made without reference to change over a dimension of time, and diachronic studies that are expressly concerned with the historical dimension. Look at the first cell of table 5 as an illustration. Typical scientific neo-Boasian studies include ones that concern classification, typologies, and description of languages. Classification studies are diachronic insofar as they are concerned with determining the family relationships of languages and the kinds of changes over time that have brought about differentiation of languages, but they can also be synchronic, as in efforts to develop criteria for classifying languages.

The same can be said of typological investigations. A cross-language typology might look for language characteristics that could be associated with one another independently of the genetic relationship of languages or the development of the characteristics; for example, the association of verb-final-word order with a noun-adjective syntactic sequence in languages (Greenberg 1966). On the other hand, a typological investigation that was concerned with the development of patterns of word order, one from the other, would be expressly diachronic (Li and Thompson 1974, Li 1977). Even descriptive grammars, which are usually thought to be synchronic investigations, may have a historical focus, as when an investigation of present-day languages is conducted with the express goal of learning the patterns of development of particular syntactic or morphological features such as inflectional systems. Similarly, interpretive neo-Boasian and both scientific and interpretive linguistic metaphorist studies accommodate both synchronic and diachronic efforts.

Table 5. Kinds of Topics Investigated under the Neo-Boasian and Linguistic Metaphorist Traditions

TRADITION	**SUBTRADITION**	
	Scientific	***Interpretive***
Neo-Boasian	Classification, including tests of linguistic relativistic hypotheses Grammatical typologies Descriptive grammars *Examples:* The Navajo: classificatory verb study; The Pear Stories project	Performance theory studies Some discourse studies Ethnography of communication The contextual effects of linguistic relativity *Example:* Performance of the *coloquio* in Tierra Blanca
Linguistic Metaphorist	"Strict" semiotics Cognitive anthropology Linguistic relativity and lexical domains *Example*: Cross-cultural studies of basic color terms	"Humanistic" (con)text-centered discourse analysis Ethnography as text Interpretivism and hermeneutics: Linguistic relativity as study of "genius" of individual languages *Example*: "Voices" in text and and discourse

The four kinds of investigations also exemplify the two persistent themes in anthropological linguistics. The extension of linguistic models to nonlanguage study is represented of course by the linguistic metaphorist tradition, with scientific and interpretive examples: the field of semiotics proper, which is scientific, and the extension of discourse analysis into ethnography as both a method and a model for ethnographers to follow, which is interpretive.

As a theme, linguistic relativity, the study of how language might affect other aspects of culture, is treated within all four of the subtraditions of investigation. As can be seen in table 5, however, studies of linguistic relativity center on examinations of different aspects of language in relation to nonlinguistic domains. Study of linguistic relativity and linguistic categories is more characteristic of neo-Boasian scientific investigation. Linguistic metaphorist scientific treatment of linguistic relativity is devoted to examination of lexical sets such as those for basic color or folk botanical terminologies where universal properties are winnowed out of the linguistic variety. Within the linguistic metaphorist interpretive framework, investigation can be exemplified by work such as that which characterizes an individual language as having a particular "genius," often seen as reflected in other aspects of the culture of the speakers of that language.

Examples

We have already discussed some of the grammatical and syntactic traits of interest to the testing of linguistic relativity including studies of grammatical categories, such as number and classification by shape or size. These exemplify the neo-Boasian scientific tradition in linguistic relativity. A classic example is the Carroll and Casagrande (1958) investigation of Navajo classificatory verbs, referred to in chapter 3 and repeated here. Recall that in Navajo, something which is the direct object of a verb will determine the verb that is appropriate. If an object is something that is long and flexible, it requires a different verb than something that is long and rigid. Thus, there are sets such as the one below for single "meanings":

šań-léh	(long and flexible object)
šań-tííh	(long and rigid object)
šań-iłóós	(flat and flexible object)

Carroll and Casagrande found differences between the way children who spoke only Navajo and children who spoke both English and Navajo discriminated simple objects on the basis of color and shape. Such a finding tended to support a position that grammatical categories do indeed affect behavior. The children who spoke only Navajo used shape as a category for grouping at an earlier age than did the bilingual Navajo children.

A second example is to be found in the Pear Stories Project (Chafe 1981). A cross-language investigation, the Pear Stories Project involved showing the same speech-free film of an incident involving the picking of pears in an orchard and the theft of the pears by a boy on a bicycle to at least 20 different speakers of each of 10 languages (English, Chinese, Japanese, Malay, Thai, Persian, Greek, German, Haitian Creole, and Sacapultec Maya). The film was always shown to speakers within their own linguistic communities so they were less likely to be influenced by being in a linguistic and cultural community other than their own. A narrative describing the events in the film was collected from each subject within 5–25 minutes after the viewing. In some instances, repeat narratives were obtained after six months and again after one year. All the materials collected were carefully transcribed and analyzed in terms of the ways different people talk about the same thing in different languages and cultures to see what similarities there might be, and also to find differences in the ways persons verbalize the same knowledge as a way of examining different discourse strategies and possible cultural influences. It was hypothesized that narratives are produced through time from points of view that parallel and express the movement of consciousness through time (Chafe 1981). Thus, there may be differences in the discourse strategies used by speakers of different languages for presentation of the events of the film, differences which at least in part may result from selection of items for presentation that are culturally relevant and culturally specific. In addition, some of the cooperating investigators found that there were cultural differences in presentation that grew out of differing definitions of "event" (Tannen 1981). Thus, American English speakers responded more to cinematic aspects in identifying "events," whereas speakers of Athenian Greek responded more to the motives and actions of characters in the film.

Study of lexical sets such as ethnobotanical terminologies and basic color terminologies cross-linguistically provide excellent examples of the studies conducted according to approaches within the linguistic metaphorist scientific tradition, as well as of research that is typical of linguistic relativity studies. In investigating the basic color terminologies of different languages, the differences in number of basic color terms first led investigators to think that color was the best known expression of a Whorfian effect. It was only after the color studies inaugurated by the Berlin and Kay (1969) comparison of a large number of color terminologies that a predictive pattern of the development of such terminologies became apparent. Thus, we have a kind of typology, which is itself relevant both synchronically and diachronically. That typology is tied to the ways speakers of different languages name a realm of language-external reality, the colors of the spectrum. Further, there is evidence that the typology shown in table 3 (see chapter 4) may reflect deeper neurophysiological facts, the operation of the opponent cells of the optic nerve to reorganize color information into four major signals (McDaniel 1972, Kay and McDaniel 1978). Those signals correspond to the primary colors: red, blue, yellow, and green.

Much of the interest in context as defining of linguistic categories and even as the central locus of language itself derives from studies within the neo-Boasian interpretive tradition. In a study of the *coloquio* genre in the town of Tierra Blanca in the Mexican state of Guanajuato, Bauman and associates (Bauman and Briggs 1990, Bauman and Rich 1994, Briggs and Bauman 1992) noted that, as might be expected, performances of these nativity plays revealed considerable variability despite the efforts of most actors to memorize and render lines faithfully. The performers of most roles drilled their parts in a serious effort to give exact renditions, even though they had difficulties of limited literacy, inadequate prompting, and so on. Of course, in any given performance, some performers suffered memory lapses, or there occurred unplanned-for circumstances that assured that the end product was not a perfect copy of some ideal performance of the genre. These less-than-perfect renditions led inevitably to a lack of fit—an intertextual "gap"—between the real and the ideal performance of the *coloquio*.

Apart from these expected deviations, one actor who took the important role of the Hermitaño (Hermit) deviated from the text constantly and on purpose. Indeed, it was a part of his role to improvise. Sometimes the departures were hilarious, even obscene. The Hermitaño never actually memorized his lines, but as he accepted prompting from the prompter during rehearsals and performances, he followed a set of conventions that prevented his performance from skidding too far off the expected. He repeated some of the words the prompter gave him; he matched phonological features of his line-final words to those of the script; he kept the distinctive intonational style of the *coloquio* intact. The Hermitaño thus maintained generic intertextuality, even as he engaged in the creativity expected of his character by purposely stretching out the intertextual gaps.

One may see intertextuality in this example as a way by which performance theory may be extended to account for variation. **Performance theory** dictates that culture *is* performance; culture is in every instance parole. Such a position eliminates the problem of relating individual variation to some general cultural statement, since culture is that variation. On the other hand, performance theorists are left with the problem of defining one culture from another. If all variation is culture, then where does one culture leave off and another culture begin? Where does some instance of it become too deviant to belong to that culture? Intertextuality is an analytic construct that may provide that general statement for a culture, since it offers an intermediate form (the intertext) to which all variants of a genre may be related. This problem should be compared to that of the cognitivists, who take culture to be located in the minds of the natives, but must provide a principled account by which variation, in both understanding and behavior, is related to that mental cultural construct. As mentioned, some of the answers to that question by cognitive anthropologists have included selecting a key informant's opinion as definitive of the culture (Goodenough 1981), defining culture as that which is shared and agreed upon among all members of the culture (consensus theory [Romney, Weller and Batcheider 1987]), identifying patterns in the variation, and including their internal relations as part of culture (Furbee and Benfer 1983; Boster 1986a, 1986b, 1987; Furbee 1989). The following example also treats the issue of variation.

Studies of "voices" (Bakhtin 1981) in texts represent a linguistic metaphorist interpretive approach to intracultural and intrainformant variation in discourse. In oral narration, changes in features of one's speech (intonation, accent, style, paralanguage, and so on) in different situational contexts signal different voices, which may be of various characters in the narrative, including the narrator at different times in the past, present, or future, or in different emotional modes. In a "voice"-centered analysis of a complex Mexicano (modern Nahuatl of Mexico) text (K. Hill 1985), J. Hill (1990) finds that the narrator speaks for 32 characters, in different voices, and that the system of voices provides an important aspect of the texture of the text. More important, however, the analysis reveals that the voices, especially the periodically weeping voice of the narrator, reveal the multilayered structure of the narrative, and the achievement of coherence in narrative and in the self of the narrators.

Great adversity has fallen upon Doña Maria, the narrator. She has left a relatively prosperous life as a market seller to enter into a common-law marriage with a man who has been abandoned by his wife. She meets with virulent hostility from her stepdaughter and her parents-in-law, but she does well by her stepsons. Her hostile stepdaughter steals from Doña Maria a large sum of money that the former market woman has been keeping for a client. Doña Maria and her husband are forced to borrow to repay the client and to pay interest on their loan at a high rate. She and her husband are reduced to poverty and must give their mule team to the creditor to settle the debt. They still owe money that they borrowed to pay the interest. In despair over the loss of the team and the many acts of persecution visited on them by in-laws and neighbors, she and her husband fall into drinking for a period during which she neglects her stepchildren.

Finally, religious petitions help her recover her sense of self-worth and aid her in returning to purposeful activity. In particular, prayers to the Virgin at Santa Maria Huitzcoma help her; the Virgin appears to her in a dream to warn her that her corn has been poisoned. Even after a year, when Doña Maria recorded the narrative as a record for her stepsons, both of her travails and of her righteousness, her neighbors continued to persecute her, but through public announcement and through her making the recording, she is recovering her good character and good opinion of herself.

J. Hill sees the coherence of the narrative as having four "wave forms": (1) The shortest is the *clause wave* which pertains to the syntactic structure and its appropriateness for the narrative. (2) The intermediate is the *plot rhythm wave* of the episodes of the narrative (represented through narration, evaluation, and reported speech). (3) A longer wave is the *theme wave* of the narrative. That theme is of Doña Maria's prosperity, the legitimacy of her marriage (which is actually only an informal one), her fitness as a mother, and her religious devotion; in short, that she is a good person, even though she has engaged in an episode of bad behavior—drinking and neglecting her stepsons. (4) There is another long *wave of selfhood* in which the Doña Maria constitutes her 'self' in accord with her experiences and in counterpoint with the third wave, the theme wave (the good person).

The episodes of full weeping occur in two places in the narrative at the intersections of the theme wave and the self-coherence wave (see figure 6). The first is just at the point in her narrative that Doña Maria begins her account of giving up the mule team which marks her fall from "good behavior" into "bad behavior," when she begins to drink and neglect her stepsons under the considerable burden of misfortune and mistreatment by her in-laws and neighbors. The second instance is where she tells of her prayers to the Virgin and the ensuing appearance of the Virgin in a dream to warn her of the poisoned corn; that is, just as she returns to "good behavior" again through appeal to the Virgin. The "weeping" voice of the narrator brackets her period of "bad self," her fall from "good self" and her return to it. In that way, the weeping functions to create a coherent self for the narrator, and for the listener.

We can see that much contradictory behavior and variety of opinion can also be understood in terms of the different voices assumed by a narrator in a text. In this instance, the voices of the narrator both help her to recover her good self-opinion and to create her self-coherence, embrac-

Figure 6 **Counterpoint of Wave Forms of Coherence**

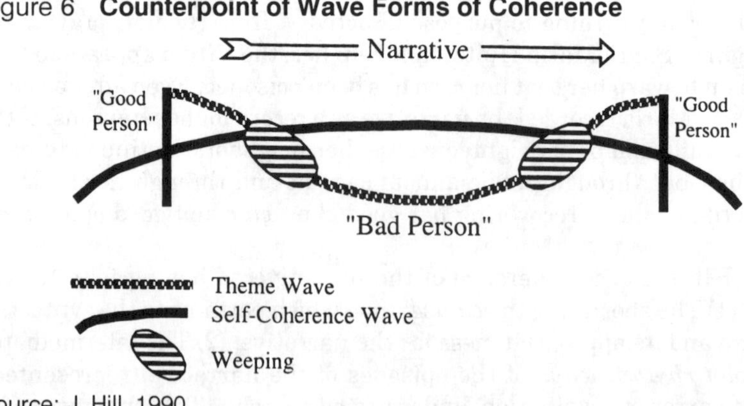

Source: J. Hill, 1990.

ing both the sadness of her former "bad" self and the construction of her present (and presumably future) "good" self, as a non-contradictory continuity.

Integration of Linguistic and Other Anthropological Studies

Many consider linguistics a part of anthropology, even though much of what can be called linguistic study is conducted outside the discipline of anthropology per se. How then does linguistic anthropology—and especially language and culture studies—integrate with activities and ideas in the larger anthropological universe? It usually does so two ways. The first kind of study that integrates linguistic anthropological endeavor with anthropology in general is one in which linguists and other anthropological specialists work together toward solving some problem of common interest which may involve, for example, issues of economic development, relations among contemporaneous peoples, or reflections of particular beliefs or practices in various systems of cultures, including language. Many of these studies concern areal investigations. Such area studies are as often across time as across space. An example is investigation of social prehistory to learn something about the lifeways of a prehistoric people and reconstruct their past ideologies (Abercrombie 1986), or to discover the homeland of a people for which there is archaeological evidence (the homeland of the Indo-Europeans, or the Keresans, for example). The linguist Dixon's studies of Australian languages had relevance for such Australian experts (Dixon 1972, 1977, 1980, 1984). Another exemplary integrative study involved the correlation of genetic, dialect, and social organizational information about the modern-day Yanomamö peoples of the Amazon basin (Chagnon 1976).

A second kind of integrative linguistic investigation is one that treats a particular theme that is of theoretical concern to anthropology. Such is the case with all linguistic relativity studies, since they concern the relation between grammar and other aspects of culture, and with use of linguistic models for nonlanguage analysis. There are other crosscutting topics too; for example, studies of classification and categorization, which are of concern as human activities to anthropologists in all subdisciplines, and the problem of integrating the individual with the collective. Similarly, any investigation concerned with the origin of language is of special interest to anthropologists who see the beginnings of language to be associated with the beginnings of humankind.

Important to sociocultural anthropology have been recent studies that concern themselves with questions of integrating individual and group variability in cultural accounts. A number of scientific linguistic metaphorist works have concerned themselves with intracultural and intraindividual variability, frequently relying on statistical and mathematical formulations. Intracultural variability led also to interpretivist explanations, many of which center on the identification and characterization of "voices" (Bakhtin) in texts and other cultural documents.

Variation and Relativity

Interpretivism challenges structuralist conventional understandings of concepts and relations by which parole (speech, message, and loosely, performance) is indicative of langue (language, code, and very loosely, competence). A postmodernist like Derrida (or even Barthes) would equate langue with writing, so language as a system for them is primarily exemplified in its written form. Saussure and his structuralist followers always regarded writing as derivative of parole, and parole as indicative of langue, but postmodernists contend that no longer does parole provide the data and langue the object of study. Whereas structuralists have used observations of parole to derive hypotheses about langue (their real object of study), many interpretivists, deconstructionists included, would privilege parole (speech) because for them a language does not exist properly except in the speech of the collective and in context.

Of course, not all interpretivism is deconstruction, but all of it privileges parole at the expense of langue to a greater or lesser degree. One may say that all linguistic anthropologists working with these ideas hold similar goals, whether they are scientific or humanistic in orientation, structuralists or interpretivists; however, they appear to start from different loci and to hold different elements as primary in their theories. Practice theory (Bourdieu 1977), for example, takes parole as both data and object of study. It generalizes and relates these observations to social and political actions. It situates meaning in the social practice as conducted in **communities of practice** (Eckert and McConnell-Ginet 1992). Such communities can be equated with the cultural groupings of other theories.

Performance theory also takes parole as both data and object of study, but it more directly equates this expression with culture. Culture is then situated in the ongoing performance. This is not to say that practice and performance-oriented approaches ignore relations to mental, cognitive, or knowledge representations. It is true, however, that the fit of performance and practice theory to psychological theory is not obvious and offers challenging and important avenues of investigation.

Cognitivists, of course, begin with assumptions about the primacy of mental representation and derive much of their motivation and argument for analyses from psychology. We can look upon the humanistic interpretive approaches and the various scientific cognitive ones as distinguished according to a conventional position from psychology that says that understanding derives from (1) an individual's previous relevant experiences plus (2) the present circumstances. Performance and discourse theories rely more on previous relevant experiences, although performance theory at least has been criticized for giving no account of history in that it situates culture in each instance of a performance. Cognitive approaches to variation, such as consensus theory and multiple pathways theory, usually concern themselves with present circumstances, at least as far as their subject of study is concerned. To give an example, scientific cognitive models do not hold that the past has no place in theory, but they do reveal preoccupations with investigations of relatively immediate problems (modeling cropping systems, formalizing the understanding of health and illness, distinguishing the contribution of a skipper to the success of a catch in fishing). The theoretical formulations deriving from such studies, on the other hand, can incorporate developments from the past, as the color studies make clear. These studies often have investigated such problems among preliterate peoples. Humanistic approaches, on the other hand, draw on theories centered in poetics and established literary traditions. Certainly, some are conducted with preliterate peoples, but often the theoretical foundation work has grown out of field studies embedded in ethnohistorical investigation (D. Tedlock 1983; Hanks 1987, 1990) or with genres that have established ties to a great tradition (Abu-Lughod 1986, J. Hill 1990).

Discourse-based approaches to language and culture (Sherzer 1987, Urban 1991) resemble performance and practice theories in important ways and differ in others. Like practice approaches, a discourse-based approach claims that discourse (parole) is the "concrete expression of the language-culture-society relationship . . . which creates, recreates, modifies, and fine tunes both culture and language and their intersection. . . ." (Sherzer 1987:296). This position reveals a sophistication that is centered less on universal concerns, but rather has shifted interest "away from a rigid dichotomization of structure and practice, focusing instead on their complex interactions" (J. Hill and Mannheim 1992:400). The formulation deviates from performance theory, however, in that the individual has no place in a discourse-centered approach as a cultural phenomenon (Urban 1991). On the other hand, the individual has a privileged position in some other interpretive formulations: the individual is seen as the site of imagination for Friedrich (1979b, 1986), and imagination can be regarded as central in studies of voice (Bakhtin 1981, 1986; J. Hill 1990).

Performance theory resembles multiple pathways theory in its efforts to relate one instantiation to another via a consideration of the contextual factors that might influence its interpretation. These factors may be the performer and audience experiences—with performance of similar genres, for example; they may include the history of the ideas and the use of the genre, the physical location of the performance, the identities of the persons taking part in the performance, or their conscious and unconscious deviations from "typical" performances, which constitutes creativity. All these are part of a framework that is built up in the social interaction of the performance. Under these considerations, a given instance of a performance may be interpreted and made congruent with previous ideas and experiences. The fit between particular utterances of a performance of a genre and their ideal models is always imperfect, leading to intertextual "gaps." Manipulation of these gaps may become in itself a part of the character of a performance; for example, a highly conventional performance would tend to minimize the distance (the gap) between itself and the generic model, but one that was particularly innovative (e.g., a Shakespearean play given in modern dress with a subtext conveying a modern political message) would attempt to widen the gap. Similarly, it may be expected of the actors performing one or more of the roles in a performance that they take liberties with the text, as was the case with the Hermitaño.

In the theory of multiple pathways, individuals may have different strategies and understandings of an event or plan that translate into the same action. They may arrive at the same point by different routes. These routes may be modeled by rules, for example, by an expert system. They may be measured against one another or against some ideal or theoretical model. Often the metaphor used is spatial. Consequently, investigators frequently use spatially situated descriptive statistical methods to model these patterns of knowledge. Phrased in terms of decisions made and actions taken, different persons may arrive at the same goal or understanding or action by different avenues according to this theory; they may also change their minds so their understandings will shift dynamically according to new knowledge and context. Context here, as in performance theory, is broadly defined: the setting in which the players find themselves; their preoccupations of the moment; immediate and more distant preceding utterances; as well as sets of assumptions about the world and its state of affairs. An important aspect of study in multiple pathway terms would be description of the processes by which these understandings are arrived at in conversations. Persons appear to create temporary frames "on-the-fly" as they converse, shifting from one view to a different one based on persuasion and evidence, or sometimes on the political necessity of the moment or in terms of social conventions of politeness.

In sum, then, these approaches tend to vary according to the elements taken as primary within them, according to the loci they assume for language and culture, and according to their treatment of relativity versus universality. Cognitive approaches privilege mental representation as a locus of language and culture. Most are concerned with the formulation of rules, schemata, strategies, scripts, or other "mental" representations of langue derived from the observation of parole for representing the mediating mechanisms of the theory or formalism. They differ as to how they integrate the individual with the whole. Some, such as earlier ethnoscience formulations, privilege the opinion of a particularly knowledgeable individual, a "key" informant (Goodenough 1957, Gardner 1976, Boster 1987). For these formulations, culture as a whole follows naturally, but the nature of the integration can be problematic. For example, consensus theory (Romney, Weller, and Batcheider 1987) makes the claim that "culture" is what is shared; it is the consensus. Multiple pathways theory (Benfer and Furbee 1989, Furbee 1989), on the other hand, attempts to integrate varying understandings in a principled manner as a part of the statement of culture. Individual variation has a coherent account and a central place in considering the whole as a work in progress. All cognitive theories accept some form of cultural and linguistic relativity but rely on universalist insights for explanation of the nature of variation. They investigate formal, neurologically associated universals of mental capacity and their reflections in cultural practice (Berlin and Kay 1969, Kay and McDaniel 1978, Furbee et al. 1996).

Interpretive theories, on the other hand, tend to situate culture and language more often in social interaction than in the mind, although occasionally they demonstrate strong mentalism also. Practice theory places culture in interaction; discourse-based theories put it in the discourse resulting from interaction; the performance approach situates culture in the performance of the text or genre (in parole). All interpretive approaches tend to be more relativistic than universalist. They may be very strongly so, refuting the possibility of generalization across cultures, or even within a culture (Taylor 1979); at their extremes, such theories deny the possibility of generalization about culture or language and appeal instead to the idea that a cultural conception lies in the mind of the interpreter. Other interpretive theories set out a theory of variation in the relating of texts (intertextuality), which calls strongly on the explanatory role of context, as a way of integrating individual in the whole (Briggs and Bauman 1992).

Today and Tomorrow

Anthropological linguistics continues in ways that often remain true to the goals and directions set by Boas nearly a century ago. The traditions, scientific and interpretivist, within language and culture studies approach one another most closely in functional theories of language and behavior. Functional linguistic theories have taken as primary goals the explanation of language use in context, and even the identification of units of analysis from language use (Hopper and Thompson 1984). Among the practitioners of these theories are linguists who would not necessarily consider themselves anthropologists, which also indicates a close association of linguistic anthropology with the field of linguistics proper. The position of descriptive grammars of unfamiliar languages recently has risen in importance to formal linguistics to a degree not seen in more than 25 years, as identified by the recent introduction of prizes for exemplar publications by both the Linguistic Society of America and the Society for the Study of the Indigenous Languages of the Americas.

A persistent theme in contemporary language and culture studies is the conscious concern for integrating the individual with the collective in analyses, and efforts to accommodate this problem can be discerned throughout both the scientific and interpretive traditions of anthropological linguistics. They represent honest attempts also to take into account the possible influence of the investigator in evaluating one's own and others' work. The most sophisticated efforts along these lines to date have been in the area of accounting for the integration of the individual with the whole. Within the interpretive tradition, we can see this integration addressed in the rigorous attempts to define different discourse styles and performance styles (Sherzer 1983, Bauman 1977). The recognition of the different voices speaking in a text, and in some instances, of the different voices taken by the narrator, is another interpretive approach to the problem of accounting for individual differences in the apparent sameness of the cultural soup (J. Hill 1990).

Within the scientific tradition, there have also been efforts to identify similarities in discourse, cross-culturally and within a culture (Chafe 1981), but the individual-collective controversy usually takes the form of debate among competing ways of explaining intracultural variation, usually employing some form of statistical modeling. As we have seen, there is considerable discussion of the best formulation for such an account. Candidates include consensus theory, which is largely derivative of psychological theory—a theory of error for anthropological data (Romney, Weller, and Batcheider 1987); a theory of variation as deviation from a modal model (Boster 1986a, 1986b, 1987; Furbee and Benfer 1983; Furbee 1989), often with an explanation for variation that is functional (Laderman 1981); a characterization of alternatives, either as rules for taking action (schemata) available within a social group (Holland and Quinn 1987) or as cognitive strategies individuals may use (Furbee 1985b). One development in this line of thinking involves making use of expert system shells to model different ways of accounting for information, either from the point of view of the analyst (Guillet 1989, Read and Behrens 1989), from the point of view of the informant (Benfer and Furbee 1989, Furbee 1989), or both (Benfer 1989).

Linguists' interest in functional approaches is shared with other areas of anthropology as well. There one finds ecology-influenced cultural anthropology and archaeology, cultural materialism, sociobiology, and numerous other contemporary theoretical frameworks which are also functionalist in orientation. It is interesting to look at discourse analysis in light of the widespread influence of functionalism in current anthropology. Discourse analysis is a central activity within linguistics proper; studies such as the Pear Stories Project (Chafe 1981) link language research conducted by linguistic anthropologists in the neo-Boasian tradition with the concerns of linguistic theorists of functional perspective who are outside anthropology. That is to say that discourse analysis is one of the primary routes by which anthropological linguistics is re-entering arenas of concern to linguistics proper, often via studies that would be called sociolinguistic as much as anthropological.

At the same time, discourse analysis can be seen to be giving to sociocultural anthropology a method for conducting investigations that is as congenial to both the scientific and the interpretivist approaches there (Marcus and Cushman 1982, Clifford and Marcus 1986). One should distinguish between **linguistic discourse analysis** such as the Pear Stories Project exemplifies and the **ethnographic discourse analysis** of many cultural anthropological endeavors (e.g., Holland and Quinn 1987). The former analyzes texts from the start point of linguistic markers such as indications of pauses, of topics, and of switch reference. Thus, for example, the patterns of information flow alluded to earlier are distinguished through association of the topics and comments with relevant linguistic elements. Ethnographic discourse analysis, on the other hand, begins with larger semantic units such as issues or metaphors mentioned in a text. In a sense, ethnographic discourse analysis extends and enriches the method of content analysis, which identifies and enumerates repeated mentions of an issue or topic, sometimes quantifying them. The statistical analysis so performed ordinarily compares the numbers of mentions of an issue with the numbers of mentions of all other issues in a text, giving a measure of saliency for that particular item. Ethnographic discourse analysis provides a means of setting such identifications of important issues or metaphors in structural or interpretive frames. Whereas content analysis will establish some issue as more salient in a text than another, ethnographic discourse analysis can identify the web of relations holding between an issue so identified and others relevant to it.

The avenues of entry for discourse analysis into ethnography have been the interpretive language and culture studies of linguistic anthropology. Interpretive work involving discourse analysis, such as that on voices by J. Hill and on past ideologies by Hanks (1986) and Abercrombie

(1986), receives a sympathetic hearing from the symbolic and interpretivist wing of sociocultural anthropology. Ethnographic discourse analysis extends many ideas from sociocultural theorists such as Geertz (1973, 1985) and Turner (1969), while conforming to a rigorous method. It is through these and similar means that linguistic anthropology as a whole, and language and culture studies in particular, can be anticipated to converse intellectually with the anthropological world at large. Consider, for example, the following statement.

> A pluralistic thinker does not retreat to the security of an exclusivist position in believing a singular truth. Nor is pluralism uncritical relativism in which all perspectives are equally good—as in the lowest common denominator. Pluralism does simultaneously recognize the significance of difference and particularity in the comparative study of social process. Commonality and difference are held in tension: an indispensable aspect of dialogue. Dialogue becomes the instrument for the creation of relationships, not for the achievement of a uniformitarian understanding of cultural evolution. (Lamberg-Karlovsky 1989:11)

This manifesto is not from the sociocultural or linguistic anthropological literature. It is from an introduction to contemporary archaeological thought; yet it summarizes all of the major concerns considered here. Such concerns, initially framed as they are by language investigation, are likely to remain central for many years to come because of the position of linguistics as the most humanistic of the sciences and the most scientific of the humanities.

Summary

Language and culture studies maintain a creative integration in spite of the considerable forces that work toward factionalizing anthropology at large. Linguistic work in anthropology achieves this coherence through integration of more humanistic approaches, many of which are informed by postmodernist critiques, with the more scientific work that is foundational to data gathering for both linguistic anthropology and theoretical linguistics itself. Linguistics as an independent discipline remains a largely scientific enterprise and works to keep practitioners of language and culture studies conversant with more scientific concerns. Thus, we can see in anthropological linguistics a grouping of studies by the character of their approaches, more scientific or more interpretivist/humanistic. Some of these are in a direct line from the neo-Boasian tradition; they may be more scientific in orientation, being concerned with classification, grammatical description, and cross-linguistic comparisons (e.g., the Pear

Stories project), or more interpretive (e.g., performance theory studies such as the analysis of the *coloquio* in Tierra Blanca). Others may follow more closely the language and culture tradition of using linguistic models for nonlanguage analysis, the linguistic metaphorist approach. Again, some of these studies are more scientific (e.g., cognitive studies such as the color studies) and others more interpretive or humanistic (e.g., analysis of "voices" in text and discourse).

Finally, one ought to keep in mind the importance of language and culture, and linguistic anthropology in general, to the field of anthropology as a whole. Although the number of linguistic anthropologists is small, the effect of language and culture studies remains strong in anthropology. The integration here centers on contributions of linguistic studies to larger efforts to understand the natural history of a people (e.g., the Yanomamö), reconstruction of the prehistory of a people (e.g., homeland studies), and to test integrative theoretical approaches relevant especially to cultural anthropology in the more restricted domain of language studies. These last efforts often return perfected models to general anthropology for further use and testing, fulfilling the semiotic role of language and culture to the discipline at large.

Discussion and Activities

1. Consider the list below:

folksy	cheesey
uppity	kooky
artsy-craftsy	sporty
kinky	iffy
horsey	funky
biggee	cutsey
kitschy	goofy
comfy	loosey-goosey

All of these terms, which are similar in form, in affective meaning, are also shifters. This means that they have lexical meaning (like other adjectives) and contextually derived meaning. In the latter instance, they point out in an actual context a particular referent's position along a continuum of the quality they designate. Some are **multiperspective** in scope (pointing out different positions on a continuum from a single vantage point), while some are **polyperspective** (pointing out a single position from different vantages).

Make a working definition of each term, and then make subgroups.

Try using each term in sentences that illustrate its range of meaning as a shifter. Which terms are multiperspective, and which are polyperspective? Do some terms belong to both groups?

Consider the semantic subgroups as domains. Is domain status correlated with type of shifter meaning or other features?

In many ways, this exercise sums up language and culture studies. The terms illustrate worldview and linguistic relativity, categorization interests, and semiotics. This is so because in isolation the terms are underdetermined (shifters need contextual reference). What does this group of terms tell about categorization?

2. Below are some expressions that go beyond naming the kind of linguistic action performed.

   sub rosa
   out of context
   to misspeak
   off the record
   just between you, me, and the lamp-post . . .
   misquote

   All of the above retract with impunity. Can you add to the list? How does a description of this set extend the analysis of linguistic action verbs? What is the linguistic ideology behind this?

Key Terms

communities of practice
ethnographic discourse analysis
functional
functional theories of grammar
interpretivist
linguistic discourse analysis
linguistic metaphorist tradition
multiperspective
neo-Boasian tradition
performance theory
polyperspective

Postscript

As we have seen, each human society has a culture that is thoroughly interwoven with at least one natural language, and it is inconceivable that human cultures would have developed without the concomitant development of human language. Yet there are no systematic relationships that simplistically relate human language with human culture, such as the scheme proposed by Marr (Thomas 1957), in his official doctrine in the former Soviet State. Marr held that agglutinative languages were to be found mainly in tribal societies with simple agriculture or pastoralism, with inflected languages being found in cultures that had developed in the context of nation states. It is equally contrary to common sense that very many language-culture near universals exist solely as expressions of a genetic coding, as Chomsky proposes. Rather, (near) universals are likely to owe their existence to the interaction of the common genetic program of human beings with factors such as shared physical environments, the physics of light and biology of vision (as in color studies), the limited number of logically possible configurations (as in kinship terminologies), and so on.

As we have seen, much of what people have identified as "language and culture" has been seen from two opposing viewpoints: (1) that of scientific linguistic anthropologists, who adopt the defining goal of science to formulate testable models of culture which are infinitely improvable upon; and (2) that of interpretivist linguistic anthropologists, who sense that they are merely making a model that parallels linguistic or cultural structure, the formulations of which may not always be testable in the scientific sense, yet the model lends insight and an understanding of the problem. What themes, ideas, methods, and terms would both camps see as central to language and culture studies? It is the purpose of this postscript to propose what this common core might be.

Certainly, in the categorization (and associated naming) of chaotic reality, we find the beginning of the creation of what we recognize as language and as culture. Probably, the debate of how things got to be named is the beginning of linguistic anthropology. A set of names, a language, creates a worldview, an "understanding of the whole world as it is thought to be, and a blueprint for the way one ought to be" (Bonvillain 1993:52). These twin questions of comparability (method) and language-culture interface (linguistic relativity) are the basic issues in any program of language and culture studies. Categorization—whether lexical, grammatical, or covert—is the focus of any systematic foray into language and culture relationships. For clarity of study, basic terms (including, for some, semantic features) and domains remain useful methodological heuristics, just as focality and the interrelations of categories are at the crux of theorizing in the field. For those with a scientific bent, the issue of universality goes beyond hermeneutic inquiry into a particular cultural practice or tradition. And, lest one miss the forest for the trees, the bird's-eye view provided by semiotics takes the analyst beyond the close scrutiny of data to the notion of holistic descriptions and cultural grammars (sets of rules or strategies, scripts, schemata, feature matrices, expert systems, and all the rest).

Ethnoscience, and its descendent cognitive anthropology, brought a microapproach in language and culture studies (examination of linguistic relativity through clearly defined and manipulated terms and domains) into conversation with the macroapproach (production of cultural grammars). In so doing, it elaborated the natural history tradition in the discipline. The obvious need to take context into account was remedied by making the unit of analysis the text, whether written or otherwise recorded. This innovation provided for partial control of the major parameters of participants, settings, and discourse topic(s). A text is a "snapshot" of a particular reality that will adhere to a given form and sets of conventions for interpretation (genre), ensuring some degree of comparability. To assist in this endeavor is the existence in all cultures of folk theories of how language is used (however appropriately); such theories of speech acts constitute the linguistic ideology of the group. To these considerations one must also list the general methods available to the social scientist: structuralism (including generativism); **comparative method**, and **historiographic method**.

The postmodern philosophy has elaborated and extended the natural history critique; it provides for deconstruction of erasures and other unstated agendas as well as for hermeneutic concern for the importance of cultural peculiarity of each domain, system, or discursive practice.

The dictum that "knowledge is power" is fundamental to political economy, which points up the structural relations of power and how power relates to crucial categories in a culture and the types of speech events and genres in which categories are used. Realizing that discourse about discourse (metadiscourse) must be self-aware and self-deconstructing, we are more free today to make analysis in linguistic anthropology a more accurate "snapshot" of reality by knowing that we are producing and editing models of idealized reality. Dialogic analysis of discourse into voices (some privileged and some not) allows otherness to be acknowledged openly and dealt with by exploring strategies by which each voice tries to get its own way, given the political economy invoked by the discursive practice in which it appears. The theoretical ramification of multivocality involves analysis using perspectives or vantages which have some systematic way of connecting different levels of themselves.

At the same time, we realize that the data we study are not chaotic reality itself, but rather systems that actual cultures and subcultures have already produced to redact chaotic reality. We are not trying to make models of reality so much as we are studying pre-existing models of reality that have been produced by the cultural participants in a social world. Given the new awareness of what goes on and what must be acknowledged in doing language and culture studies, as well as the actual nature of our data, we are in less trouble than radical postmodernists would suggest.

Key Terms

comparative method
historiographic method

Appendix I
Phonetics

Speech is produced by the human **vocal tract**. The pressure of air expelled from the lungs, or for some sounds pulled back toward the lungs, moves across the apparatus of the vocal tract and is shaped and constricted by the actions of **articulators**, the active moving vocal organs such as the tongue, against **points of articulation**, the targets of the articulation. This characteristic of speech sound as being produced by the actions of the articulators upon the points of articulation, along with the associated **manner of articulation** (for example, voicing vs. nonvoicing of a sound, closure vs. nonclosure of the air stream, and so on) provides the basis of **articulatory phonetics**. Articulatory phonetics is a system for describing all possible sounds in all human languages.

Figure 7 presents a diagrammatic view of the vocal tract. In it one can see the active articulators (lips, tongue, and glottis) and their points of articulation (lips, teeth, alveolar ridge, hard palate, soft palate [also called velum], uvula, pharynx, and glottis). The movement of an articulator toward or upon a point of articulation, along with the manner of articulation, provides the foundation of the classification system by which speech sounds are described. For example, a bilabial voiced **stop** is a sound articulated by the lips upon the lips (bi 'two,' labial 'lip') which is voiced and produced with complete closure (in other words, stops are sounds that involve complete closure of the articulator with the point of articulation, sealing off the air stream at least momentarily) and with vibration of the vocal chords producing the 'voicing'; we write that with the symbol [b]. A labiodental voiceless **fricative** (or **spirant**), on the other hand, is articulated with the lower lip (labio) upon the upper teeth (dental) and is produced without complete closure (spirants are sounds that involve constriction of the air stream but not complete closure) and without the vibration of the vocal chords (hence 'voiceless'); we write this sound as [f].

All sounds can be described according to point of articulation in the vocal tract and manner of articulation. These principles underlie the classification system called the International Phonetic Alphabet (figure 8),

Figure 7 **Diagram of Human Vocal Tract Showing Articulatory Apparatus**

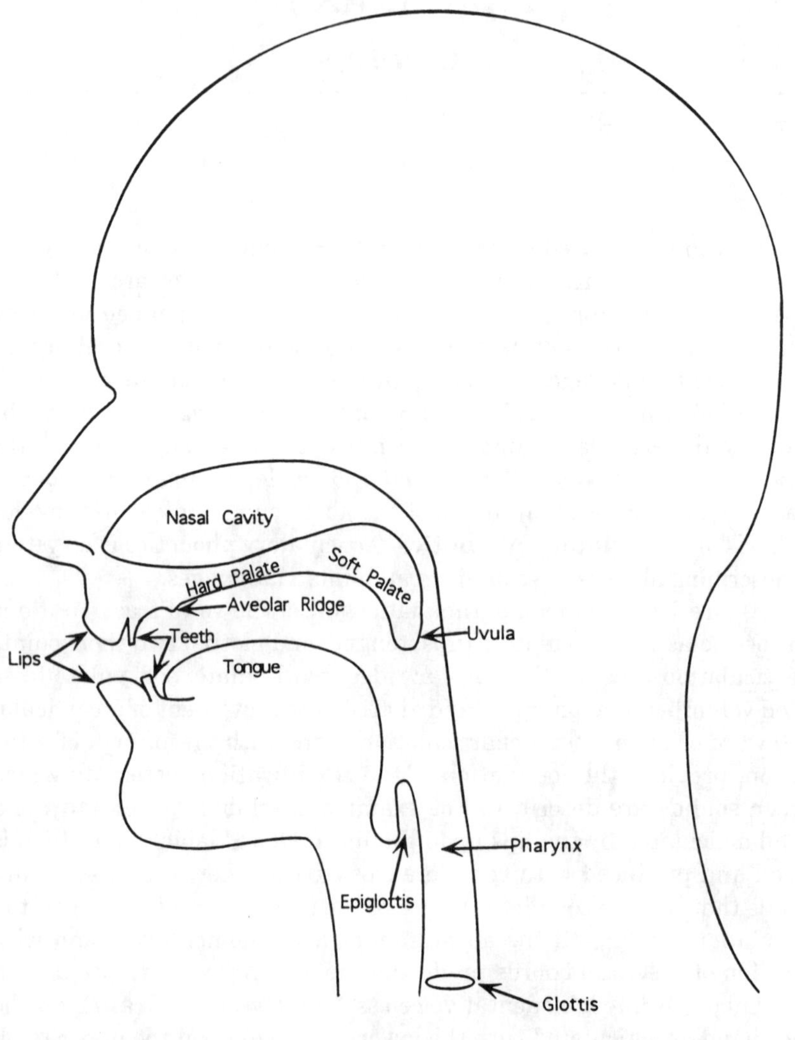

often abbreviated as the IPA. The IPA provides a symbol for every potenial human sound when one considers also the diacritic markings that can be used to show modifications of sounds. For example, sounds that are customarily voiced, such as [n], may occasionally be unvoiced; such a situation is signaled by use of a diacritic—[n̥].

Articulations include Bilabial, Labiodental, Dental (tongue upon back of teeth), Dentoalveolar (tongue upon back of teeth and alveolar ridge), Palatal (tongue upon hard palate), Velar (tongue upon soft palate, also called velum), Uvular (tongue upon uvula), Pharyngeal (tongue upon pharynx), and Glottal (vocal chords, also called vocal bands, in glottis closing or constricting upon one another).

Vowel sounds, like consonant sounds, are written according to their point and manner of articulation. Since vowel sounds are **open** in most cases (that is not involving either **nasality** or complete **closure** of articulation), the parameters have more to do with the placement of articulation in the mouth according to features of **high** (also called closure), **mid** (both closed and open versions), and **low** (open) along the vertical dimension and features of **front**, **central**, and **back** along the horizontal dimension. Vowel modifications also can be described with diacritics.

By comparing figures 7 and 8, one can see that the transcription system in figure 8 is a model of the left-facing diagrammatic cut-away drawing of the vocal tract in figure 7. Thus, the IPA chart has been constructed according to an anatomical template for representing the articulators and their points of articulation, enhanced by a set of principles that can be used to express the manner of articulation, including deviations from the unusual given through the diacritics. Such a system of transcription allows one to write accurately the sounds of all the world's languages.

Americanists have customarily used some phonetic symbols that differ from those employed in the IPA system. Those most frequently substituted are [š ž č ǰ t͡s ñ] for the symbols represented in IPA as [ʃ ʒ ʧ ʤ ʦ ɲ].

Ladefoged (1990, 1993) provides an excellent guide to phonetics for readers seeking additional information.

Key Terms

articulators
articulatory phonetics
back
central
closure
fricative
front
high
low
manner of articulation
mid
nasality
open
points of articulation
spirant
stop
vocal tract

Figure 8 **The International Phonetic Alphabet** (revised to 1993, corrected 1996)

CONSONANTS (PULMONIC)

	Bilabial	Labiodental	Dental	Alveolar	Postalveolar	Retroflex	Palatal	Velar	Uvular	Pharyngeal	Glottal
Plosive	p b			t d		ʈ ɖ	c ɟ	k g	q ɢ		ʔ
Nasal	m	ɱ		n		ɳ	ɲ	ŋ	ɴ		
Trill	ʙ			r					ʀ		
Tap or Flap				ɾ		ɽ					
Fricative	ɸ β	f v	θ ð	s z	ʃ ʒ	ʂ ʐ	ç ʝ	x ɣ	χ ʁ	ħ ʕ	h ɦ
Lateral fricative				ɬ ɮ							
Approximant		ʋ		ɹ		ɻ	j	ɰ			
Lateral approximant				l		ɭ	ʎ	ʟ			

Where symbols appear in pairs, the one to the right represents a voiced consonant. Shaded areas denote articulations judged impossible.

CONSONANTS (NON-PULMONIC)

Clicks		Voiced implosives		Ejectives	
ʘ	Bilabial	ɓ	Bilabial	ʼ	Examples:
ǀ	Dental	ɗ	Dental/alveolar	pʼ	Bilabial
ǃ	(Post)alveolar	ʄ	Palatal	tʼ	Dental/alveolar
ǂ	Palatoalveolar	ɠ	Velar	kʼ	Velar
ǁ	Alveolar lateral	ʛ	Uvular	sʼ	Alveolar fricative

VOWELS

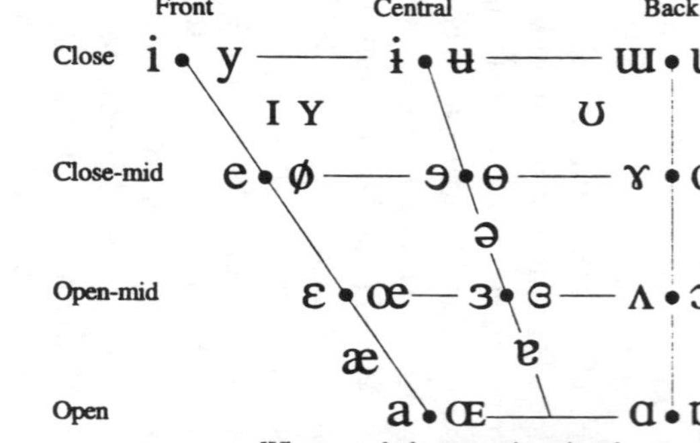

Where symbols appear in pairs, the one to the right represents a rounded vowel.

OTHER SYMBOLS

ʍ	Voiceless labial-velar fricative	ɕ ʑ	Alveolo-palatal fricatives
w	Voiced labial-velar approximant	ɺ	Alveolar lateral flap
ɥ	Voiced labial-palatal approximant	ɧ	Simultaneous ʃ and x
ʜ	Voiceless epiglottal fricative		
ʢ	Voiced epiglottal fricative		
ʡ	Epiglottal plosive		

Affricates and double articulations can be represented by two symbols joined by a tie bar if necessary. k͡p t͡s

DIACRITICS

Diacritics may be placed above a symbol with a descender, e.g. ŋ̊

̥	Voiceless	n̥ d̥	̤	Breathy voiced	b̤ a̤	̪	Dental	t̪ d̪
̬	Voiced	s̬ t̬	̰	Creaky voiced	b̰ a̰	̺	Apical	t̺ d̺
ʰ	Aspirated	tʰ dʰ	̼	Linguolabial	t̼ d̼	̻	Laminal	t̻ d̻
̹	More rounded	ɔ̹	ʷ	Labialized	tʷ dʷ	̃	Nasalized	ẽ
̜	Less rounded	ɔ̜	ʲ	Palatalized	tʲ dʲ	ⁿ	Nasal release	dⁿ
̟	Advanced	u̟	ˠ	Velarized	tˠ dˠ	ˡ	Lateral release	dˡ
̠	Retracted	e̠	ˤ	Pharyngealized	tˤ dˤ	̚	No audible release	d̚
̈	Centralized	ë	̴	Velarized or pharyngealized ɫ				
̽	Mid-centralized	e̽	̝	Raised	e̝ (ɹ̝ = voiced alveolar fricative)			
̩	Syllabic	n̩	̞	Lowered	e̞ (β̞ = voiced bilabial approximant)			
̯	Non-syllabic	e̯	̘	Advanced Tongue Root	e̘			
˞	Rhoticity	ə˞ a˞	̙	Retracted Tongue Root	e̙			

SUPRASEGMENTALS

ˈ	Primary stress	
ˌ	Secondary stress	ˌfoʊnəˈtɪʃən
ː	Long	eː
ˑ	Half-long	eˑ
̆	Extra-short	ĕ
|	Minor (foot) group	
‖	Major (intonation) group	
.	Syllable break	ɹi.ækt
‿	Linking (absence of a break)	

TONES AND WORD ACCENTS

LEVEL			CONTOUR		
e̋ or	˥	Extra high	ě or	˩˥	Rising
é	˦	High	ê	˥˩	Falling
ē	˧	Mid	e᷄	˦˥	High rising
è	˨	Low	e᷅	˩˨	Low rising
ȅ	˩	Extra low	e᷈	˧˦˧	Rising-falling
ꜜ		Downstep	↗		Global rise
ꜛ		Upstep	↘		Global fall

Courtesy: International Phonetic Association, http://web.uvic.ca/ling/

Appendix II
Glossary

active. a grammatical category (active voice) of the verb and by extension the sentence in which the semantic role of actor is expressed as the grammatical subject. Sentences that are active are usually considered to express the fundamental or primary situation and those that are passive are often regarded as derived from them; see **passive**.

actor. the semantic (pragmatic) role of a term in a proposition or sentence usually expressed through the grammatical subject; a common synonym is agent; see **goal**.

adjective. a word that expresses a state or quality; *ex.* blue, tall, happy.

adverb. a word that expresses a state or condition (time, manner, place) of the action of a verb or adjective. *ex.* fast, later, roughly, here.

affective meaning. meaning that is related to or affects an emotional response; *ex. policeman* vs. *cop* vs. *pig* (the term *policeman* has the least affective meaning).

agent. syn. of actor.

alliteration. repetition of the same initial consonant in succeeding words; *ex.* wild and wooly.

animacy. refers to whether the referent of a noun is a living thing or not; this category often excludes plants, and most usually includes animals.

anthropological linguistics. the practice of linguistics (description of the structure of a language, how language changes over time, etc.) but with some reference to cultural concerns; cf. **linguistic anthropology**.

anthropology. the study of humankind across all time and all space; the systematic study of the human species, seen from the perspective of culture rather than society.

antirationalism. not an irrational stance, but the philosophical position that there is no objective reality and that systematic inquiry such as science is limited in scope.

antithesis. an opposing idea, often the direct opposite of an initial idea; see **thesis**, **synthesis**.

arbitrary. the position that the form of a word has no connection with what it means; an important exception is onomatopoeia.

areal linguistics. the study of how languages from different families in the same geographic area come to be similar through mutual contact; see **language family.**

articulator. the active part of the vocal tract, such as the tongue, that constricts the column of air against the point of articulation to form a speech sound.

articulatory phonetics. study and classification of speech sounds based on the point of articulation and the manner of articulation of each.

aspect. with verbs, a grammatical category that indicates the relative manner of the action such as completed, ongoing, momentary, etc., as opposed to the relative time at which the action takes place (tense); compare (English): is *reading a book* to *reads a book* / was *reading a book* with *read a book*.

autochthony. considerd as having earthy not celestial origin; *ex.* the symbolic value of snakes vs. birds..

autonomous. the notion that an entity is self-contained and nonreferential to other related systems for its operation.

autonomous linguistics. the position that a natural language, with the obvious exception of the lexicon, is relatively self-contained and not related to culture or society.

autonomous syntax. only reflecting reality, not actually linked to it.

back. an articulatory feature used in the classification of speech sounds; sounds generally are considered back if they are articulated on or behind the hard palate; *ex.* [k], [g], [h], [o], [u].

base (component). a rule set (component) in early generative grammatical theory that defined phrase and sentence structure.

basic color category. the range of color in the visible spectrum labeled by a basic color term.

basic color term. one of the color names in a language that in general are (1) a single lexeme (not *hot pink*), (2) not a metaphor (not *plum*), and not a borrowed word (not *ecru*).

basic term. a word in a language referring to a fundamental thing or concept that is typically monomorphemic, not a metaphor and not a loan word, that names a primary category in a domain; see **key term**, **generic term**, **specific term**.

binary features. features that differentiate by their presence or absence only and do not allow for scalar representations.

binary oppositions. the presence or absence of traits, used to define or differentiate categories or words; *ex.* using [+ fruit] or [- fruit] as a way of distinguishing produce.

blurb. a short prose composition designed to inform, advertise and entice a reader in a product (or larger piece of prose).

canonization. creating style(s) and/or genre(s) that reflect a single ideology; see **political economy**.

case. a grammatical category that relates a noun to a verb or another noun such as subject, direct object, indirect object or possessor; *ex. I* vs. *me* vs. *my*.

categories. the fundamental elements of a system of linguistic or cultural meaning.

categorization. the process by which reality, especially particular linguistic and sociocultural domains, is organized according to native ideas and folk theories as opposed to classification.

causer. the grammatical role of the actor that in a transitive construction causes some action or event.

central. in articulatory phonetics, a feature of some speech sounds, especially of some vowels, that they are articulated near the center of the mouth on a dimension of front to back.

centrifugal. moving away from a center; in Bakhtin's discourse analysis, any factors promoting variety in public discourse creating heteroglossia.

centripetal. moving toward a center or axis; in Bakhtin's discourse analysis, the trend toward canonization resulting from discourse practices and genres of the elite in the political economy of linguistic practice.

chaotic reality. the view that the physical reality of the world is overwhelming in its detail and variety so as to defy categorization or classification; see **reality**.

classification. arrangement of elements or entities in a domain according to a set of externally motivated criteria; *ex.* the International Phonetic Alphabet is a system for classifying speech sounds according to the feature of the mouth and vocal tract.

clause. a verb and nouns, other clauses, or adverbs associated with it; *ex.* the duck ate, the duck at the bread, the duck wants to eat the bread, the duck ate the bread noisily.

closure. in articulatory phonetics, pertains to the complete blocking of the movement of the column of air by an articulator against a point of articulation.

code. 1. a system for conveying message(s). 2. the use of such a system to express things in or out of context, but outside the language system being used.

code-switching. alternation between two or more codes (typically different languages or dialects) in the same communicative event; usually the shift is dictated by context or topic.

co-extensive semantics. situation in which the same category has more than one lexicalization.

co-extensivity. the occurrence of at least one category focus within the range of another category; see **near-synonymy**.

cognate. a word in two or more related languages that have the same root from the ancestral language; *ex.* English *three* and Spanish *tres* are cognates, while *three* and German *drei* are closer cognates.

cognate set. a set of cognates from different members of a language family that have the same root word or morpheme.

cognitive anthropology. the outgrowth of ethnographic semantics; an approach to language and culture studies seeking to produce cultural grammars that have formal elegance and economy of explanation, eventually taking context as a factor to be considered in analysis.

collocation. the arrangement of words in a phrase in a conventional order; *ex.* black and blue, not *blue and black.

communication. the transfer of information through a message; this implies a system of meanings and a medium for sending meaning.

communicative competence. the linguistic and sociocultural knowledge needed to use a language appropriately in all social situations.

communitas. the ideal of a society or smaller social group as uniform and the feeling of solidarity within a community fostered by such an image as well as participation in important cultural rituals.

communities of practice. social groups having common linguistic and/or cultural practices.

comparative linguistics. the study of elements and processes in several languages, especially in a group of genetically related languages.

comparative method. the systematic study of similarities, such as between those related languages of a language family or other comparable systems.

competence. the linguistic knowledge of an idealized speaker-hearer, as opposed to the use of such knowledge in an actual situation (performance); cf. **langue**.

component. a rule set within early generative grammar; *ex.* base component, phonological component, transformational component.

componential analysis. the use of binary features in a feature matrix to model the semantic or phonetic differences between words or other lexemes.

compound term. a term made of two or more parts; *ex.* dining room chair.

compound word. a compound word is made up of two free-standing words, as opposed to morphemes which must be bound (see **derivation**); *ex. doghouse* is a compound word, but not the nonsense forms *dogify* or *undogly*.

confidence factor. a judgment, usually of the expert(s), as to the likelihood of a rule's firing in an expert system.

connotation. the aspects of the meaning of a lexeme that are associated with it, especially emotional aspects, rather than its literal, central meaning; *ex.* in *that sly old dog*, the connotative meaning of *dog* is clearly shown.

consensus theory. the averaging of opinions of natives as to what a cultural category, domain, or even a whole culture is, creating a model or statement that is a consensus.

consonant. a speech sound made by partial or complete constriction of the flow of air in the vocal tract, as opposed to a vowel.

constraint. a condition that restricts use of a rule or morpheme; *ex.* English *not* is constrained if there is another negative word in the same clause: *the televisions do not work* is okay, but not **none of the televisions don't work*.

context. the environment, linguistic as well as sociocultural, in which communicative events take place and from which they may derive part of their meaning.

context sensitive. any use of a word or expression that is tied to particular context(s); a good example are the "four-letter words" of colloquial English which are quite natural to many speakers, but not in all contexts.

continuum (pl. continua). a coherent whole made up of a progression of elements or values ordered by their relation to two extremes; *ex.* the range of meaning between two polar opposites such as *good* and *bad*.

conversational analysis. the discourse analysis of conversation, especially with reference to turn-taking, structuring the information, and showing degrees of politeness and degrees of solidarity.

counterfactuals. linguistic devices or constructions that indicate hypothetical events or events contrary to fact; *ex.* were I to go, I'd need a couple of days.

covert. unnamed, especially when speaking of categories that are logically possible within a system or domain, but not named with a single word; *ex.* there is no specific word for heterosexual couples who deliberately choose not to have children.

critical species. plant or animal species that define a discrete geographic area in which a proto-language might have been spoken.

cultural. pertaining to a specific culture, or to the study of cultures in general.

cultural anthropology. the branch of anthropology that deals with culture, as opposed to archaeology (which studies the material remains of past cultures) and physical anthropology (which relates how culture interacts with human biology); cultural anthropology is close to linguistic anthropology, but lacks the pervading concern about languages that guides the latter.

cultural grammar. a set of rules, array, design or other device made to predict normative, native-like behavior; theoretically, this may refer to the whole of a culture, but in practice is limited to modeling particular domains within a culture.

cultural meaning. meaning of a communicative event derivable largely from culture and cultural context.

cultural relativism. see **cultural relativity**.

cultural relativity. the view or degree of how cultures are independent of each other in content, giving rise to the philosophical position that all cultures are equivalent and have equally valid ways of seeing reality.

cultural schemata. conventional plans for understanding or for meaning creation that are appropriate for a culture.

culture. sets of beliefs, knowledge, and worldview which guide behavior creating a group life-style that may be transmitted to succeeding generations.

culture history. the ideographic background and development of a language, language family, or culture.

decenter. to remove from universal relevancy.

deconstruction. production of a counterargument (antithesis) by pondering what assumptions an argument, idea, or thesis has left unstated and unacknowledged.

deep. refers to knowledge, as opposed to actual speech or behavior, which is, by metaphor, surface.

deep structure. implicit knowledge of a language or other cultural domain shown by actual performance (and inferred from it).

deictic. Greek for 'pointer'; a grammatical category of this type refers to something outside language itself in the speech context; *syn.* shifter; examples include pronouns, tense, and modals.

deixis. the phenomenon or study of deictics.

denotation. the literal meaning of a lexeme, which refers directly to something in the physical or sociocultural world; *ex. hog* is the denotation of *pig*; see **connotation**.

deontic modal. a modal referring to obligation and permission, as opposed to epistemic modality; *ex. must* in the clause *you must buy it* or *may* in the clause *you may buy it*; by extension, the same modals *may* and *must* can express conditions that are asserted or implied to exist, in which case they are considered to be epistemic modals: *may* suggests the possibility of the condition(s) expressed by the clause to be true, and *must* guarantees the condition(s) to be true; *ex. you may be tired from all that swimming* as opposed to *you must be tired from all that swimming.*

derivation. 1. the part of morphology that creates new words from other words; derivational morphemes are the commonest way this is done; *ex.* the suffix *-ize* 'to actively make or do' derives verbs from nouns: *harmony* --> *harmonize*; *-ness* makes new nouns from adjectives: *kind* --> *kindness*; 2. a word created according to the process of derivation; *ex. kindness* (from *kind*); 3. a form (especially a word or morpheme) that is the historical product or descendent of an earlier form in the language; see **reflex**.

descriptive cultural relativism. according to Spiro (1986), a position grounded in a theory of cultural determinism; given that social and psychological characteristics are produced by a culture, then descriptive cultural relativism is a corollary to the fact that cultures vary.

determined. the quality of an utterance pertaining to the degree to which it can be understood apart from its context; *ex.* the sentence, *you've done a beautiful job* is somewhat determined, because it codes part of context in *beautiful*; see also **overdetermined** and **underdetermined**.

deterministic. the philosophical position that one thing absolutely causes or brings about another thing; *ex.* "The ideas named by the words of one's native language determine how one perceives and thinks about reality."

diachronic. pertaining to a language or other cultural tradition over time; cf. **synchronic.**

diachrony. the (pre)history of a language or other cultural tradition; the study of such trajectories.

dialect. a variety of a language, mutually intelligible with other varieties of that language; dialects are usually characteristic of geographic regions or social classes.

dialogic. 1. in the discourse analysis of Bakhtin, the fundamental assumption that discourse is structured in the give-and-take fashion of spoken or written conversation, whether this is reflected in the actual (surface) structure of a discourse; for example, a reader might use voices to analyze the implicit conversation (even if it is restricted to the authoritarian, expert voice and the reader's own passive voice; see **voice**. 2. philosophical idea that reality consists of contexts in which people interact.

dichotomy. a division into two opposites; this was used as a rhetorical device by Saussure, whose Saussurian dichotomies are fundamental theoretical ideas in twentieth century linguistics: *synchrony* vs. *diachrony; syntagmatic* vs. *paradigmatic; langue* vs. *parole* (very similar to Chomsky's *deep* vs. *surface, competence* vs. *performance*); and *signifier* vs. *signified*.

diphthong. a cluster of two vowels that function within a single syllable.

direct object. the grammatical category that expresses the actual or potential immediate affectee of the action specified by the verb; *ex.* the direct object in the clause, *the boy walked the dog*, is *dog* even though the subject (*boy*) is not actually moving the dog's legs.

discourse. linguistic and social events of communication, often identifiable by genre, that form the fundamental subject matter of much linguistic and ethnographic study.

discourse analysis. the study of how different kinds of discourse are structured and used in a culturally appropriate way.

domain. a related set of terms such as those for plants, animals, family members, colors, and the like; the focus and methodological convenience of studying smaller, definable portions of actual cultures has made the concept of domain a fundamental one in linguistic anthropology.

duality of patterning. the characteristic of language whereby units from the sound pattern are intertwined with units from the semantic pattern into one single stream of speech.

economy of explanation. see **formal elegance**.

-eme. a suffix meaning 'unit of analysis.'

emic. analysis that claims to represent the point of view of the native participants in a language or culture; this idea comes from theoretical units (phonemes, morphemes) that designate native categories.

empiricism. philosophical position which accepts both the independent existence of reality (positivism) and the practical possibility of discovering it.

epistemic modal. a modal that asserts or implies that the conditions specified by a clause are known or believed; for an example, see **deontic modal**.

epistemological cultural relativism. according to Spiro (1986), a strong form of cultural relativism that accepts the claim that all knowledge comes to the individual through culture.

epistemology. the branch of philosophy that questions how we know what we know and what is knowable.

erasure. 1. what a text omits (it is finite and cannot possibly be definitive). 2. an issue or fact deliberately left unsaid or not considered; *ex.* the failure of history textbooks to comment on Washington or Jefferson as slave owners, or the half-caste children fathered by Jefferson on his estate.

ethnographic discourse analysis. analysis of descriptive and behavioral texts from a start point of issues or metaphors that recur and are therefore assumed to be culturally important; the practice of discourse analysis which pays particular attention to context and discourse participants.

ethnographic semantics. the use of lexical semantics, especially componential analysis, to model cultural domains; more or less synonymous with ethnoscience.

ethnography. the systematic description of a culture or subculture, or a discrete part (domain) of one.

ethnography of communication. an approach to study of a language in which emphasis is given to the sociocultural contexts in which linguistic interaction takes place.

ethnography of speaking. see **ethnography of communication**.

ethnolinguistics. see **linguistic anthropology**.

ethnoscience. an approach to the study of cultural domains influenced by linguistic models; using chiefly lexical data, componential analysis is applied to make a cultural grammar of the domain.

etic. any systematic analysis that relies on categories, but is external to the language/culture under study; the categories of an etic system for analysis are ideally independent of specific cultures; examples include biological classification, the chemical elements, and the International Phonetic Alphabet; see **emic**.

evaluation section. in narratives of American or European origin, a section near the end of the story that emphasizes its worthiness as a story; *ex.* the lesson explicitly taught in a fable.

experiential. philosophical idea that reality is experienced rather than independent or secondhand.

expert system. a computer program designed to imitate expert judgment in a specific domain or set of knowledge.

expert system shell. a programming environment for the computer, which provides logical operators and reasoning strategies, into which a knowledge base may be added to produce an expert system.

extralinguistic. anything that accompanies the use of language, such as gestures or social distance; see **kinesics** and **proxemics**.

family resemblances. a set or grouping based upon resemblances, as in a family.

feature. any typical or noticeable property of a speech sound, morpheme, syntagm, or other linguistic or cultural unit, especially one(s) used to distinguish between units (speech sounds, morphemes, etc.) on the same level of analysis; features may be binary or multivalent, and are noted by the use of square brackets ([ ]); *ex.* [+/- feline].

feature matrix. a set of binary features specified plus or minus used to define or distinguish members of a domain.

flow chart. a chart that illustrates the steps used in making a decision or a procedure for doing a particular task.

focus. the best example of a category.

folk classification. classification of a domain according to general knowledge of common folk rather than according to some set of scientific principles.

folk theory. an analytic account of a linguistic or cultural phenomenon that is consistent with the native point of view, following from basic, stated cultural premises; a folk theory, however, may or may not be within native awareness.

folklore. 1. any emotive material (often a story, belief, song, or design) that is passed from person to person informally; *ex.* a joke or photocopy lore. 2. the study of folklore.

folktales. a tale or story told by word of mouth by the common folk; an oral story; a story handed down as part of the traditions of a group.

form. the actual shape or design of a linguistic or cultural category; opposed to function. There is usually no relationship between the actual pronunciation of a morpheme as a string of consonants and vowels and its meaning; *ex.* the English words *to*, *two*, and *too* have the same forms but different meanings.

formal elegance. the degree to which a rule or hypothesis can be stated in a math- or logic-like, formal representation; this is held to make expression exact (if it can't be formalized, it is not defined enough to be tested empirically).

frame. 1. a syntagmatic frame for language analysis, such as a frame sentence into which items may be substituted; *ex.* the grammatical category of tense in English may be attached to the verb, in a clause: in *the man walk-**ed** to town*, the suffix *-ed* marks the verb, and other words that could be substituted for *walk* would presumably be verbs, so *the man strutt**ed** to town* is okay; as in any analysis, there will be exceptional cases as in *the man catapult**ed** to town*. 2. a stored mental scenario which is a recipe for a given type of procedure; *ex.* introducing two people, ordering dinner in a fancy restaurant; see *script*. 3. an analytic orientation that follows from a philosophical position; *ex.* the postmodern frame in linguistic anthropology vs. the scientific frame interpretation in the same.

fricative. a kind of speech sound that involves constriction between the articulator and the point of articulation but not complete closure between them; *ex.* [s], [f]; see also **spirant**.

front. in articulatory phonetics, a feature of some speech sounds, especially of some vowels, that describes them as articulated near the front of the mouth on a dimension of front to back.

function(s). 1. the particular job(s) a linguistic or cultural category has to do; as opposed to form. 2. for folktales, "Stable, constant elements [events] in a tale, independent of how and by whom they are fulfilled" (Propp 1928 [1968:21]); *ex.* the fairy godmother in fairy tales is a function.

functional. 1. system(s) of knowledge seen from the point of view of their (interrelated) functions. 2. an analytic perspective or method which is based on the function(s) of each part of a system and the overall functioning of the system as a whole.

functional theory of grammar. a theory of grammar that has to do with deriving grammatical categories according to the behavior (function) of grammatical elements in actual language use, rather than the use of *a priori* grammatical categories for analysis of linguistic structure and behavior; the description of language's structure which takes context and discourse purpose into account.

functionalist. having to do with the analytic perspective or method based on the function(s) of each part of a system and the overall functioning of the system as a whole.

fuzziness. the belonging of a category to more than one domain because of overlap; lack of clear boundaries between categories.

fuzzy set. a domain or set of categories that lack clear boundaries and intersect.

generalization. after Vygotsky, a means of building concepts whereby an idea is placed within two continua, one representing objective content and the other acts of thought-apprehending content.

generative. an approach to stating how a language works and consisting of a set of rules which are explicitly stated and intended to produce all and only grammatical combinations of the language's elements.

generativism. of or pertaining to generative linguistic approaches in linguistics, and in other cultural studies that are influenced by generative grammar and theory.

generic term. a term that names things in general; it is necessarily semantically vague, and is monomorphemic; it may be grammatically unusual; *ex.* the word *tree* or *plant* would be used generically to categorize an oak tree, with the word *oak* being a basic term (having more semantic content), and a term like *live oak* being a specific term; see also **key term**.

genetic relation. different languages that closely resemble each other may stand in a familial relation to one another by virtue of their derivation from a common mother tongue; *ex.* Indo-European.

genre. a type of discourse distinguished by characteristic form and/or content; *ex.* a joke has a punch line; recipes begin by listing the ingredients in order of use and use a headline style for giving directions; letters and formal speeches begin with a salutation.

glossolalia. speaking in tongues, a phenomenon of a possessed participant in a religious exercise speaking in a language unknown to his or her fellow humans.

goal. the semantic (or pragmatic) role of a term in a proposition or sentence that is acted upon or receives the action of the verb, usually expressed as a grammatical direct object; see **direct object**.

grammar. a systematic description of a language, the linguistic equivalent of ethnography; such description may be of the standard variety of a language or a nonstandard variety or dialect.

grammatical. conforming to a specified description of a language; 1. acceptable to a native speaker. Ungrammatical instances are indicated by placing a star or asterisk (*) in front; questionable instances are indicated by a preceding question mark; *ex. the man pole-vaulted to town* is an "okay" English sentence (at least in terms of the form rather than the meaning), while **the man to town pole-vaulted* is not and ?*the man towned by pole-vault* is too odd to give a clear grammaticality judgment. 2. pertaining to the grammar.

grammatical category. the categories of a language that interrelate nouns, verbs, adjectives and adverbs in terms of their grammatical relations in expressions; examples include animacy, aspect, case, modals, number, and tense. cf. **lexical category**.

grammaticality. the condition of being grammatical.

habitus. customary modes of action, feeling, and interpretation that promote psychological comfort; see **practice theory**.

hedge. a linguistic qualifier indicating that something is a less than perfect example of or fit; *ex. sort of.*

Heisenberg uncertainty hypothesis/principle. a hypothesis of a famous physicist that holds that the act of observation inherently distorts what is observed.

helping verb. a verb that is used to indicate grammatical categories for a main verb; *ex.* use of *be* and *have* in English: *he is helping me this morning* vs. *he has helped me in the past.*

hermeneutics. concerned with careful readings of and explications of texts, including cultural texts.

heteroglossia. in the discourse analysis of Bakhtin, the multiplicity of voices in a text; *ex.* an epic novel depicting the fortunes of a family for over five centuries would have a high degree of heteroglossia, while a monologic novel about what happened to a single person during the course of a day, which is written in one voice would have little heteroglossia; *syn.* polyphony.

high. in articulatory phonetics, a feature of some speech sounds, especially of some vowels, that all share the property of being articulated with the tongue high in the mouth; see also **closure**.

historical linguistics. the study of the history and development of individual languages and of languages in general.
historiographic method. any method of systematic investigation that is organized around the historical development of a given institution, cultural practice, or intellectual movement, including attention to the background and cultural context of the main concepts or ideas.
homeland studies. the practice of using the reconstructed morphemes for critical species to pinpoint the geographic range in which a proto-language might have been spoken.
honorific. a word or morpheme that signals grammatically the relative status between speaker and addressee.
humanistic. an analytical stance centered on human interests and values, asking what the nature of humankind is.
hypothesis. a tentative assumption about a phenomenon for empirical testing.
icon. any sign that directly represents or imitates its referent; *ex.* a design of a single flame is an icon of 'fire', while the presence of smoke is an index of 'fire'.
ideographic. what is unique about a culture or language.
idiolect. the variety of a language spoken by one individual; there are as many idiolects of a language as there are living speakers.
idiom. a phrase that has a conventional meaning which is not apparent from its literal meaning; *ex.* it's raining cats and dogs.
image. an iconic relation used as a model of a category; *ex.* the words *by* and *to* must be understood to involve motion along a path which creates an image of actual locomotion.
imperative. the grammatical category expressing a command.
indeterminacy. the view that language is arbitrary, so meaning must be created or negotiated in context; removed from context, a text loses some of its total meaning.
index. a sign that signals association of some word or action with some other piece of knowledge; *ex.* a ring of the doorbell indexes the presence of a visitor.
indexical. meaning is tied to context, as with shifters, deictics, and modals.
indirect object. grammatical category that labels the actual or potential secondary affectee of the action specified by the verb; usually the indirect object is the noun that is the recipient of the noun that is coded as the direct object in a clause; *ex.* the indirect object in *Bill gave the book to Sam* is *Sam*, since it is *Sam* who receives *the book* which is the direct object of the verb *give*; see **direct object, object**.
indirection. a linguistic strategy of speaking that employs an indirect way of stating something; *ex.* would you mind closing the window? instead of, close the window!.

inflection. the use of morphemes that express grammatical categories to show how words are related grammatically to other words.

interjection. a grammatical category expressing emotion, also called exclamation; *ex.* English *oh!*, *drat!*, *zounds!* are examples of outdated interjections.

interpretivism. any method or theory relying on context as a factor in analysis and explanation; see **scientific**.

interpretivist. 1. a scholar who proceeds from the position of interpretivism. 2. an analysis that is guided by interpretivism.

intertext. the product of an analysis using the concept of intertextuality; an intermediate form to which various versions of a text may be related.

intertextuality. the association of related texts, pointed up when their relations are shown in a formal model.

intonational. the quality of the pitch contour or melody of an utterance; compare *please sit down!* with *sit down, turkey!* noting that even though they both have imperative intonation, they are still slightly different.

key terms. words or phrases that are repeated in context because they are important to the topic being pursued or the genre being performed and thus a source of data for analysis; key terms are either basic or specific (rarely generic).

key words. words in conversation that signal the primary topic or domain under discussion.

language. 1. the capacity for human communication, typically by speaking, but also by writing or other recording. 2. the combining of a sound pattern with a meaning pattern for such communication; see **duality of patterning, langue**. 3. any actual system of natural language; *ex.* English, French, Spanish, German, etc. 4. by extension, any systematic way of using signs for communication that is not a natural language or a representation of one.

kinesics. the study of gestures, especially how they relate to language and communication.

language and culture studies. the branch of linguistic anthropology that investigates the relationship of language and culture through studies in categories and semiotics.

language family. a group of related languages that came from a single, common ancestor, which often must be reconstructed through the use of cognate sets with their systematic correspondences and inherited irregularities.

language games. see **word games**.

langue. the linguistic system shared by speakers as deep knowledge; opposed to actual language use (parole).

level. hierarchical organization of a language's sound pattern and semantic pattern; *ex.* in phonology there is the phoneme level, the syllable level, the level of the phonological word, and the intonation level.

lexeme. a vocabulary item, typically a word; see **collocation**, **compound**, **derivation**, **idiom**, **root**.

lexical category. one of the categories of a language that define and distinguish the vocabulary items of that language; cf. **grammatical category**.

lexical domain. a group of lexemes that have similar meanings and pertain to a semantically related set of terms; *ex.* the domain of kin terms.

lexical gap. a possible word (from the point of view of the sound pattern) but which is not actually a word in the lexicon; *ex.* the sound combination *glarf* sounds like an English word, but isn't.

lexical semantics. the meaning system of the vocabulary (lexemes) of a language and the study of these phenomena.

lexical universals. universals of the lexicon or vocabulary; *ex.* every language has a lexeme for 'sun' and 'moon.'

lexicon. the vocabulary of a language (see **lexeme**), or of a domain; *syn.* vocabulary.

linear structuralism. a semiotic (structural) system that is organized in linear fashion; spoken language is an example of a linear structuralism; see **nonlinear structuralism**.

linguistic. pertaining to language in general, a specific language, or the study of languages.

linguistic action verb. a verb for which the act of saying it is itself a performance or example of the action named by the verb; *ex.* promise, declare, command.

linguistic anthropology. the pursuit of anthropology using linguistic data as the primary source of information, consisting of language and culture studies, sociolinguistics, paralinguistics, discourse analysis, origin of language, and historical linguistics; syn. ethnolinguistics. Sometimes distinguished from anthropological linguistics.

linguistic category. fundamental units of a linguistic system; may be a lexical category (pertaining to the vocabulary or lexicon) or grammatical category (pertaining to the relations of nouns, verbs, adjectives, adverbs, and so on, in expressions, or to the part of speech identities of words).

linguistic determinism. the doctrine that a language, because of its idiosyncratic lexicon (and possibly grammatical categories), determines how a native speaker of the language perceives reality and thinks.

linguistic discourse analysis. analysis of texts proceeding from an identification of linguistic markers (such as indications of pauses), of topics, and of reference that structure the flow and focus of information.

linguistic ideology. a culturally recognized way of using language; *ex.* the lack of some function words and inflection is appropriate (and obligatory) in several contexts of English usage, among them recipes, headlines, telegraphs, and even coded messages sent by code.

linguistic meaning. the meaning of a communicative event derivable largely from language.

linguistic metaphorist tradition. a tradition of study in language and culture by which analysis is less concerned with individual languages or cultures and more interested in semiotics and linguistic relativity; see **neo-Boasian**.

linguistic particularism. the doctrine that each language can only really be understood on its own terms, that it is unique in its way of coding and considering chaotic reality; linguistic particularism is the basis of linguistic relativity.

linguistic relativism. see **linguistic relativity**.

linguistic relativity. the idea that the grammatical and lexical categories of a language can influence one's perception and thinking; *syn.* Whorfian hypothesis.

linguistic repertory. the language(s) and/or dialects used within a particular speech community; *ex.* the possible use of Standard American English and African American Vernaculer English by blacks in appropriate contexts.

linguistic universals. properties of form or content that are the same across all languages.

linguistics. the systematic study of human language(s), often pursued from an autonomous point of view; see **linguistic anthropology**.

loaded term. a lexeme, the literal meaning of which is subordinate to connotations and/or assumptions tied to the word or expression.

loanwords. words borrowed from one language to another.

logocentrism. the view of myth in Western culture that language is an absolute, a kind of ultimate truth.

long-distance relations. in historical linguistics, the grouping of language families into larger genetic groupings such as phyla and even families of phyla.

low. in articulatory phonetics, a feature of some speech sounds, especially of some vowels, that all share the property of being articulated with the tongue in a low position in the mouth; see **open**.

manner of articulation. the means by which a speech sound is produced; *ex. voicing* vs. *nonvoicing*, *closure* vs. *nonclosure of the airstream*, and so on.

mass inspection. looking at the words of many languages to find a limited set of similar lexical items to generate hypotheses about long-distance relations.

meaning. 1. broadly speaking, anything intended to be communicated by some conventional means such as a semiotic system like a language. 2. more narrowly, the entity, quality, action, or relationship inferred by a sign. 3. by extension, the intellectual and/or emotional impact of experience on an individual or group of persons.

mediate. a factor or feature that connects two elements in a model, especially seeming contradictions.

medium. the form a message takes; *ex.* language may be expressed through spoken, written, or gestured means.

meta-. more comprehensive, transcending, of greater scope.

metaphor. 1. figurative language in which one thing is likened to another (A is like B; *ex.* new love is (like) a fresh, red rose) or in which one thing is substituted for another (*ex.* drowning in money). 2. broadly speaking, any figurative use of language.

method. in the social sciences and humanities, the general means of pursuing systematic study: comparative method, historiographic method, structuralism, and collocational method.

metonym. figurative language in which one thing is used in association with another thing (*ex. their right hand man* or *Sage and Sand* as a name for a motel located in a desert area), or in which one thing names an attribute of another (in *their plan was put on the back burner*, a stove's burner is used to suggest an intellectual gulag into which plans may be consigned to languish).

mid. in articulatory phonetics, a feature of some speech sounds, especially of some vowels, that all share the property of being articulated with the tongue in a mid position in the mouth so they are neither high nor low.

minimal pairs. two linguistic forms which are identical except for one segment or feature and therefore have two different meanings or functions; minimal pairs are typical in phonology as a test for phoneme status (*ex. Tish* and *dish* are identical except for the initial consonant), but which may extend to different levels: compare *the man walks to town* with *the man walked to town*.

modal. a grammatical category expressing probability, likelihood, veracity, intent, and desire; *ex.* In English, some modals are adverbs (*perhaps*, *probably*, *evidently*) and others are helping verbs (*may*, *can*, *must*, etc.).

model. any deliberate representation of a system to explain its structure or function.

modifier. anything that acts to modify the meaning of another entity or sign, but which does not change its basic meaning; *ex.* compare *book* with *Chairman Mao's little red book* which has three modifiers; in models, modifiers may be used like features to differentiate or point up a particular element or part of the model.

monologic. a characteristic of a text that has only one voice; *ex.* the performance of a stand-up comic.

monomorphemic. a lexeme or term that consists of a single morpheme.

morpheme. the smallest unit of meaning; *ex.* the English word *elephant* consists of a single morpheme, while the word *undeniable* contains three.

morphology. 1. the study of the way the morphemes of a language are arranged to make up words. 2. the study of word structure in human languages in general.

morphosyntax. the view that the inflectional morphology and syntax of a language form a larger, more comprehensive system.

multiperspective. pointing to or selecting different points along a continuum from a variety of vantages; see **polyperspective**.

multiple pathways theory. view of culture as a whole, derived from a variety of opinions, which accommodates different views of culture; *ex.* consider jazz musicians; each musician has his or her own individual style and ideally plays each piece differently each time because he or she improvises, yet there is a common set of cultural values and practices that define jazz; see **consensus theory**.

mutual intelligibility. the criterion of whether speakers of one linguistic variety can understand speakers of another variety: if both sets of speakers can understand each other, they may be considered to be speakers of dialects of a single language; this may be constrained by political considerations (*ex.* Swedish and Norwegian are mutually intelligible, but considered separate languages because they are spoken in two different countries.

myth. a belief or set of beliefs expressed in a story; *ex.* myths are about the creation of the world and humankind's place in it; the term may be extended to include any statement or story that expresses fundamental cultural values or beliefs.

mytheme. a part of a myth that is of fundamental importance (i.e., the myth would not be complete without it); *ex.* the beanstalk in *Jack and the Beanstalk*.

naive thinking. thinking that is not self-reflective, but rather spontaneous, natural, and unmonitored by the speaker.

nasality. in articulatory phonetics, indicates the passage of air through the nasal passages; sounds such as [m] and [n] are characterized by the feature nasality.

native knowledge. the deep, intuitive knowledge of a linguistic or cultural system (its langue) represented by a grammar or cultural grammar, and evidenced from actual behavior (parole).

near synonymy. in color studies, categories having overlapping ranges but separate foci in their respective range; see **co-extensivity**.

near-universals. generalizations about language or culture that are true of almost all languages/cultures, but which have exceptions; near universals are statistical statements; *ex.* nearly all languages have a formal distinction between nouns and verbs, but in Chinese and many other Pacific and Asian languages, this is not a valid statement; see **universals**.

neo-Boasian traditions. approaches to linguistic anthropology that involve concerns that fall well within the traditional goals of the program of investigation conceptualized by Franz Boas, the father of American anthropology.

New Ethnography (the). *syn.* ethnoscience, ethnographic semantics.

nominal style. the use of nouns, especially from Latin or Greek, to create a static, serious, "scientific" style; see **verbal style**.

nomothetic. pertaining to abstract, general, or universal generalizations; admitting law-like statements; see **ideographic**.

nonlinear structuralism. 1. any simultaneous array or display or use of signs; *ex.* in American Sign Language, two or even three signs may be used all at once, creating the effect of a simultaneous clause. 2. a sign system which favors such an arrangement or which must operate in this way; *ex.* a Christmas tree, where each decorative element contributes to the total effect.

norm. 1. an average or median. 2. by extension, what a person(s) is likely to do in a given context; the proper or appropriate behavior for a given context.

normative. pertaining to a norm.

normative cultural relativism. according to Spiro (1986), this represents a position that one cannot make value judgments about the merits of individual cultures because all standards are culturally constituted.

noun. a substantive; a word used to designate a creature or thing, real or imaginary (city, man, theory).

number. the category that marks quantity, typically of entities (nouns) or referents; *ex.* English has singular and plural: the *boy eat***s** *cake* vs. *the boy***s** *eat cake*.

object. the grammatical category that expresses the primary or secondary, actual or potential affectee of the action specified by the verb; cf. **direct object** and **indirect object**.

onomatopoeia. words or utterances that supposedly imitate the sound of their referent; *ex. babble*, *hiss*, *buzz*, and *bow-wow*; sometimes onomatopoeia is involved with rhyme (*ex.* "double, double, toil and trouble/fire burn, and cauldron bubble").

ontological. related to being or existence.

open. in articulatory phonetics, indicates lack of interruption in the air column; opposite of closure.

otherness. the emotive and intellectual feeling of being separate from another language or culture; see **native knowledge**.

overdetermined. the quality of an utterance or sentence that is easily understood without any context; *ex.* the sentence, *Cats purr*, is overdetermined since it requires little or no context for interpretation.

overt. a category named by a word or expression in a language or domain; *ex.* the English word *parents* identifies a set of biological and/or sociological partners in producing and rearing children.

paradigm. 1. a substitution set in which one item may be substituted for another; *ex.* in English verb morphology, the grammatical category of tense is added as a suffix, and only one suffix may be used at a time: *walk*, *walk*-**s**, *walk*-**ing**, *walk*-**ed**. 2. by extension, any substitution set in a semiotic system; *ex. soup* or *salad* precedes the main course in a formal dinner. 3. reigning academic project, or dominant theoretical formulation.

paradigmatic. pertaining to a substitution set of a linguistic or cultural paradigm that occurs as part of a syntagm.

paralanguage. aspects of speaking not directly part of a language, such as voice quality.

paralinguistic. 1. having to do with the study of paralanguage. 2. more broadly, related to the study of communication systems that accompany language use: paralanguage, kinesics, proxemics.

parole. 1. actual instances or examples of language use, as opposed to knowledge of how to use a language (grammar, lexicon, sound pattern); *syn.* speech, performance. 2. an instance of use of linguistic competence. 3. the occurrence of a conventional event, especially one framed according to a particular genre; see **performance**, **speech**.

particularism. the ideographic position that each language and/or culture must be understood in terms of itself.

passive. a grammatical category of the verb (passive voice) and by extension the sentence, in which the goal becomes the grammatical subject and the actor an oblique object; cf. **active**; *ex. The ants raided the picnic* is active; the passive equivalent is *The picinic was raided by ants.*

performance. an actual use of occurrence of language (and by extension culture); *syn.* parole.

performance theory. an approach to the analysis of culture that is text and genre based and grounded in folklore, in which a particular performance is considered a cultural expression.

person. the grammatical category that labels participants in a context of language usage or referents not present: first person includes the speaker(s) ('I', 'we'); second person identifies the hearer(s) ('you'); third person codes nonparticipants in the speech events ('s/he', 'it', 'they').

phenomenology. a philosophical position that sees human beings as being meaning-creating and that values especially their subjectivity in the process of creating meaning; accepts that social and cultural phenomena are the products of the consciousness of interacting individuals.

phonaestheme. a sequence of sound smaller than a syllable which may be assigned a vague denotative meaning, but which also has connotative meaning as well; *ex.* the *bl-* in *blat*, *blech*, *bleet*, and *blah* indicates making an irritating, high pitched sound and suggests nausea, while the *bl-* in *blaring* and *bleary* has a nonvocalizing denotation that suggests indistinct or *blurred* visual or aural outlines.

phone. a speech sound.

phoneme. a fundamental unit of sound (in the sound pattern), each natural language having a set of phonemes which are assumed to have psychological reality for speakers of the language; *ex.* English */I/* and */a/* as in */tit/* vs. */tat/*; cf. **minimal pair**.

phonemics. the study of the phonemes of a particular language.

phonetics. the study of the production of speech sounds, including means of recording and representing them.

phonological. pertaining to phonology.

phonology. 1. the study of the sound pattern of a particular language. 2. the study of sound patterns in general. 3. the sound system of a language; *ex.* the phonology of Urdu.

phrase. a grouping of words.

phyla (sing. phylum). language families grouped into a larger genetic group believed to have come from a single, remote linguistic ancestor; see **long-distance relations**.

plural. the grammatical category indicating more than one entity or referent; see **number**.

point of articulation. the place in the vocal tract against which or forward toward which the articulator moves in the production of a speech sound; the target of the articulation.

politeness. the degree to which difference is shown, or to which appropriate cultural norms are observed; clearly an important factor in conversations, it can be extended for analysis in discourse analysis in general; *ex.* the word *nigger* is not appropriate in most conversational or written contexts, as its use would violate accepted norms of language use in most networks of educated English speakers; see **solidarity**.

political economy. the ecology of power relations, especially with reference to language use; having to do with access to resources, and how they are used and controled, which is partly credited to being able to communicate in the appropriate discourses and contexts used/maintained by the controlling elite.

polyperspective. pointing out a single position on a continuum from different vantages; see **multiperspective**.

polyphony. *syn.* of heteroglossia.

polysemy. situation in which two or more distinct but related meanings are associated with a single lexeme; *ex.* bachelor.

positivism. philosophical position which accepts the independent existence of reality.

possessive. the grammatical category that shows ownership of an entity; *ex.* the word *my* is possessive, as is *-'s*.

postmodernism. broadly, the antirational movements that question the possibility of obtaining absolute truth through systematic study or empirical investigation, succeeding the paradigms of structuralism and generativism.

practice. following Bourdieu, a series of contexts with common themes and/or motivations; this implies genres, although Bourdieu preferred to think of culture in terms of strategies.

practice theory. a theory (of Bourdieu) that holds that culture is a series of games, each of which has strategies which, if mastered, serve to foster positive emotions (habitus); see **communitas**.

pragmatics. the study of meaning in context; the study of language usage (beyond the scope of literal meaning), including shifters and deitics.

pronoun. a deictic that codes the categories of person in a text or discourse.

proto-language. the model that is made of the ancestor of a language family by means of reconstruction using systematic correspondences.

prototype. original or archetypical, showing essential and defining traits; in language and culture studies, a set of traits, each of which is ranked as to the contribution of each to the overall goodness of fit of an example to the category.

proxemics. the phenomenon and study of social distance.

psychological reality. the idea that linguistic and cultural categories have a real existence in a person's mind.

puns. plays on words usually involving a rhyme.

reality. 1. the totality of real experience and events. 2. a selective filtering (via art, language, culture) of reality; see **chaotic reality**.

reconstruction. a model or hypothesis about an earlier linguistic or cultural form or system.

reductionism. 1. use of categories to reduce chaotic reality. 2. use of a theory or model to provide a simple yet hopefully comprehensive account of a phenomenon; use of a theory or model to efficiently account for a phenomenon; see **economy of explanation, formal elegance**.

reduplication. the doubling of a linguistic unit (phoneme, morpheme, etc.) to signal grammatical or lexical meaning.

referent. that which is labeled or referred to by a lexeme.

referential. referring to something else; see **sign**.

reflex. a linguistic form that is the direct descendent of an earlier one; *ex.* English and French *p* are both reflexes of Indo-European **p*: compare French *pere* with English *father*; reflexes are found in cognate sets.

relation. *syn.* relationship.

relationship. the association (or bond) holding between two elements, especially between two *signs* or *categories* in a structure; *syn.* relation.

relativism. the position that a generalization is only partly true, or true only to a degree; see **determinism**.

respelling. a deliberate nonstandard spelling of a word for emotive impact; *ex. shoppe* for a store that sells kitsch, *Kowboy Kountry Klub* for a cowboy bar, *kwik* for any commercial process that is efficient and thus saves the customer money or provides convenience.

ritual. 1. the enactment of a myth (in the cosmological sense). 2. any procedure that is repeated in the same way so as to create habitus.

role. 1. the function of someone or something in a given context. 2. the function or orientation of a speaker in a speech event or other cultural context.

root. a morpheme that refers to the world outside language; *ex.* the English words *dog* and *cat* are roots, but not prefixes like *un-* or suffixes like *-ing*.

rule. a formal account of a relationship between or among processes and forms, formulated as a general statement; *ex.* tense is marked in English by adding a suffix to the verb or helping verb in a clause; see **strategy**.

scene. *syn.* of frame (sense 2).

schema (pl. schemata). a design or array that models a domain or experience (as opposed to a procedural account of mental knowledge); cf. **frame, scene**.

scientific. pertaining to systematic inquiry to derive general statements about how the natural and social worlds behave through hypothesis formation and empirical testing.

script. the sense of frame as a procedural account of mental knowledge extended to the point of suggesting stored dialogue to be used in the activity; *ex.* not only does the stored procedure for greeting someone contain a sequence of actions prototypically done, but conventional strings of language as well; see also **schemata**.

script-frame. a type of schema that is concerned with procedures; a form of analysis used in cognitive anthropology.

semantic feature. a feature, usually binary, used as a means of modeling the distinguishing features of meaning of a lexeme, particularly those that set it off from other categories in the same domain; see **componential analysis**.

semantic pattern. the way of combining the lexemes of a language into a coherent message; see **morphosyntax**.

semantics. 1. the meaning pattern of a language or culture, usually considered from overt and covert categories. 2. the study of meaning from a linguistic or cultural point of view.

semiology. *syn.* of semiotics.

semiotics. 1. a system of sociocultural meaning, and a formal study of one. 2. extension of linguistic models to account for sociocultural meaning.

setting. the time and place in which a communicative event takes place.

shifter. *syn.* of deictic.

sign. the relation holding between the signifier and signified; signs are understandable and describable but the meaning attached to them is dynamic; see **icon**, **index**, and **symbol**.

sign system. a related set of signs that communicate similar messages; comparable to a domain or paradigm (sense 2); *ex.* a traffic light, the dance of honey bees, an entire language.

signified. the concept or meaning signaled by the signifier in a communicative event.

signifier. the elements (acoustic in the case of spoken language) that identify the signified.

singular. a grammatical category indicating a single entity or referent.

slips of the tongue. unwitting mistakes where parts of a syllable, word or phrase are produced out of order; *ex.* spoonerisms such as *sons of toil* for *tons of soil*, or *half-warmed fish* for *half-formed wish*.

slotmates. members of a substitution set in a paradigm; *ex.* *-s* and *-ed* are slotmates.

social. pertaining to society.

social contract. presumed agreement among individual persons of a society to define and limit the rights and duties of each member; see **role** and **status**.

society. an enduring and cooperative group of people with an established organization and conventional behavior patterns; see **social contract**.

sociolinguistics. systematic study of how sociocultural factors correlate with language use; *ex.* it could be easily shown that English speakers use *-in* for *-ing* in informal circumstances, while speakers of Scots (the closest relative of English) use it as the default since this form of the suffix is standard in their language.

sociology. the systematic study of society and subgroups within societies; traditionally, sociology has relied on statistics to define norms of social behavior.

solidarity. the degree to which participants in a communicative event feel comfortable with each other as members of the same culture or social group; *ex.* the word *nigger* which violates politeness in most situations may be used by some African Americans as a term that fosters solidarity in certain contexts; see **communitas** and **habitus**.

sound correspondences. the regular reflexes of sound change; *ex.* *p* corresponds to German *pf* as in the words *path* and *Pfad* and this correspondence is found throughout the lexicons of both languages in a systematic way.

sound pattern. the organization of speech sounds in a language, typically thought of as a set of phonemes drawn from the total set of speech sounds producible by humans, the means of organizing these into syllables, and the syllables into phonological words; intonation patterns are superimposed over utterances as the most complex level of the sound pattern; see **duality of patterning**.

sound symbolism. the use of sounds, including speech sounds and intonation as symbols; examples include onomatopoeia, phonaesthemes, interjections (especially negative ones such as *yuck*, *ouch*, and *shit*); sound symbolism may also be paralinguistic (*ex.* the tone of voice when angry as opposed to sad, or happy), and single sounds may have a symbolic value in a language (*ex.* the use of *th* (as in the word *thing*) as a substitute for *s* as the stereotypical marker of male homosexuals: *I can't thit for long, or I feel real thilly*).

sounds. see **speech sounds**.

species term. a term for a classificatory group of animals or plants that belong to a genus; a term that labels specific members under the *generic term* level.

specific term. a term that has more semantic detail than a generic or basic term, and is almost never monomorphemic.

speech. instances of verbal communication composed according to the system of language or langue.

speech act. doing a single, specific thing with language; *ex.* promises, commands, greetings, or threats as single events within a larger discourse that accomplish a single thing; speech acts may be seen as miniature genres and analyzed as frames or scenes.

speech community. a social group that shares a linguistic repertory which may be limited (*ex.* teenage slang is limited in the numbers of items in its lexicon) or quite extensive (*ex.* a bilingual village that code-switches according to the particular context).

speech event. a complete spoken discourse made up of a series of speech acts (*ex.* a conversation) made and shared by participants (possibly with shifting roles and voices) in a specific setting; a recorded speech event (a text) or a discourse that was originally written as a text may be analyzed as a speech event, but this is a theoretical/methodological matter for discourse analysis.

speech sounds. those sounds that are produced by the vocal tract and are involved in linguistic communication.

spirant. a kind of speech sound that involves constriction between the articulator and the point of articulation but not complete closure between them; *ex.* [s], [f]; see also **fricative**.

status. the relative rank or prestige of a person in a given context and/or society; see **role**.

stop. a kind of speech sound made by the complete closure of the air stream by the action of the articulator against the point of articulation; *ex.* [p], [t].

strategy. an alternative way of thinking about rules; instead of making law-like statements, a strategy shows the typical way of handling a given situation; a strategy is a scenario with interaction and emotional involvement, and genres and other cultural categories are thought of as games with participants interacting according to conventions (rules); *ex.* pre-planned ways of breaking up a fight or diffusing an argument could be described as a set of ordered rules, but might more profitably be seen as a plan or procedure for doing a particular task; see **speech act**, **practice theory**, **genre** and **frame** (sense 2).

structural method. analysis that shows how different paradigmatic sets may occur in different slots of a syntagm (conventional combination).

structuralism. 1. an analytic method which shows how the meaningful elements of a sign system are arranged into possible combinations. 2. a sign system that has elements that may be used in conventional combinations to create meaning.

structuralist. of or pertaining to structuralism as an analytic method and as a theory of human behavior.

structure. an arrangement of signs; *syn.* sign system.

style. 1. a distinctive manner of expression. 2. conforming to the conventions or requirements of a genre.

subject. prototypically, the actual or potential agent of an action (*ex.* the subject in *the boy walked to town* is *the boy*), but a subject may also be a purely grammatical category that is not the agent of the action (*ex.* the subject in *Suzi is sick with the flu bug* is not really an agent, nor is the subject in *the boy was bitten by a rabid skunk* an agent); see **object**, **clause**,

suffix. a morpheme that cannot stand alone and that attaches after the root of the word.

surface. refers to actual, observable and recordable behavior; see **parole, performance.**

surface deconstruction. a term or expression that explicitly directs the reader's or hearer's attention to assumptions and/or affective meanings that must usually be deconstructed for most lexical terms.

surface structure. the actual form of an utterance or sentence; for examples, see **transformation**.

syllable. a grouping of sounds into a phonological unit built around a vowel (or vowel cluster) with or without surrounding consonants.

symbol. a sign that has no formal resemblance to or connection with its referent; see **icon** and **index**.

synchronic. having to do with analysis of linguistic or cultural phenomena without consideration of its history or development; see **diachrony**.

synchrony. a linguistic or cultural system's state at any given point in time, usually the present; *ex. Old English* vs. *Middle English*.

synecdoche. use of part to symbolize a whole (*ex. two farm hands* for *workers*), a whole to symbolize a part (*ex. society* for *high society*), or the material a thing is made of for the item (*ex. tread the boards* for *walk on the stage as an actor*); this form of verbal symbolism is closely related to metonymy which uses associated things or attributes as symbols for a referent.

synonym. one of a set of words that share the same lexical meaning; *ex. chum* and *buddy*.

syntagm. a conventional combination of signs or morphemes; *ex.* the English syntagm for marking tense is *root* plus *suffix*, as in the combinations *walk-s* and *walk-ed*.

syntagmatic. relating to the linear or other arrangement of signs in a combination; see **paradigmatic**.

syntax. the organization of words into phrases, clauses, and sentences.

synthesis. putting together into a new whole, the final step of the process of analysis by using a thesis and antithesis.

systematic correspondences. regular correspondences shared by daughters of the same linguistic ancestor or proto-language; these may be sounds (see **sound correspondences**, **reflex**) or grammatical categories (*ex.* German *-te*, English *-ed*, and Scots *-it* are all past tense markers) or grammatical patterns (*ex.* German *sing/sang/gesungen* and Scots *sing/sang/sungit* correspond to English *sing/sang/sung*).

tautology. a repetition of the same term, idea, or argument; *ex. necessary essentials* is a tautology, especially when compared to *absolute essentials*.

taxonomy. the orderly classification of entities, especially plants and animals.

tense. the grammatical category marking relative time, usually present, past and future; *ex.* tense in English is expressed with suffixes and "helping verbs": is reading the book/reads the book, has read the the book, will read the book.

text. 1. any recorded discourse, especially one that is written; recorded discourses become artifacts, taking on a life of their own, being removed from an actual speech event. 2. the underpinnings of a discourse, a model of speaker turn taking, topic shift, etc.

theme. subject or topic of a discourse, especially one that is focused or distinctive; see **mytheme**.

thesis. 1. an initial hypothesis to be subjected to empirical tests and/or a counter idea (antithesis) to produce an expanded hypothesis (synthesis). 2. a position or proposal taken for the sake of debate on an issue.

time depth. in historical studies, the relative amount of time that has passed between the synchronic stage being studied and some time in the past.

time perspective. the trajectory or development of a particular linguistic or cultural trait (or whole language or culture) over a period of time; see **diachronic**.

transformation. an operation that changes input into a transformed output; *ex.* the sentence, *flying planes can be dangerous* as an output can have to different inputs: (a) *for someone to fly planes can be dangerous* and (b) *planes that are flying can be dangerous*; a transformation raising the object *planes* to be the subject of *be dangerous* accounts for (a), while a transformation raising the subject *planes* as the subject of *can be dangerous* accounts for (b).

transformational. of or pertaining to transformations or the grammatical theories employing them.

underdetermined. the quality of an utterance whose meaning is not clear from context; *ex.* the sentence, *I see that you've really done it now,* is underdetermined, because it refers to something that must be supplied by context.

underlying form. the sequence of phonemes or morphemes that make up a surface form, but which do not distinctly appear in the surface form; *ex.* the word *don't* has the underlying form *do not*; *dunno* is underlyingly *I don't know*.

universals. generalizations that are true for all languages or cultures; *ex.* all cultures and languages have some kind of kinship terminology; all cultures have some kind of music; see **law** and **near universals**.

validation section. the section of a story, usually near the end, that validates the story by emphasizing why it is worth telling (i.e., its story worthiness).

vantage. a perspective or viewpoint; used analytically, vantage suggests that there are different ways of looking at the same domain within a single culture (culture is not shared equally) and that this is the source of change; *ex.* candy seen from a child's point of view vs. that of an adult.

variation theory. a linguistic approach that accounts for variation in language by assigning probabilities of occurrence to rules corresponding to their actual occurrence in different contexts and in different dialects and styles.

verb. a word that expresses an action (*ex. run, sing, do*) or a state of being (*sleep, love*); in many languages, there is no formal distinction between verbs and adjectives.

verbal style. the use of more verbs than nouns in a discourse which creates a dynamic style less "serious" in tone than the nominal style.

vocabulary. *syn.* of lexicon.

vocal tract. the organs involved in the production of speech sounds, including the lips, mouth, pharynx, and glottis.

voice. in the discourse analysis of Bakhtin, the different viewpoints that are contained in a piece of writing and by extension speech event; *ex.* in a ghost story, there are the voices of the persons experiencing the ghost, the intrusive voice of the author or storyteller to provide the setting and mood, and, by implication, the voice of the ghost (even though s/he may not be actually heard speaking).

vowel. a speech sound that is characterized by openness of the vocal tract and lack of constriction of the air as it passes through; see **consonant**.

Whorf(ian) hypothesis. *syn.* of linguistic relativity.

word. a free-standing morpheme or group of morphemes with an independent meaning.

word games. the idea of Wittgenstein that a word's value and meaning comes from the way it is used, not its literal meaning; *ex.* what is the meaning of the word *good*?; see **context** and **interpretivism**.

worldview. the general perspective that an individual or culture has on the reality or chaotic reality; one's fundamental beliefs and essential values that derive from them.

Bibliography

Abercrombie, Thomas Alan. 1986. The Politics of Sacrifice: An Aymara Cosmology in Action. Unpublished Ph.D. Dissertation, Department of Anthropology, The University of Chicago.

Abu-Lughod, L. 1986. *Veiled Sentiments: Honor and Poetry in a Bedouin Society*. Berkeley and Los Angeles: University of California Press.

Agar, Michael. 1981. Whatever Happened to Ethnoscience: A Partial View. *Human Organization* 41:82–86.

Albert, Roy, and David Leedom Shaul. 1985. *A Concise Hopi and English Lexicon*. Amsterdam: John Benjamins.

Atran, Scott. 1990. *Cognitive Foundations of Natural History: Towards an Anthropology of Science*. Cambridge: Cambridge University Press.

Au, T. K. 1983. Chinese and English: Counterfactuals and the Sapir-Whorf Hypothesis Revisited. *Cognition* 15:155–87.

_____. 1984. Counterfactuals: In Reply to Alfred Bloom. *Cognition* 17:289–302.

Bachrach, Ira. 1983. How to Choose and Use and Trademark. *Nation's Business*, March, 1983: 71–72.

Bakhtin, Mikhail. 1981. *The Dialogic Imagination*. Austin: University of Texas Press.

_____. 1986. Speech Genres and Other Late Essays. Trans. by V. W. McGee, ed. by C. Emerson and M. Holquist. Austin: University of Texas Press.

Barthes, R. 1970. *Writing Degree Zero, and Elements of Semiology*. Trans. by Annette Lavers and Colin Smith. Boston: Beacon Press.

_____. 1972. *Mythologies*. Trans. by Annette Lavers. New York: Hill and Wang.

Basso, Keith H. 1967. Semantic Aspects of Linguistic Acculturation. *American Anthropologist* 69:471–77.

Basso, K. H., and H. Selby, eds. 1976. *Meaning in Anthropology*. Albuquerque: University of New Mexico Press.

Bastien, Joseph W. 1985. Quollahuaya-Andean Body Concepts: A Topographical-Hydrolic Model of Physiology. *American Anthropologist* 87:598–611.

Bastien, Joseph, W. 1987. *Healers of the Andes, Kallawaya Herbalists and Their Medicinal Plants*. Salt Lake City: University of Utah Press.

Bateman, R., I. Goddard, R. O'Grady, V. A. Funk, R. Mooi, W. J Kress and P. Cannell. 1990. Speaking of Forked Tongues: The Feasibility of Reconciling Human Phylogeny and the History of Language. *Current Anthropology* 31:1–24.

Bauman, Richard. 1977. *Verbal Art as Performance*. Prospect Heights, IL: Waveland Press, 1984.

_____ and Charles L. Briggs. 1990. Poetics and Performance as Critical Perspectives on Language and Social Life. *Annual Review of Anthropology* 19:59–88.

_____ and Pamela Rich. 1994. Informing Performance: Producing the *Coloquio* in Tierra Blanca. *Oral Traditions* 9(2): 255–80.

Beherns, Clifford A. 1986. Relationships between Shipibo and Western Soil Classification: Changes in Land Use Patterns with Cash Cropping. Paper presented to the Symposium on Ecology, Culture, and Development at the 85th Annual Meeting of the American Anthropological Association, Philadelphia.

_____. 1987. KAES: An Expert System for the Algebraic Analysis of Kinship Terminologies. Part I. Paper presented at the Symposium on Computers in Anthropology at the 86th Annual Meeting of the American Anthropological Association, Chicago.

Benfer, Robert A. 1989. Individual Differences in Rule-based Systems of Knowledge with Behavioral Implications. *Anthropology Quarterly* 62:69–81.

_____, Edward E. Brent, Jr., and Louanna Furbee. 1991. *Expert Systems*. Newbury Park, CA: Sage Publications.

_____ and Louanna Furbee. 1989. Knowledge Acquisition in the Peruvian Andes. *AI Expert* 4:22–29.

Berlin, Brent. 1972. Speculations on the Growth of Ethnobotanical Nomenclature. *Language in Society* 1:51–86.

_____. 1973. The Relation of Folk Systems to Biological Classification and Nomenclature. *Annual Review of Systematics and Ecology* 4:259–71.

_____. 1990. The Chicken and the Egg Revisited: Further Evidence for the Intellectualist Bases of Ethnobiological Classification. In D. A. Posey and William Leslie Overal, et al., eds., *Proceedings of the First International Congress of Ethnobiology*, 1:19–33. Belén, Brazil: Museu Paraense Emílio Goeldi.

Berlin, Brent, and Eloise Ann Berlin. 1975. Aguaruna Color Categories. *American Ethnologist* 2:661–87.

Berlin, Brent, D. C. Breedlove, and Peter Raven. 1968. Covert Categories and Folk Taxonomies. *American Anthropologist* 70:290–99.

_____. 1973. General Principles of Classification and Nomenclature in Folk Biology. *American Anthropologist* 75:214–42.

Berlin, Brent, and Paul Kay. 1969. *Basic Color Terms: Their Universality and Evolution*. Berkeley: University of California Press.

Berne, E. 1964. *Games People Play*. New York: Ballantine Books.

Bernstein, Basil. 1975. *Class, Codes and Control: Theoretical Studies Towards a Sociology of Language*. New York: Shocken.

Birdwhistle, R. L. 1952. *Introduction to Kinesics: An Annotation System for Analysis of Body Motion and Gesture*. Washington, DC: Foreign Service Institute.

Bloom, A. H. 1981. *The Linguistic Shaping of Thought: A Study in the Impact of Language on Thinking in China and the West*. Hillsdale, NJ: Erlbaum.

_____. 1984. Caution—the Words You Use May Affect What You Say: A Response to Au. *Cognition* 17:275–87.

Bloomfield, Leonard. 1933. *Language*. New York: Holt, Rinehart & Winston.

Blossom Hill Collection. 1995. [Blurb on wine bottle.] Madera, CA: Blossom Hill Collection.

Blount, Ben G., ed. 1995. *Language, Culture and Society: A Book of Readings*. 2d edition. Prospect Heights, IL: Waveland Press.

_____ and Paula Schwanenflugel. 1993. Cultural Bases of Folk Classificational Systems. In J. Altarriba, ed., *Cognition and Culture: A Cross-cultural Approach to Cognitive Psychology*, pp. 3–22. New York: Elsevier.

Boas, Franz. 1911. *Introduction to The Handbook of American Indians*. Bureau of American Ethnology, Bulletin 40. Part 1, pp. 1–83. Washington, DC: Smithsonian Institution. Reprint: University of Nebraska Press, 1966.

Bonvillain, Nancy. 1993. *Language, Culture, and Communication: The Meaning of Messages*. Englewood Cliffs, NJ: Prentice Hall.

Bornstein, M. H. 1973a. Color Vision and Color Naming: A Psychological Hypothesis of Cultural Difference. *Psychological Bulletin* 80:257–85.

_____. 1973b. The Psychophysiological Component of Cultural Difference in Color Naming and Illusion Susceptibility. *Behavior Science Notes* 8:41–101.

_____. 1975. The Influence of Visual Perception on Culture. *American Anthropologist* 77:774–98.

Boster, James S. 1986a. Exchange of Varieties and Information Between Aguaruna Cultivators. *American Anthropologist* 88:428–36.

_____. 1986b. Can Individuals Recapitulate the Evolutionary Development of Color Lexicons? *Ethnology* 15:61–74.

_____. 1987. Requiem for the Omniscient Informant: "There's Life in the Old Girl Yet." In Janet W. D. Dougherty, ed., *Directions in Cognitive Anthropology*, pp. 177–97. Urbana and Chicago: University of Illinois Press.

_____ and Roy D'Andrade. 1989. Human and Natural Sources of Cross-Cultural Agreement in Ornithological Classification. *American Anthropologist* 91:132–42.

Bourdieu, Pierre. 1962 [1958]. *The Algerians*. Trans. by C. M. Ross. Boston: Beacon Press.

_____. 1977. *Outline of a Theory of Practice*. Trans. by R. Nice. Cambridge, England: Cambridge University Press. (Original published in French in 1972.)

Bridgeman, P. W. 1929. *The Logic of Modern Physics*. New York: Macmillan.

Briggs, Charles L., and Richard Bauman. 1992. Genre, Intertextuality, and Social Power. *Journal of Linguistic Anthropology*:131–72.

Brown, Cecil H. 1977. Folk Botanical Life-forms: Their Universality and Growth. *American Anthropologist* 79:317–42.

_____. 1979. Folk Zoological Life-forms: Their Universality and Growth. *American Anthropologist* 81:791–817.

_____. 1984. *Language and Living Things: Uniformities in Folk Classification*. New Brunswick, NJ: Rutgers University Press.

Brown, Cecil H. 1992. British Names for American Birds. *Journal of Linguistic Anthropology* 2:30–50.

_____, John Kolar, Barbara J. Torrey, Tipawan Truong-Quang, and Phillip Volkman. 1976. Some General Principles of Biological and Non-Biological Folk Classification. *American Ethnologist* 3:73–85.

Brown, Penelope, and Stephen C. Levinson. 1978. Universals in Language Use: Politeness Phenomena. In E. Goody, ed., *Questions and Politeness: Strategies in Social Interaction*. Cambridge: Cambridge University Press, pp. 56–311.

Brown, Roger. 1956. Language and Categories. Appendix in J. S. Bruner, J. J. Goodnow, and G. A. Austin. *A Study of Thinking*, pp. 247–321. New York: John Wiley.

_____. 1976. Reference. *Cognition* 4:125–53.

_____ and A. Gilman. 1960. The Pronouns of Power and Solidarity. In T. Sebeok, ed., *Style in Language*, pp. 253–76. Cambridge, MA: MIT Press.

Bruner, J. S., J. Goodnow, and G. A. Austin. 1956. *A Study of Thinking*. New York: John Wiley.

Buechel, Eugene. 1970. *A Dictionary of the Teton Dakota Sioux Language*. Vermillion: University of South Dakota.

Burgess, D. W., Willett Kempton, and Robert MacLaury. 1983. Tarahumara Color Modifiers: Category Structure Presaging Evolutionary Change. *American Ethnologist* 10:133–49.

Burke, Kenneth. 1957. *The Philosophy of Literary Form*. New York: Vantage Books.

Burling, Robbins. 1964. Cognition and Componential Analysis: God's Truth or Hocus-Pocus? *American Anthropologist* 66:20–28.

Carroll, J. B., and J. B. Casagrande. 1958. The Function of Language Classifications in Behavior. In E. E. Maccoby, T. M. Newcomb, and W. L. Hartley, eds., *Readings in Social Psychology*, pp. 18–31. 3d edition. New York: Holt, Rinehart and Winston.

Casagrande, Joseph, and Kenneth Hale. 1967. Semantic Relationships in Papago Folk-Definitions. In Dell H. Hymes and William E. Bittle, eds., *Studies in Southwestern Ethnolinguistics: Meaning and History in the Languages of the American Southwest*, pp. 165–93. The Hague: Mouton.

Cassirer, Ernst. 1946. *Language and Myth*. Trans. by S. K. Langer. New York: Harper and Brothers.

Chafe, Wallace L. 1981. The Deployment of Consciousness in the Production of a Narrative. In W. L. Chafe, ed., *The Pear Stories*, pp. 9–50. Norwood, NJ: Ablex.

Chagnon, Napoleon A. 1976. Genealogy, Solidarity and Relatedness: Limits to Group Size and Patterns of Fissioning in an Expanding Population. *Yearbook of Physical Anthropology, 1975*. 19:95–110.

_____. 1992. *Yanomamö: The Last Days of Eden*. New York: Harcourt Brace Jovanovich.

Cheng, P. W. 1985. Pictures of Ghosts: A Critique of Alfred Bloom's *The Linguistic Shaping of Thought*. *American Anthropologist* 87:917–22.

Chomsky, Noam A. 1957. *Syntactic Structures*. The Hague: Mouton.

_____. 1965. *Aspects of the Theory of Syntax*. Cambridge: MIT Press.

_____. 1981. *Lectures on Government and Binding*. Dordrecht: Foris.

Chomsky, Noam A. 1982. *Concepts and Consequences of the Theory of Government and Binding*. Cambridge: MIT Press.

_____. 1986a. *Barriers*. Cambridge: MIT Press.

_____. 1986b. *Knowledge of Language: Its Nature, Origin, and Use*. New York: Praeger.

_____. 1995. Bare Phrase Structure. In G. Webelhuth, ed., *Government and Binding Theory and the Minimalist Program*, pp. 383–439. Oxford: Basil Blackwell.

Clifford, James, and George Marcus, eds. 1986. *Writing Culture: The Politics of Ethnography*. Berkeley: University of California Press.

Clyne, P. R., William F. Hanks, and Carol C. Hofbauer, eds. 1979. *The Elements: A Parasession on Linguistic Units and Levels*. Chicago: Chicago Linguistic Society.

Colby, B. N. 1973. A Partial Grammar of Eskimo Folktales. *American Anthropologist* 75:645–62.

_____. 1975. Cultural Grammars. *Science* 187:913–19.

_____. 1985. Toward an Encyclopedic Ethnography for Use in "Intelligent" Computer Programs. In J. W. D. Dougherty, ed., *Directions in Cognitive Anthropology*, pp. 269–90. Urbana and Chicago: University of Illinois Press.

Coleman, Linda, and Paul Kay. 1981. Prototype Semantics. *Language* 57:26–44.

Comrie, Bernard. 1981. *Language Universals and Linguistic Typology*. Chicago: University of Chicago Press.

Conklin, Harold C. 1955. Hanunoó Color Categories. *Southwestern Journal of Anthropology* 11:339–44.

_____. 1972. *Folk Classification*. New Haven: Yale University, Department of Anthropology.

Cooper, R. L., and B. Spolsky, eds. 1991. *The Influence of Language on Culture and Thought*. Berlin: Mouton de Gruyter.

Cowan, W., M. K. Foster and K. Koerner, eds. *New Perspectives in Language, Culture, and Personality*. Amsterdam and Philadelphia: John Benjamins.

Crocker, J. Christopher. 1977. The Social Function of Rhetorical Forms. In J. D. Sapir and J.C. Crocker, eds., *The Social Use of Metaphor*, pp. 33–66. Washington, DC: American Anthropological Association.

Culler, J. 1976. *Ferdinand de Saussure*. New York: Penguin.

_____. 1982. *On Deconstruction: Theory and Criticism after Structuralism*. Ithaca, New York: Cornell University Press.

_____. 1983. *Roland Barthes*. New York: Oxford University Press.

D'Andrade, Roy. 1990. Some Propositions about the Relations between Culture and Human Cognition. In J. W. Stigler, R. W. Shweder, and G. Herdt, eds., *Cultural Psychology: Essays on Comparative Human Development*, pp. 65–129. New York: Cambridge University Press.

Darnell, Regna. 1990. *Edward Sapir: Linguist, Anthropologist, Humanist*. Berkeley: University of California Press.

Deane, Paul D. 1988. Polysemy and Cognition. *Lingua* 75:325–61.

Derbyshire, Desmond C. 1985. *Hixkaryana and Linguistic Typology*. Dallas: Summer Institute of Linguistics.

_____ and G. K. Pullum. 1981. Object-Initial Languages. *International Journal of American Linguistics* 47:192–214.

Derrida, J. 1976. *Of Grammatology*. Trans by G. C. Spivak. Baltimore: Johns Hopkins Press.

DeValois, Russell L., Israel Abramov, and Gerald H. Jacobs. 1966. Analysis of Response Patterns of LGN Cells. *Journal of the Optical Society of America* 56:966–77.

____ and G. H. Jacobs. 1968. Primate Color Vision. *Science* 162:533–40.

Dixon, R. M. W. 1972. *The Dyirbal Language of North Queensland*. Cambridge, England: Cambridge University Press.

____. 1977. *A Grammar of Yidiny*. Cambridge, England: Cambridge University Press.

____. 1980. *The Languages of Australia*. Cambridge, England: Cambridge University Press.

____. 1984. *Searching for Aboriginal Languages: Memoirs of a Field Worker*. St. Lucia, London, New York: University of Queensland Press.

Dorian, Nancy. 1981. *Language Death: The Life Cycle of a Scottish Gaelic Dialect*. Philadelphia: University of Pennsylvania Press.

Dougherty, Janet W. D. 1975. A Universalist Analysis of Variation and Change in Color Semantics. Ph.D. Dissertation, University of California, Berkeley.

____. 1977. Color Categorization in West Futunese: Variability and Change. In B. Blount and M. Sanches, eds., *Sociocultural Dimensions of Language Change*, pp. 103–18. New York: Academic Press.

____, ed. 1985. *Directions in Cognitive Anthropology*. Urbana and Chicago: University of Illinois Press.

____ and C. M. Keller. 1982. Taskonomy: A Practical Approach to Knowledge Structures. In Janet W. D. Dougherty, E. Ohnuki-Tierney, J. W. Fernandez, and N. E. Whitten, special issue eds. *Symbolism and Cognition II. American Ethnologist*, 9:763–74.

Duranti, Alessandro, and Elinor Ochs. 1990. Genitive Constructions and Animacy in Samoan Discourse. *Studies in Language* 14:1–23.

Eastman, Carol M. 1979a. 'Culture-loaded' Vocabularies and Language Resurrection (Research Note). *Current Anthropology* 20:401–2.

____. 1979b. Language Reintroduction: Activity and Outcome Language Planning. *General Linguistics* 19(3): 99–111.

Eckert, Penelope, and Sally McConnell-Ginet. 1992. Think Practically and Look Locally: Language and Gender as Community-Based Practice. *Annual Review of Anthropology* 21:461–90.

Ellen, R. F. 1987. Review of *Language and Living Things* (New Brunswick, NJ: Rutgers University Press) by C. H. Brown. *Language in Society* 16:123–31.

Ellis, John M. 1989. *Against Deconstruction*. Princeton, NJ: Princeton University Press.

Emery, Olga B. 1985. *Language and Aging*. South Harbor, ME: Beech Hill Publishing.

Ervin-Tripp, Susan. 1967. In D. I. Slobin, ed., *A Field Manual for Cross-cultural Study of Communicative Competence*. Berkeley: Language-Behavior Research Laboratory, University of California, Berkeley.

Felperin, Howard. 1985. *Beyond Deconstruction*. Princeton: Princeton University Press.

Fisher, Mary J., Bernard Ewigman, James Campbell, Robert Benfer, Louanna Furbee, and Steven Zweig. 1991. Cognitive Factors Influencing Women to Seek Care During Pregnancy. *Family Medicine* 23:443–46.

Foucault, Michel. 1973a [1965]. *Madness and Civilization: A History of Insanity in the Age of Reason*. Trans. by R. Howard. New York: Vintage Books.

_____. 1973b [1970]. *The Order of Things: An Archaeology of the Human Sciences*. New York: Vintage Books.

_____. 1975. *The Birth of the Clinic: An Archaeology of Medical Perception*. New York: Vintage Books.

_____. 1980 [1972]. *The Archaeology of Knowledge, and the Discourse on Language*. New York: Pantheon Books.

_____ and Colin Gordon. 1980. *Power/Knowledge:Selected Interviews and Other Writings, 1972–1979*. New York: Pantheon Books.

Friedrich, Paul. 1970. Shape in Grammar. *Language* 46:379–407.

_____ 1979a. The Symbol and Its Relative Non-Arbritrariness. In *Language, Context, and the Imagination: Essays by Paul Friedrich*. Selected and Introduced by Anwar S. Dil. pp. 1–61. Stanford: Stanford University Press.

_____. 1979b. Poetic Language and the Imagination: A Reformulation of the Sapir Hypothesis. *Language, Context, and the Imagination: Essays by Paul Friedrich*. Selected and Introduced by Anwar S. Dil. pp. 441–512. Stanford: Stanford University Press.

_____. 1986. *The Language Parallax: Relativism and Poetic Indeterminacy*. Austin: University of Texas Press.

_____. 1989. Language, Ideology and Political Economy. *American Anthropologist* 91:295–312.

Fromkin, Victoria. 1991. Forum Lecture. LSA Linguistic Institute, Santa Cruz.

Furbee-Losee, Louanna. 1976. *The Correct Language, Tojolabal: A Grammar with Ethnographic Notes*. New York: Garland.

Furbee, Louanna. 1985a. New Developments in Linguistics. Lecture given to the Society for Anthropology in Community Colleges at the 84th Annual Meeting of the American Anthropological Association, Denver.

_____. 1985b. Loss of Basic Color Terminology. Paper presented to the Symposium on Archeology, Evolution, and the Brain at the 84th Annual Meeting of the American Anthropological Association, Denver.

_____. 1986. Linguistics in Anthropology. Paper presented to the Symposium on Language in Anthropology at the 85th Annual Meeting of the American Anthropological Association, Philadelphia.

_____. 1989. A Folk Expert System: Soils Classification in the Colca Valley, Peru. *Anthropology Quarterly* 62:83–102.

_____. 1992. Effect of Eye Color on Perception. Paper presented to the 91st Annual Meeting of the American Anthropological Association, San Francisco.

Furbee, Louanna, and Robert A. Benfer. 1983. Cognitive and Geographic Maps: Intracultural Variation among Tojolabal Mayans. *American Anthropologist* 85:305–34.

_____. 1989. Validation in Expert Systems. Paper presented to the Symposium on Use of Expert Systems in Cultural Anthropology at the 88th Annual Meeting American Anthropological Association, Washington, DC.

Furbee, Louanna, Kelly Maynard, J. Jerome Smith, Robert A. Benfer, Sarah Quick, and Larry Ross. 1996. The Emergence of Cognition from Perception. *Journal of Linguistic Anthropology* 6(2): 223–40.

Gadamer, Hans Georg. 1976. *Philosophical Hermeneutics*. Trans. by E. Linge. Berkeley: University of California Press.

Gal, S. 1989. Language and Political Economy. *Annual Review of Anthropology* 18:345–67.

Gardín, Jean-Claude. 1988. *Artificial Intelligence and Expert Systems: Case Studies in the Knowledge Domain of Archaeology*. Chichester, West Sussex, England: Ellis Horwood Limited.

Gardner, P. M. 1976. Birds, Words, and a Requiem for the Omniscient Informant. *American Ethnologist* 3:446–68.

Gatewood, J. B. 1983. Loose Talk: Linguistic Competence and Recognition Ability. *American Anthropologist* 85:378–87.

_____. 1985. Actions Speak Louder than Words. In Janet W. D. Dougherty, ed., *Directions in Cognitive Anthropology*, pp. 199–210. Urbana and Chicago: University of Illinois Press.

Gazdar, Gerald, Ewan Klein, Geoffrey K. Pullum, and Ivan Sag. 1985. *Generalized Phrase Structure Grammar*. Cambridge: Harvard University Press.

Geertz, C. 1973. *Interpretations of Culture*. New York: Basic Books.

_____. 1985. *Local Knowledge: Further Essays in Interpretive Anthropology*. New York: Basic Books.

Gersh, Harry. 1971. *When a Jew Celebrates*. New York: Behrman.

Goldman, Lawrence. 1983. *Talk Never Dies: The Language of Huli Disputes*. London: Tavistock.

Goodenough, Ward H. 1957. Cultural Anthropology and Linguistics. In P. Garvin, ed., *Seventh Annual Roundtable Meeting on Lingusitics and Language Study*. Washington, DC: Georgetown University, pp. 167–73.

_____. 1981. *Culture, Language, and Society*. Menlo Park, CA: Benjamin Cummings.

Golla, Victor, ed. 1984. *The Sapir-Kroeber Correspondence: Letters between Edward Sapir and A. L. Kroeber, 1905–1925*. Berkeley: Survey of California and Other Indian Languages.

Gould, Lewis L. 1988. *Wyoming: A Political History*. New Haven: Yale University Press.

Grace, George W. 1987. *The Linguistic Construction of Reality*. London: Croon Helm.

Greenberg, Joseph. 1966. *Language Universals, with Special Reference to Feature Hierarchies*. Janua Linguarum, Series Minor 59. The Hague: Mouton.

_____. 1987. *Language in the Americas*. Palo Alto: Stanford University Press.

_____, C. G. Tuner, and S. L. Zegura. 1986. The Settlement of the Americas: A Comparison of the Linguistic, Dental and Genetic Evidence. *Current Anthropology* 27:477–99.

Guillet, David. 1989. A Knowledge-Based-System Model of Native Soil Management. *Anthropology Quarterly* 62:59–67.

Gumperz, J. J. 1982. Conversational Code Switching. In J. J. Gumperz, ed., *Discourse Strategies*. Cambridge, England: Cambridge University Press, pp. 59–99.

Gumperz, J. J., and Stephen C. Levinson. 1991. Rethinking Linguistic Anthropology. *Current Anthropology* 32:613–23.

Hall, Edward T. 1959. *The Silent Language*. Garden City, NY: Anchor Press/Doubleday & Co., 1973.

_____. 1963. A System for the Notation of Proxemic Behavior. *American Anthropologist* 65:1003–26.

_____. 1974. *Handbook for Proxemic Research*. Washington, DC: Society for the Anthropology of Visual Communication.

Halliday, M. K. 1987. Arguments between Language and Literature. Language and the Order of Nature. In Nigel Fabb, Derek Attridge, Alan Durant, and Colin MacCabe, eds., *The Linguistics of Writing*, pp. 135–54. New York: Methuen.

Hammond-Tooke, W. D. 1981. *Patrolling the Herms: Social Structure, Cosmology and Pollution Concepts in Southern Africa*. 18th Raymond Dart Lecture. Johannesburg: Witwatersrand University Press.

Hanks, William F. 1986. Authenticity and Ambivalence in the Text: A Colonial Maya Case. *American Ethnologist* 13:721–44.

_____. 1987. Discourse Genres in a Theory of Practice. *American Ethnologist* 14:668–92.

_____. 1989. Text and Textuality. *Annual Review of Anthropology* 18:95–127.

_____. 1990. *Referential Practice: Language and Lived Space Among the Maya*. Chicago: University of Chicago Press.

Harkness, Sarah. 1973. Universal Aspects of Learning Color Codes: A Study of Two Cultures. *Ethos* 1:175–200.

Harris, Zellig. 1951. *Methods in Structural Linguistics*. Chicago: University of Chicago Press.

Harris, Randy Allen. 1993. *The Linguistics Wars*. New York: Oxford University Press.

Hatano, G. 1982. Cognitive Barriers in Intercultural Understanding. *Contemporary Psychology* 27:819–20.

Haywood, Charles. 1966. *Folk Songs of the World*. New York: John Day Company.

Heath, Shirley Brice. 1982. What No Bedtime Story Means: Narrative Skills at Home and School. *Language in Society* 11:49–76.

Heider, Karl G. 1988. The Rashomon Effect: When Ethnographers Disagree. *American Anthropologist* 90:73–81.

Heider [Rosch], Eleanor. 1972a. Probabilities, Sampling and Ethnographic Method: The Case of Dani Colour Names. *Man* (NS) 7:448–466.

_____. 1972b. Universals in Color Naming and Memory. *Journal of Experimental Psychology* 93:10–20.

Heidegger, Martin. 1969. *Identity and Difference*. Trans. by J. Stambaugh. New York: Harper and Row.

Heisenberg, W. 1927. Über den anschaulichen Inhalt der quantentheoretischen Kinematik und Mechanik. *Zeitschrift für Physik* 43:172–98.

Henning, H. 1916. *Der Gruch*. Leipzig: Barth.

Hering, Ewald. 1920. *Grundzüge der Lehre vom Lichtsinn*. Berlin: Springer. English translation: *Outline of a Theory of the Light Sense*. Trans. by L. M. Hurvich and D. Jameson. Cambridge: Harvard University Press, 1964.

Hill, Jane H. 1984. The Voices of Don Gabriel. Paper presented at the 83rd Annual Meeting of the American Anthropological Association, Washington, D.C.

_____. 1986a. The Refiguring of the Anthropology of Language. *Cultural Anthropology* 1:89–102.

_____. 1986b. Language, Culture and World View. In F. Newmeyer, ed., *Linguistics: The Cambridge Survey*, 4:14–35. Cambridge: Cambridge University Press, pp. 14–36.

_____. 1990. Weeping as a Meta-signal in a Mexicano Woman's Narrative. In E. B. Basso, ed., *Native Latin American Cultures through Their Discourse*, pp. 29–49. Bloomington: Indiana University Press and the Folklore Institute.

_____ and Kenneth C. Hill. 1986. *Speaking Mexicano*. University of Arizona Press.

_____ and Bruce Mannheim. 1992. Language and World View. *Annual Review of Anthropology* 21:381–406.

Hill, Kenneth C. 1985. Las Penurias de Doña María: Un Análisis Sociolingüístico de un Relato del Náhuatl Moderno. *Tlalocan* 10:33–115.

Hinton, Leanne. 1994. *Flutes of Fire: Essays on California Indian Languages*. Berkeley, CA: Heyday Books.

Hoijer, H. 1848. Linguistic and Cultural Change. *Language* 24:335–45.

Holland, Dorothy, and Naomi Quinn, eds. 1987. *Cultural Models in Language and Thought*. New York: Cambridge University Press.

Hopper, P., and S. A. Thompson. 1984. The Discourse Basis for Lexical Categories in Universal Grammar. *Language* 50:703–52.

Hudson, R. A. 1980. *Sociolinguistics*. New York: Cambridge University Press.

Hughes, Phyllis, ed. 1977. *Pueblo Indian Cookbook*. Albuquerque: University of New Mexico Press.

Humboldt, Wilhelm von. 1988. *On Language: The Diversity of Human Language Structure and Its Influence on the Mental Development of Mankind*. Trans. by Peter Heath. London: Cambridge University Press.

Hunn, Eugene. 1982. The Utilitarian Factor in Folk Biological Classification. *American Anthropologist* 84:830–47.

Husserl, E. G. A. 1927. Phenomenology. *Encyclopedia Britannica*, 14th edition, 17:699–702.

Hymes, Dell H. 1964. A Perspective for Linguistic Anthropology. In Sol Tax, ed., *Horizons in Anthropology*, pp. 92–107. Chicago: Aldine.

_____. 1966. Two Types of Linguistic Relativity. In William Bright, ed., *Sociolinguistics*, pp. 14–17. The Hague: Mouton.

_____. 1971. Sociolinguistics and the Ethnography of Speaking. In E. Ardener, ed., *Social Anthropological Linguistics*, pp. 47–93. Association of Social Anthropologists, Monograph 10. London: Tavistock.

Illich-Svitych, Vadislav M. 1971. *Opyt Sravneniia Norstratichestikh Iazykov*. [*The Experience of the Comparison of Norstratic Languages*.] Moscow: USSR Academy of Science, Institute for Slavistics and Balkinistics.

Jakobson, Roman. 1941. Child Language, Aphasia, and Phonological Universals. Trans. by A. R. Keiler. In *Roman Jakobson: Selected Writings*, Vol. 1: *Phonological Studies*, pp. 328–401. The Hague: Mouton, 1968.

_____. 1957. Shifters, Verbal Categories, and the Russian Verb. In *Roman Jakobson, Selected Writings*, Volume 2: *Word and Language*, pp. 130–147. The Hague: Mouton, 1971.

Kaiser, M., and V. Shevoroshkin. 1988. Nostratic. *Annual Review of Anthropology* 39:309–29.

Kant, Immanuel. 1965. *On History*. Trans. by L. W. Beck. New York: Bobbs-Merrill.

Kay, Paul. 1975. Synchronic Variability and Diachronic Change in Basic Color Terms. *Language in Society* 4:257–70.

_____, Brent Berlin, and William Merrifield. 1991. Biocultural Implications of Systems of Color Naming. *Journal of Linguistic Anthropology* 1:12–25.

_____ and Willett Kempton. 1984. What Is the Sapir-Whorf Hypothesis? *American Anthropologist* 86:65–79.

_____ and Chad K. McDaniel. 1978. The Linguistic Significance of the Meanings of Basic Color Terms. *Language* 54:610–46.

Keesing, R. L.. 1972. Paradigms Lost: The New Ethnography and the New Linguistics. *Southwestern Journal of Anthropology* 28:299–332.

Kempton, W. M. 1978. Social Correlates of Informant Variation in Folk Classification. In Donald M. Lance and Daniel Gulstad, eds., *Proceedings of the Mid-American Linguistics Conference, 1977*, pp. 130–47. Columbia: University of Missouri.

_____. 1981. *The Folk Classification of Ceramics: Fuzziness and Subcultural Differences*. San Diego: Academic Press.

Koerner, E. F. 1992. The Sapir-Whorf Hypothesis: A Preliminary History and a Bibliographic Essay. *Journal of Linguistic Anthropology* 2:173–98.

Kroeber, A. L. 1917. The Superorganic. *American Anthropologist* 19:163–213.

_____. 1948. White's View of Culture. *American Anthropologist* 50:409–14.

_____ and J. Richardson. 1940. Three Centuries of Women's Dress Fashions: A Quantitative Analysis. *University of California Anthropological Records*, 5(2): 111–54. (Reprint: A. L. Kroeber, ed., *The Nature of Culture*, pp. 358–72. Chicago: University of Chicago Press, 1952.)

Kuhn, Thomas. 1970. *The Structure of Scientific Revolutions*. 2d edition, revised. Chicago: University of Chicago Press.

Kultgen, John. 1975. Phenomenology and Structuralism. *Annual Review of Anthropology* 4:371–87.

Labov, William. 1966. *The Social Stratification of English in New York City*. Washington, DC: Center for Applied Linguistics.

_____. 1969. Contraction, Deletion and Inherent Variability of the English Copula. *Language* 45:715–62.

_____. 1973. *Sociolinguistic Patterns*. Philadelphia: University of Pennsylvania Press.

_____. 1982. Objectivity and Commitment in Linguistic Science: The Case of the Black English Trial in Ann Arbor. *Language in Society* 11:165–201.

_____ and J. Waletzky. 1967. Narrative Analysis: Oral Versions of Personal Experience. In J. Helm, ed., *Essays in the Verbal and Visual Arts*, pp. 12–44. Seattle: University of Washington Press.

Ladefoged, Peter. 1990. Some Reflections on the IPA. *Journal of Phonetics* 18:335–46.

_____. 1993. *A Course in Phonetics*. 3d edition. New York: Harcourt, Brace.

Laderman, C. 1981. Symbolic and Empirical Reality: A New Approach to the Analysis of Food Avoidances. *American Ethnologist* 8:468–93.

Laitin, David L., and Guadalupe Rodriguez Gomez. 1992. Language, Ideology and the Press in Catalonia. *American Anthropologist* 4:9–30.

Lakoff, George. 1987. *Women, Fire, and Dangerous Things: What Categories Reveal About the Mind*. Chicago: The University of Chicago Press.

_____ and Mark Johnson. 1980. *Metaphors We Live By*. Chicago: University of Chicago Press.

Lamberg-Karlovsky, C. C. 1989. Introduction. In C. C. Lamberg-Karlovsky, ed., *Archaeological Thought in America*, pp. 1–16. Cambridge: Cambridge University Press.

Lancy, D. F. and A. J. Strathern. 1981. "Making Twos": Pairing as an Alternative to the Taxonomic Mode. *American Anthropologist* 83:773–95.

Lardiere, Donna. 1992. On the Linguistic Shaping of Thought: Another Response to Alfred Bloom. *Language in Society* 21:231–51.

Larson, T. A. 1965. *History of Wyoming*. Lincoln: University of Nebraska Press.

Lenneberg, Eric, and John Roberts. 1956. The Language of Experience, a Study in Methodology. Memoir 13. *International Journal of American Linguistics*. Indiana University Publications in Anthropology and Linguistics. Baltimore: Waverly Press.

Levi-Strauss, Claude. 1963. The Structural Study of Myth. In *Structural Anthropology*, pp. 206–31. Trans. by C. Jacobson and B. Grundfest-Schoetf. New York: Basic Books.

_____. 1966. *The Savage Mind*. Trans. by J. Weightman and D. Weightman. Chicago: University of Chicago Press.

_____. 1969. *The Raw and the Cooked: Introduction to a Science of Mythology*. Volume I. Trans. by J. Weightman and D. Weightman. Chicago: University of Chicago Press.

_____. 1973. *From Honey to Ashes: Introduction to a Science of Mythology*. Volume II. Trans. by J. Weightman and D. Weightman. Chicago: University of Chicago Press.

Li, Charles N., ed. 1977. *Mechanisms of Language Change*. Austin: University of Texas Press.

_____ and Sandra A. Thompson. 1974. An Example of Word Order Change: SVO to SOV. *Foundations of Language* 12:201–14.

Lucas, Donald. 1968. Euripedes. *Encyclopedia Britannica* 8:829–35.

Lucy, John A. 1985. Whorf's View of the Linguistic Mediation of Thought. In E. Mertz and R. J. Parmentier, eds., *Semiotic Mediation*, pp. 73–77. New York: Academic Press.

_____. 1992a. *Language Diversity and Thought*. Cambridge, England: Cambridge University Press.

_____. 1992b. *Grammatical Categories and Cognition*. Cambridge, England: Cambridge University Press.

_____ and R. A. Shweder. 1979. Whorf and His Critics: Linguistic and Nonlinguistic Influences on Color Memory. *American Anthropologist* 81:581–615.

MacLaury, Robert E. 1987a. Color-category Evolution and Shuswap Yellow-in-Green. *American Anthropologist* 89:1–18.

_____. 1987b. Co-extensive Semantic Ranges: Different Names for Distinct Vantages of One Color. In A. Bosch, B. Need and E. Schiller, eds., *Papers form the 23rd Regional Meeting, Chicago Linguistic Society*, pp. 268–82. Chicago: Chicago Linguistic Society.

_____. 1991. Exotic Color Categories: Linguistic Relativity to What Extent? *Journal of Linguistic Anthropology* 1:26–51.

_____. 1992a. From Brightness to Hue: An Explanatory Model of Color Category Evolution. *Current Anthropology* 33:127–86.

_____. 1992b. Karuk Color: A Close Look at the Yellow-Green-Blue Category of Northern California. Paper presented at the 91st annual meeting of the American Anthropological Association, San Francisco.

_____. 1997. Color and Cognition in Mesoamerica: Constructing Categories as Vantages. Austin: University of Texas Press.

_____ and Brent D. Galloway. 1988. Categories and Color Qualifiers in Halkomelem, Samish, Lushootseed, Nooksack, and Yakima. 23rd Annual Meeting of Salishan and Neighboring Languages. University of Oregon, Eugene.

Malotki, Ekkehart. 1979. *Hopi Raum*. Tübingen: Gunther Narr.

_____. 1983. *Hopi Time*. Berlin: Mouton.

Malony, H. N., and A. Adams Lovekin. 1985. *Glossolalia: Behavioral Science Perspectives on Speaking in Tongues*. New York: Oxford University Press.

Mamis, Robert. 1984. Name-Calling. *INC* July:67–73.

Maranz, A. 1995. The Minimalist Program. In G. Webelhuth, ed. *Government and Binding Theory and the Minimalist Program*, pp. 349–82. Oxford: Basil Blackwell.

Marcus, George, and R. Cushman. 1982. Ethnographies as Texts. *Annual Review of Anthropology* 11:25–69.

Martin, Laura. 1986. "Eskimo Words for Snow": A Case Study in the Genesis and Decay of an Anthropological Example. *American Anthropologist* 88:418–23.

McDaniel, Chad K. 1972. Hue perception and Hue Naming. A. B. Honors thesis, Harvard University.

Merbs, S. L., and J. Nathans. 1992. Absorption Spectra of Human Core Pigments. *Nature* 356:433–35.

Mervis, Carolyn, Jack Catlin, and Eleanor Rosch. 1975. Development of the Structure of Color Categories. *Developmental Psychology* 11:554–60.

Miller, Wick R. and Irvine Davis. 1963. Proto-Keresan Phonology. *International Journal of American Linguistics* 29:310–30.

Mollon, J. 1992. Worlds of Difference. *Nature* 356:378–79.

Moravcsik, Edith A., and Jessica R. Wirth, eds. 1980. *Current Approaches to Syntax*. New York: Academic Press.

Morrow, D. H. 1986. Grammatical Morphemes and Conceptual Structure in Discourse Processing. *Cognitive Science* 10:423–55.

Murphy, Robert I. 1990. The Dialectics of Deeds and Words: Or, Anti-the-Antis (and the Anti-Antis). *Cultural Anthropology* 5(3): 331–37.

Nabhan, Gary, C. W. Weber, and J. L. Berry. 1979. Legumes in the Papago-Pima Diet and Ecological Niche. *The Kiva* 44:173–90.

Natanson, M. A., ed. 1973. *Phenomenology and the Social Sciences*. 2 volumes. Evanston, IL: Northwestern University Press.

Nettl, Bruno. 1989. *Blackfoot Musical Thought*. Kent, OH: Kent State University Press.

Newman, Stanley. 1958. Zuni Dictionary. *International Journal of American Linguistics* 24(1), Part II.

Newmeyer, Frederick J. 1986. *The Politics of Linguistics*. Chicago: University of Chicago Press.

Ortega y Gasset, José. 1957 [1932]. *The Revolt of the Masses*. New York: W.W. Norton & Co.

Palmer, Gary B. 1988. The Language and Culture Approach in the Coeur D'Alene Language Preservation Project. *Human Organization* 47(4): 307–17.

Peirce, Charles S. 1940. *The Philosophy of Peirce*. Ed. by J. Buchler. New York: Harcourt and Brace.

Perry, Edgar, C. Z. Quintero, C. Davenport, and C. B. Perry. 1972. *Western Apache Dictionary*. Fort Apache, AZ: White Mountain Apache Cultural Center.

Phillip Morris Inc. 1994. [sales brochure.] No place given: Phillip Morris Inc.

Pike, K. L. 1967. *Language in Relation to a Unified Theory of the Structure of Human Behavior*. The Hague: Mouton.

Pokorny, Julius. 1959. *Vergleichendes Wörterbuch des Indogermanischen Sprachen*. Ed. by A. Walde. Berlin: DeGruyter.

Popper, Karl R. 1965. *Conjectures and Refutations: The Growth of Scientific Knowledge*, 2d edition. New York: Basic Books.

Pratt, M. L. 1977. *Toward a Speech Act Theory of Literary Discourse*. Bloomington: Indiana University Press.

Propp, V. 1928. *Morphology of the Folktale*. Trans. by L. Scott. Austin: University of Texas Press, 1968.

Pukui, Mary Kawena, and Samuel H. Elbert. 1965. *Hawaiian Dictionary*. Honolulu: University of Hawaii Press.

Pullum, Geoffrey K. 1989a. Topic . . . Comment: Formal Linguistics Meets the Boojum. *Natural Language & Linguistic Theory* 7:137–43.

_____. 1989b. Topic . . . Comment: The Great Eskimo Vocabulary Hoax. *Natural Language & Linguistic Theory* 7:275–81.

Rabinow, Paul, and William M. Sullivan, eds. 1979a. *Interpretive Social Science: A Reader*. Berkeley: University of California Press.

_____. 1979b. The Interpretive Turn: Emergence of an Approach. In Paul Rabinow and William M. Sullivan, eds., *Interpretive Social Science: A Reader*, pp. 1–21. Berkeley: University of California Press.

Ramanujan, A. K. 1971. The Indian Oedipus. *Seminar of Indian Literature*. Sinla, India: The Indian Institute for Advanced Studies. Reprinted in Lowell Edmunds and Alan Dundes, eds., *Oedipus: A Folklore Case Book*. New York: Garland Publishing Co.

Read, Dwight. 1987. KAES: An Expert System for the Algebraic Analysis of Kinship Terminologies. Part II. Paper presented at the Symposium on Computers in Anthropology at the 86th Annual Meeting of the American Anthropological Association, Chicago.

_____ and Clifford Behrens. 1989. Modeling Folk Knowledge as Expert Systems. *Anthropology Quarterly* 62:107–20.

Reed, A. W. 1948. *Concise Maori Dictionary*. Wellington: A. H. and A. W. Reed.

Ricoeur, Paul. 1967. *The Symbolism of Evil*. Boston: John Wiley.

Rice, G. E. 1980. On Cultural Schemata. *American Ethnologist* 7:152–72.

Roche, M. 1973. *Phenomenology, Language and the Social Sciences*. London: Routledge & Kegan Paul.

Romney, A. Kimball, Susan C. Weller, and W. H. Batcheider. 1987. Recent Applications of Consensus Theory. *American Behavioral Scientist* 31:163–77.

Room, Adrian. 1982. Introduction. *Dictionary of Trade Name Origins*. London: Rutledge and Kegan-Paul.

Rosaldo, M. 1984. Toward an Anthropology of Self and Feeling. In R. Shweder and R. LeVine, eds., *Culture Theory*, pp. 137–57. Cambridge: Cambridge University Press.

_____. n.d. Toward an Anthropology of Self and Feeling. Manuscript.

Rosch, Eleanor. 1973. Natural Categories. *Cognitive Psychology* 4:328–50.

_____. 1981. Prototype Classification and Logical Classification: The Two Systems. In E. Scholnick, ed., *New Trends in Cognitive Representation: Challenges to Piaget's Theory*, pp. 73–86. Hillsdale, NJ: Erlbaum.

Rose, M. D., and A. K. Romney. 1979. Cognitive Pluralism or Individual Differences: A Comparison of Alternative Models of American English Kin Terms. *American Ethnologist* 6:752–62.

Rumsey, Alan. 1992. Wording, Meaning and Linguistic Ideology. *American Anthropologist* 92:346–61.

Ryan, Gery. 1991. Can Expert Systems Really Help Us Model Decisions in the Field: Testing Artificial Intelligence on Infantile Diarrhea Management. *Cultural Anthropology Methods Newsletter* 3(1): 5–7.

Sacks, J. S. 1967. Recognition Memory for Syntactic and Semantic Aspects of Connected Discourse. *Perception and Psychophysics* 2:437–42.

Sankoff, Gillian. 1971. Quantitative Analysis of Sharing and Variability in a Cognitive Model. *Ethnology* 10:389–408.

_____. 1973. Above and Beyond Phonology in Variable Rules. In C. J. N. Bailey and R. H. Shuy, eds., *New Ways of Analyzing Variability in English*, pp. 44–66. Washington, DC: Center for Applied Linguistics.

Sankoff, David, and Gillian Sankoff. 1973. Sample Survey Methods and Computer Assisted Analysis in the Study of Grammatical Variation. In R. Darnell, ed., *Canadian Languages in Their Social Context*, pp. 7–63. Edmonton: Linguistic Research, Inc.

Sapir, Edward. 1921. *Language: An Introduction to the Study of Speech*. New York: Harcourt, Brace and World.

_____. 1931. Conceptual Categories in Primitive Languages. *Science* 74:578.

_____. 1933. La Réalité Psychologique des Phonèmes. *Journal de Psychologie Normale et Pathologique* 30:247–65. English translation: The Psychological Reality of Phonemes. In V. B. Makkai, ed., *Phonological Theory: Evolution and Current Practice*, pp. 22–31. New York: Holt, Rinehart and Winston, 1972.

_____. 1936 Internal Evidence Suggestive of the Northern Origins of the Navaho. *American Anthropologist* 38: 224–35.

_____ and Maurice Swadesh. 1946. American Indian Grammatical Categories. *Word* 2:103–12.

Sapir, J. David. 1977. The Anatomy of Metaphor. In J. D. Sapir and J. C. Crocker, eds., *The Social Use of Metaphor*, pp. 3–32. Washington, DC: American Anthropological Association.

Sapir, J. David, and J. C. Crocker, eds. 1977. *The Social Use of Metaphor*. Washington, DC: American Anthropological Association.

Saussure, Ferdinand de. 1959 [1916]. *Cours de linguistique générale*. Charles Bally and Albert Sechehaye, in collaboration with Albert Reidlinger. 3d ed. Lausane: Payot.

_____. 1966. Course in General Linguistics. Trans. by W. Baskin. New York: McGraw-Hill.

Saville-Troike, M., ed. 1977. *Linguistics and Anthropology. Georgetown University Roundtable, 1977*, pp. 139–51. Washington, DC: Georgetown University.

_____. 1982. *The Ethnography of Speaking: An Introduction*. Oxford, England: Basil Blackwell.

Schank, R. C., and R. P. Abelson. 1977. *Scripts, Plans, Goals, and Understanding*. Hillsdale, NJ: Lawrence Erlbaum Associates.

Schlesinger, I. M. 1991. The Wax and Wane of Whorfian Views. In R. L. Cooper and B. Spolsky, eds., *The Influence of Language on Culture and Thought*, pp. 7–44. Berlin: Mouton de Gruyter.

Schneider, David M. 1976. Notes Toward a Theory of Culture. In K. H. Basso and H. Selby, eds., *Meaning in Anthropology*, pp. 197–220. Albuquerque: University of New Mexico Press.

_____. 1962, 1963, and 1964. *Collected Papers*. The Hague: Nijhoff.

Shaul, D. L. 1985. Review of *Hopi Raum* (Tübingen: Gunther Narr, 1979) and *Hopi Time* (Berlin: Rinehart, 1983) by E. Malotki. *Language* 61:481–84.

_____. 1988. Topic and Information Structure in a Hopi Radio Commercial. *International Journal of American Linguistics* 54:96–105.

_____. 1992. A Hopi Song-poem in 'Context.' In B. Swann, ed., *On the Translation of Native American Literatures*, pp. 228–41. Washington, DC: Smithsonian Institution Press.

_____, R. Albert, C. Golstan, and R. Satory. 1987. The Hopi Coyote Story as Narrative: The Problem of Evaluation. *Journal of Pragmatics* 11:17–39.

Sherzer, Joel. 1983. *Kuna Ways of Speaking: An Ethnographic Perspective*. Austin: University of Texas Press.

_____. 1987. A Discourse-centered Approach to Language and Culture. *American Anthropologist* 89:295–309.

Shore, Bradd. 1991. Twice-Born, Once Conceived: Meaning Construction and Cultural Cognition. *American Anthropologist* 93:9–27.

Shweder, Richard A. 1984. Anthropology's Romantic Rebellion Against the Enlightenment. In R. A. Shweder and R. A. LeVine, eds., *Culture Theory: Essays on Mind, Self, and Emotion*, pp. 22–66. Cambridge: Cambridge University Press.

_____. 1990. Cultural Psychology: What Is It? In J. W. Stigler, R. A. Shweder and G. Herdt, eds., *Cultural Psychology: Essays on Comparative Human Development*, pp. 1–43. New York: Cambridge University Press.

Silverstein, Michael. 1976. Shifters, Linguistic Categories, and Cultural Description. In K. Basso and H. Selby, eds., *Meaning in Anthropology*, pp. 11–55. Albuquerque: University of New Mexico.

_____. 1977. Cultural Prerequisites to Grammatical Analysis. In M. Saville-Troike, ed., *Linguistics and Anthropology. Georgetown University Roundtable, 1977,* pp. 139–51. Washington, DC: Georgetown University.

Silverstein, Michael. 1979. Language Structure and Linguistic Ideology. In P. R. Clyne, W. F. Hanks, and C. C. Hofbauer, eds., *The Elements: A Parasession on Linguistic Units and Levels*, pp. 193–248. Chicago: Chicago Linguistic Society.

_____. 1981. Language and the Culture of Gender: At the Intersection of Structure, Usage, and Ideology. In E. Mertz and R. J. Parmentier, eds., *Semiotic Mediation: Sociocultural and Psychological Perspectives*, pp. 219–59. Orlando, FL: Academic Press.

_____. 1986. The Diachrony of Sapir's Synchronic Linguistic Description, or, Sapir's "Cosmographical" Linguistics. In W. Cowan, M. K. Foster and K. Koerner, eds., *New Perspectives in Language, Culture, and Personality*. Amsterdam and Philadelphia: John Benjamins.

Slobin, D. I., ed. 1967. *A Field Manual for Cross-Cultural Study of the Acquisition of Communicative Competence*. Berkeley: Language-Behavior Research Laboratory, University of California, Berkeley.

Smith, J. Jerome. 1993. Using ANTHROPAC 3.5 and a Spreadsheet to Compute a Free List Salience Index. *Cultural Anthropology Methods Newsletter* 5(3): 1–3.

_____, Louanna Furbee, Kelly Maynard, Sarah Quick, and Larry Ross. 1995. Salience Counts: A Domain Analysis of English Color terms. *Journal of Linguistic Anthropology* 5(2): 203–16.

Spiro, Melford E. 1986. Cultural Relativism and the Future of Anthropology. *Cultural Anthropology* 1:259–86.

Spradley, J. P., ed. 1972a. *Culture and Cognition: Rules, Maps, and Plans*. San Francisco: Chandler.

_____. 1972b. Foundations of Cultural Knowledge. In J. P. Spradley, ed., *Culture and Cognition: Rules, Maps, and Plans*, pp. 3–38. San Francisco: Chandler.

Stanlaw, Stanley James. 1987. Color, Culture, and Contact: English Loanwords and Problems of Color Nomenclature in Modern Japanese. Dissertation, University of Illinois at Urbana-Champaign.

Starbucks Coffee Company. 1995. *Starbucks Summer Catalog 1995*. Seattle: Starbucks Coffee Company.

Stigler, J. W., R. A. Shweder, and G. Herdt, eds. 1990. *Cultural Psychology: Essays on Comparative Human Development*. New York: Cambridge University Press.

Steinthal, H. H. 1881. *Einleitung in der Psychologie und Sprachwissenschaft*. 2d edition. Berlin.

Stoller, Paul, and Cheryl Olkes. 1986. Bad Sauce, Good Ethnography. *Cultural Anthropology* 1:336–52.

Strasser, S. 1963. *Phenomenology and the Human Sciences*. Pittsburgh: Duquesne University Press.

Stross, Brian. 1974. Speaking of Speaking: Tenejapa Tzeltal Metalinguistics. In R. Bauman and Joel Sherzer, eds., *Explorations in the Ethnography of Speaking*, pp. 213–39. Cambridge: Cambridge University Press.

Sweetzer, E. E. 1987. The Definition of *lie*: An Examination of the Folk Theories Underlying a Semantic Prototype. In D. Holland and N. Quinn, eds., *Cultural Models in Language and Thought*, pp. 43–66. New York: Cambridge University Press.

Tannen, Deborah. 1981. A Comparative Analysis of Oral Narrative Strategies: Athenian Greek and American English. In W. L. Chafe, ed., *The Pear Stories*, pp. 51–88. Norwood, NJ: Ablex.

Taylor, Charles. 1979. Interpretation and the Sciences of Man. In Paul Rabinow and William M. Sullivan, eds., *Interperetive Social Science: A Reader*, pp. 25–72. Berkeley: University of California Press.

Tedlock, Dennis. 1983. *The Spoken Word and the Work of Interpretation*. Philadelphia: University of Pennsylvania Press.

Thomas, Lawrence L. 1957. *The Linguistic Theories of N. J. Marr*. University of California Publications in Linguistics, Volume 14. Berkeley and Los Angeles: University of California Press.

Trachtenberg, Jeffrey. 1985. Name that Brand. *Forbes* April:128–30.

Trudgill, Peter. 1974. *Sociolinguistics: An Introduction*. Harmondsworth, England: Penguin.

Turner, Victor. 1969. *The Ritual Process: Structure and Anti-Structure*. Chicago: University of Chicago Press.

Tversky, Amos. 1977. Features of Similarity. *Psychological Review* 84:327–52.

_____ and I. Gati. 1978. Studies of Similarity. In Eleanor Rosch and Barbara Lloyd, eds., *Cognition and Classification*, pp. 79–98. Hillsdale, NJ: Lawrence Erlbaum Associates.

Tyler, Edward B. 1871. *Primitive Culture: Researches into the Development of Mythology, Philosophy, Religion, Art and Custom*. London: John Murray.

Tyler, S. A., ed. 1969. *Cognitive Anthropology*. New York: Holt, Rinehart, and Winston.

_____. 1984. The Vision Quest of the West, or What the Mind's Eye Sees. *Journal of Anthropological Research* 40:23–89.

_____. 1986. Post-Modern Ethnography from Document to Occult to Occult Document. In James Clifford and George E. Marcus, eds., *Writing Culture: The Poetics and Politics of Ethnography*, pp. 122–40. Berkeley: University of California Press.

Urban, Greg. 1991. *A Discourse-Centered Approach to Culture*. Austin: University of Texas Press.

Viberg, A. 1983. The Verbs of Perception: a Typological Study. *Linguistics* 21:123–62.

Vygotsky, Lev S. 1962. *Thought and Language*. Cambridge: The MIT Press.

Watkins, Calvert. 1985. *The American Heritage Dictionary of Indo-European Roots*. Boston: Houghton-Mifflin.

Webelhuth, G., ed. 1995. *Government and Binding Theory and the Minimalist Program*. Oxford: Basil Blackwell.

Weigand, Hans. 1990. *Linguistically Motivated Principles of Knowledge Base Systems*. Holland/Providence, RI: Dordrecht.

White, J. P., and D. A. Thomas. 1972. What Mean These Stones? Ethnotaxonomic Models and Archaeological Interpretation in the New Guinea Highlands. In D. L. Clarke, ed., *Models in Archaeology*, pp. 275–308. London: Methuen.

Whorf, Benjamin Lee. 1956. *Language, Thought, and Reality: Selected Writings of Benjamin Lee Whorf*. J. Carroll, ed. Cambridge: The MIT Press.

Wierzbicka, Anna. 1989. Soul and Mind: Linguistic Evidence for Ethnopsychology and Culture History. *American Anthropologist* 91:41–58.

Wierzbicka, Anna. 1991. *Cross-Cultural Pragmatics: the Semantics of Human Interaction*. Berlin: de Gruyter.

Winserickx, J., D. T. Lindsey, E. Sanocki, D. Y. Teller, A. G. Motulsky, and S. S. Debb. 1992. Polymorphism in Red Photopigment Underlies Variation in Color Matching. *Nature* 356:431–33.

Witherspoon, Gary. 1977. *Language and Art in the Navajo Universe*. Ann Arbor: University of Michigan Press.

_____. 1980. Language in Culture and Culture in Language. *International Journal of American Linguistics* 46:1–13.

Witkowski, Stanley R., and Cecil H. Brown. 1977. An Explanation of Color Nomenclature Universals. *American Anthropologist* 79:50–57.

Wittgenstein, L. 1958. *Philosophical Investigations*. 3d edition. Trans. by G. E. M. Anscombe. New York: Macmillan. (Original publication in 1953.)

Wright, Robert. 1991. Quest for the Mother Tongue. *Atlantic Monthly* April, 1992:39–68.

Zadeh, Lofti. 1965. Fuzzy Sets. *Information and Control* 8:338–53.

Zubin, D. A., and K. M. Koepcke. 1981. Gender: A Less than Arbitrary Grammatical Category. *CLS 17 (Regional Meeting of the Chicago Linguistic Society)*: 439–49.

Index